THE ENNEAGRAM CONNECTION

THE ENNEAGRAM CONNECTION

Using the Enneagram and Emotional Intelligence to Transform Work and Personal Relationships

Robert J. Tallon

FOREWORD BY STEVE CHANDLER
BESTSELLING AUTHOR OF *REINVENTING YOURSELF*

ALSO BY ROBERT J. TALLON

Awareness to Action, The Enneagram, Emotional Intelligence, and Change
by Robert Tallon and Mario Sikora (2006: University of Chicago Press)

Tallon, Robert, J –
The Enneagram Connection: Using the Enneagram and Emotional Intelligence to Transform Personal and Work Relationships by Robert J. Tallon
ISBN: 1512315656
ISBN 13: 9781512315653

PRAISE FOR *THE ENNEAGRAM CONNECTION*

"The *Enneagram Connection* demonstrates how easy and effective it is to use the enneagram and emotional intelligence with friends, family, boss, peers, and subordinates. Read *The Enneagram Connection* and you will soon find yourself growing greatly in areas that make a real difference in your life."

Joseph Dillard, PhD, author of *Waking Up,* and *Integral Deep Listening, Assessing Your Inner Compass*

"Bob Tallon has written a compelling book on using the enneagram and emotional intelligence in relationships in business and personal life. He identifies six main areas of successful relationships and lays out a precise practice for improving in each one. This is a stimulating and useful book. I highly recommend it to anyone trying to master their effectiveness with others."

Jay Earley, Ph.D., author of *Self-Therapy: A Step-by-Step Guide to Creating Wholeness Using IFS*

"Bob Tallon's new book, *The Enneagram Connection* is a perfect companion to his first book, *Awareness to Action.* He shows you new ways to pay attention to yourself, to your intentions with others, and to the opportunities and challenges that present themselves. I'm happy to endorse this wonderful, well thought-out book. *The Enneagram Connection* is a road map for better relationships and a better life."

Kathy Cramer, Ph.D., Emmy Award winner and bestselling author of *Lead Positive,* and *Change the Way You See Everything Through Asset-Based Thinking.*

"In *The Enneagram Connection,* Bob Tallon weaves together his more-than two decades of front-line experience with the Enneagram and provides a wealth of practical advice on how to break down the barriers that stand between people. Bob demonstrates that the Enneagram is not a dead or calcified model standing in isolation, but that it is a living, breathing system that can be used in new and surprising ways."

Mario Sikora, co-author, *Awareness to Action: The Enneagram, Emotional Intelligence, and Change;* 2011-2012 president of the International Enneagram Association; president, Awareness to Action International.

"The enneagram, the subject of Bob Tallon's first book, *Awareness to Action,* is an effective tool to understand what drives us to be who we are. In his latest book, *The Enneagram Connection*, he takes the next step in blending the Enneagram Strategies with EQ concepts to present us with the standard work on how to become a more balanced person and to improve our relationships with those around us. Industry has many tools and concepts to improve the efficiency of accomplishing work together. *The Enneagram Connection* provides the methodologies to maximize the value of our most important process, how we communicate and relate with each other."

Dave Sharkis, Supreme Council, Ancient Accepted Scottish Rite, Northern Masonic Jurisdiction, and Co-Founder of the *Children's Dyslexia Center of Connecticut*

"Bob Tallon is a gifted drummer and writer and he's got the rhythm right in this book. His theme of *The Enneagram Connection* is nicely voiced by the sections on the Enneagram personality styles, the emotional intelligences of each style, and the communication patterns among all the styles. *The Enneagram Connection* is a fine reference book, a piece that can be taken out and played over and over whenever you encounter a different type. You will find Bob's book both enjoyable and enlightening."

Jerome Wagner, Ph.D., author of *Nine Lenses on the World: the Enneagram Perspective,* and *The Enneagram Spectrum of Personality Styles: an Introductory Guide.*

"*The Enneagram Connection* combines the richness of the enneagram, the wisdom and necessity of emotional intelligence, and what Tallon calls the Six Practices—tools that transform the ways we work and thrive with others. We enthusiastically recommend *The Enneagram Connection* for anyone who wants to create powerful work teams and fulfilling personal relationships."

Stan Sherman and Kathy Garret, Ph.D., Co-Founders of *The Propel Consulting Group*

"Bob Tallon and I are members of The ManKind Project, a men's organization dedicated to gaining deeper levels of self-awareness and translating that into missions of service in the community. *The Enneagram Connection* has enabled me to discover more about myself, and has helped me understand others in new ways. The discovery process outlined in *The Enneagram Connection* is a must-have tool for individual development. It also offers innovative ways for teams to reach new levels of effectiveness and accomplish powerful results together. If learning, growth, and service are important to you, then this book will be a significant resource."

John Davis, Senior Consultant, *The Cramer Institute*

"*The Enneagram Connection* marries the enneagram and emotional intelligence (EQ) to guide us through the confusing maze of relationship building. I appreciate the comprehensive resource guide that *The Enneagram Connection* is. Read this book and keep it by your side to improve how you interact with the people in your life."

Andrea Isaacs, creator of EnneaMotion, host of the "What We Need To Know" Radio Program, and co-founding editor/publisher of the *Enneagram Monthly*

"Bob Tallon suggests a different paradigm for understanding the enneagram in his new book, *The Enneagram Connection*. He reveals how our life can be a journey filled with rich relationships, an adventure of promise and joy. *The Enneagram Connection* presents an inviting vision of what mature, integrated relationships can be, written with the author's signature clarity and insight.

Do the exercises in this book. They will change the way you see, understand, and act with others."

James Hughes, CFP, CLU, CHP, President and Founder, *Financial Planning Directions*

"*The Enneagram Connection* offers solid advice on building and improving personal and work relationships. The Six Practices are worth the price of the book. They provide an accurate and user friendly map to more successful relationships."

Don Johnson, US Director of Sales, *Insights*

"Bob Tallon hits the nail on the head with *The Enneagram Connection*. Successful relationships in life and business involve a variety of factors. Tallon does us a favor by narrowing those factors down to six: being aware, establishing trust, dealing with conflict, making a commitment, being accountable, and achieving mutual goals. Keep this gem of a book handy if you want to improve all of your relationships."

Helene Meisler, Wall Street technical analyst, contributor for *Real Money*, and author of *The Streets Top Stocks*

"Bob Tallon suggests that we need to refine our relationship skills if we want to enrich our lives and the lives of others, and I wholeheartedly agree. His emphasis on mindfulness and emotional intelligence strikes a strong cord with me. Filled with wisdom and clarity, *The Enneagram Connection* is a powerful guidebook that will transform your life, and the lives of those you touch."

Dick Goldberg, President of *The Goldberg Group*, and former Executive Director of the *Mankind Project USA*

"*The Enneagram Connection* demonstrates how we can use our emotions and our personality as opportunities to increase satisfaction, performance, and bottom-line results. Bob Tallon's work is as thorough as it is thought-provoking."

Elliot Weiler, News Anchor, KTVI-TV/KPLR-TV, Host "Hancock & Kelley," and "Post Scripts"

For my wife, Robyn
my support, my strength, my love

Table of Contents

Part One: Strategies

Part Two: Practicing

Part Three: Connecting

Acknowledgements

I began studying the enneagram in 1988. My first formal teachers were Don Riso and Russ Hudson. Their first book, *Personality Types,* woke me up like the whack of a Zen master's stick. It described my personality's gifts and foibles with pinpoint accuracy. Don and Russ were, as they say, greater than the sum of the parts. In early workshops they would challenge each other, testing their personal theories and experiences. Each brought a different perspective to the emerging enneagram field. Their spirited discussions inspired each other and their students, and true to George Gurdgieff's Law of Three, their affirming and negating perspectives inevitably led to reconciliation, which they later called the Insight Approach. I was lucky to be one of the first people to become certified by Don and Russ back in 1992, and taught with them for two years in their certification program. The three of us became students together in the Ridhwan School where we further explored the nature of personality, essence, and reality. I'm forever grateful to Don and Russ, for their books and teachings, for all they brought to the study of the enneagram, and for all they brought to me.

I'm grateful to Patrick Lencioni, whose bestselling book, *The Five Dysfunctions of a Team,* changed the way I taught and facilitated team building. His book inspired me to combine my version of the enneagram with his Five Dysfunctions. His influence can be seen in the structure and content of this book.

I'm profoundly thankful to Steve Chandler, whose many books, podcasts, and CD programs changed the way I connect with people. I first listened to

Steve's CD program, *Mind Shift*, eight years ago and it transformed my life as a coach, a trainer, and as a person. It made my relationships richer, my work more fulfilling, and my focus clearer. I found in Steve a successful teacher, life coach, and business consultant who shared my perspective—that work should be emotionally and spiritually fulfilling. His grasp of human nature and motivation zeroes in on the essence of being productive and being happy. He taught me that the true measure of our success is how effectively we serve others. Steve's ability to take people from this awareness to meaningful action is unsurpassed in its simplicity and clarity. I'm honored that Steve agreed to write the Forward to this book.

I'm also thankful to some very special people: to Mario Sikora, my nephew and co-author of my first book, *Awareness to Action*, who developed the strategy approach to the enneagram with me and who has contributed so much to the growth of the enneagram through his leadership in the International Enneagram Association, and by bringing his enneagram-based business to a global audience; to John Davis, a tireless warrior and servant leader who got me involved in the transforming work of the ManKind Project and whose impact on men is an inspiration to so many; to Kathy Cramer, who's development of Asset-Based Thinking, and her numerous books and teaching on positive psychology have helped me focus on possibilities; to my brother, Dennis Tallon, management consultant and enneagram teacher, who read many drafts of this book, and served as an untiring cheerleader; to my dear friend and spiritual mentor, Patricia Wintyr, whose guidance and love have lifted me up and brought me insight and energy; to Ken Sheer, who got me off my butt after a long injury and back onto the court playing competitive tennis and focused on the ball (read "here and now"); to Steve Pidgeon, webmaster, photographer, and videographer, who designed the book's cover and graphics and continues to indulge my appetite for long discussions on philosophy, religion, and psychology; to Jane Friesz, who meticulously proofed the manuscript; to Dave Sharkis, engineer, untiring caregiver, and inspiring leader, who, with his wife Cheryl, founded and runs the Children's Dyslexia Center of Connecticut. Dave has hired me throughout the years to teach the enneagram to both business and charitable groups. To my father-in-law, Jack

Helmer, who read what I thought was a final proof of this book and found two mistakes in the first 20 pages. His eagle eye and Eight tenacity inspired me to re-read and re-edit the manuscript one last time. And what a difference that made! A special thanks to my children, Aaron and Lauren, who are always there and always supportive, and lastly, to my greatest support, my wife, Robyn Helmer-Tallon, whose counsel, intelligence, and resilience helped me keep my nose to the grindstone. Her love, patience, and compassion always amaze and inspire me.

Foreword

The Underrated Power of Understanding
By
Steve Chandler

Somewhere deep into this rich and rewarding field guide for creating great relationships, I am stopped by a quote that Robert Tallon drops in like an artist affixing the brightest tile in a mosaic. It is a quotation from Dale Carnegie that points out the value of being interested in others. It's a principle borrowed by more modern social philosophers, like Stephen Covey, but it sounds the bell for why this book, *The Enneagram Connection,* connected with me. Carnegie says that we can make more friends in two months by being interested in others than we can in two years by trying to make ourselves interesting to others.

This book is the ultimate master key to open the door to a fulfilling, profound, comprehensive understanding of, and interest in, other people. By explaining and applying the wisdom and the utility of the enneagram, Tallon gives us a way to be intrigued by our differences instead of threatened by them. Despite our free will and creativity, patterns and styles of thinking are real. The more we understand them, the faster we connect with others and the less fear we feel in interpersonal relationships.

This book is powerful for people in the professional world, especially those who negotiate, sell and create relationships all day. Because the number one reason buyers give for wanting to buy from a certain person is "he gets us. He understands what we are up to."

True, too, in personal relations. In family, in romance, in any attempt at an intimate connection, when a person feels heard and feels understood, true love sets in. How sweet when we hear someone talk about finding a soul mate and saying, "He gets me."

The beauty of this book is that those kinds of connections don't have to be mysterious anymore. They don't have to be a matter of chemistry, or a certain sales person's "charisma." Right here is a logical, clear and exciting guide for "getting" and thereby connecting with another person. Too often in this age we demean the intellect and honor the gut feeling. We brag about "getting an intuitive hit" during a vital conversation.

But I think we were given our brains for a reason. And I've always observed in my coaching and training of people and teams over the years that people become happier, more productive and better at collaborating when their level of understanding improves.

Ever since I read Colin Wilson's book about Gurdjieff, *The War Against Sleep*, I have been a student and advocate of the enneagram. There are many deep, dense books about it. Why it works isn't always clear (until now) but its power to capture and explain various thinking patterns in people is uncanny. But to date no book has delivered the teaching with such clarity and utility. Robert Tallon is to be thanked for a long time to come for this rich, strong work.

I recommend clearing a nice amount of time for yourself to relax into this book. Find the silence and solitude it deserves, and then read to learn about people, and how and why they think and behave the way they do. You'll get a feeling that you're seeing the human beings in your world almost for the first time. And your path to understanding them and connecting with them will also be made surprisingly clear.

Steve Chandler is the author of 30 books that have been translated into over 25 languages. His personal success coaching, public speaking, and business consulting have been used by CEOs, top professionals, major universities, and over 30 Fortune 500 companies. He has twice won the national Audio of the Year award from King Features Syndicate. A popular guest on TV and radio talk shows, Steve Chandler has recently been called "the most powerful public speaker in America today." He is a master coach who has trained countless coaches to transform many lives and businesses.

Preface

"Consider the following. We humans are social beings. We come into the world as the result of others' actions. We survive here in dependence on others. Whether we like it or not, there is hardly a moment in our lives when we do not benefit from others' activities. For this reason it is hardly surprising that most of our happiness arises in the context of our relationship with others."

The Dalai Lama

My previous book, *Awareness to Action,* was first published in 2004, followed by a revised edition in 2006. It described the nine types of the enneagram in the context of 16 emotional competencies. It presented for the first time, the *Awareness to Action Process,* a three-step change model that is the cornerstone of my work in coaching and training people to become more effective employees, managers, and leaders. *Awareness to Action* has an introspective and individual focus, and addresses how each personality type can improve performance in the workplace.

Since the publication of *Awareness to Action* an increasing number of clients and readers have requested a companion piece—a book that goes beyond individual behavior and addresses how each of the personality types can best interact with others on work teams and in personal relationships. Readers wanted to know how a person could relate more effectively with each of the other types; for example, how a Type One can best relate with another Type One, a Type Two, a Type Three, and so forth. This seemed like a good reason to write a second book.

But there are two other reasons I decided to write *The Enneagram Connection*; the first is the joy I experience when I see people resolve conflicts and relate with acceptance and understanding when they realize that their problems, so often based on biases, fears, and misunderstandings, can be solved by a deeper understanding of different personality styles and emotional intelligence. Countless times I've heard people say, "I always thought my neighbor was impossible to get along with. Now I realize he just sees things differently. He's just got a different personality style." This style also includes different motivations, blind spots, and perspectives—and a unique level and expression of emotional intelligence. When we become mindful of our own and another's personality style, compassion fills the heart, understanding informs the mind, new relationships are born, and old ones transformed.

The additional reason for writing this book was my growing recognition of the importance and necessity of people being connected—*really connected*—not via Facebook, Twitter, or LinkedIn—but face to face, and feelings to feelings. In connecting with individuals, couples, and teams, I've been dismayed by how technology has encouraged people to drift further apart, even as it has helped them grow closer. I'm sure we've all seen couples on a date, parents with their children, and workers in the lunch room texting messages or checking emails on their smart phones—together but disconnected. Our emotional life suffers when we're not connected, and our effectiveness to build solid relationships and achieve mutual goals suffers as well. We are all ultimately connected and interdependent, and we ignore this reality at our peril.

In his book *Social Intelligence: The New Science of Human Relationships*, Daniel Goleman describes how discoveries in neuroscience and biology establish that we are hardwired for connection and that our relationships influence our biology and our personal experiences. He writes, "Even our most routine encounters act as regulators in the brain, priming our emotions, some desirable, others not. The more connected we are with someone emotionally, the greater the mutual force." In *The Gifts of Imperfection*, Brené Brown writes,

"It's amazing—yet perhaps not surprising—that the connectedness we experience in our relationships impacts the way our brain develops and performs."

What would your relationships be like if you were better connected? How much healthier, more authentic, loving, and productive would relationships be if you were connected in a deeper, more personal way? How would your work life, marriage, and family life improve? What does it mean to be connected, and what skills are required?

In *Everyone Communicates, Few Connect* John C. Maxwell writes: "What do we mean when we say 'connect'? Connecting is the ability to identify with people and relate to them in a way that increases your influence with them. Why is that important? Because the ability to communicate and connect with others is a major determining factor in reaching your potential. To be successful, you must work with others. And to do your absolute best you must learn to connect." Maxwell describes that connecting begins when the other person feels valued. People feel valued when we make the effort to know and understand them, which begins with awareness.

My first book was called *Awareness to Action* for good reason. As a consultant, coach, and trainer, I realized that no learning and no growth could happen without first being aware of reality. Before we can take our first step toward change, toward creating fulfilling relationships and rewarding teams, we have to see where we are. We must become self-aware and accurately perceive the territory right here and now. We must become self-observers—witnesses of our strengths, weaknesses, unproductive habits and blind spots—of what's working and not working in our lives and relationships. It's my hope that this book will help us connect with others and ourselves with compassion, courage, and understanding.

Introduction

"Whereas average individuals often have not the slightest idea of what they are, of what they want, of what their own opinions are, self-actualizing individuals have superior awareness of their own impulses, desires, opinions, and subjective reactions in general."

Abraham Maslow

CONNECTION BEGINS WITH AWARENESS

Studies conducted over the last 10 years show how practicing awareness, also called mindfulness, creates positive effects on the brain by building new neural connections among brain cells. Mindfulness helps us rewire the brain, and with each new neural connection, the brain is learning. Over time, mindfulness practice thickens the region of the brain responsible for self-observation, optimism, compassion, possibility thinking, and a sense of well being. This area is also associated with creativity, an increased sense of curiosity, and the ability to be reflective and observe how our mind works. All this positivity helps us to avoid being dominated by the part of the brain that is associated with fear, depression, anxiety, and pessimism. As a result, our self-awareness, emotional stability, and sense of self-worth increase as our negative judgments of others and ourselves decrease.

By developing a daily practice of awareness we train and master the mind and open ourselves to better relationships and a more fulfilling life. Many of the studies that demonstrate the positive effects of mindfulness focus on meditation. However, growing research shows that the same results can be achieved through other practices, such as the suggestions found in the *Wake-Up Call* and the *Take Action* sections in this book.

When we are aware we are learning. Awareness enables us to create rather than react to situations. Awareness gets us off the "victim of circumstance" treadmill. Becoming more aware means being a "learner" rather than a "reactor."

- Learners are aware of their behavior; reactors are not.
- Learners reflect on their observations and realize things about themselves and their environment. Reactors stay in a trance, rejecting self-reflection.
- Learners accept new, resourceful information even when it contradicts their existing beliefs. Reactors grasp stubbornly to the status quo.
- Learners more easily assume accountability, resolve conflicting commitments, and expand their thinking. Reactors rationalize, make excuses, blame others, and find ways to remain unconscious—still blind to their blind spots, still limited by their limiting beliefs.
- Learners learn to overcome fear, to make conscious decisions, to manage and to communicate with awareness, compassion and precision. Reactors resist learning, and continue to make the same poor decisions based on fear, habit and reactivity.

Connecting With Others Without Losing Ourselves

The founder of the Ridhwan School, Hameed Ali, teaches an awareness practice called Sensing, Looking, and Listening. It is a body scan exercise were we begin with eyes closed, sense the left foot, left calf, left thigh, and progressively sense the entire body, then lastly, we allow our focus to settle on the arms and legs. Next, while still being mindful of our arms and legs, we expand our awareness to listening. Then we open the eyes and let our awareness see the world around us. The idea is to maintain our sense of ourselves—our own presence—while sensing, looking, and listening to the environment and to others. This can be difficult; we are easily distracted, and it takes an act of will to resist being spellbound by the sounds and images around us. Many of us are aware of being so captivated by someone that we "lose" ourselves. When we are lost in another, we are not really connected. When we lose connection with our own self, we can't be connected in a powerful and meaningful way with another. The way I use the word connection in this book does not involve merging with someone, nor does it mean surrender to another. It involves being open to others while maintaining our own physical and emotional boundaries. It requires openness, acceptance, and personal autonomy. Being aware of yourself while being aware of another, (also known as *divided attention*), takes practice.

In *The Unfolding Now*, Hameed Ali (under his pen name A.H. Almaas) writes:

"You need to practice awareness as much as possible. What you need to remember about your practice is that at all times—whether sitting in meditation or having a meal or talking with a friend or listening to a lecture—you can be present and aware. You can remember to be present to what is going on. Learning to be real must begin with recognizing what is real in our experience, and that always begins with being aware of where we are in the present moment."

FOCUS OF ATTENTION

Daniel Goleman writes in *Focus, The Hidden Driver of Excellence*, "Attention, from the Latin *attendere*, which means to reach toward, connects us with the world, shaping and defining our experience. 'Attention,' cognitive neuroscientists Michael Posner and Mary Rothbart write, provides the mechanisms 'that underlie our awareness of the world and the voluntary reaction of our thoughts and feelings.' Ann Treisman, a dean of this research area, notes that how we deploy our attention determines what we see. Or as Yoda says, 'Your focus is your reality'."

Helen Palmer would agree with Yoda and Goleman about the power of focus; she notes how each enneagram type has a specific *focus of attention*. These can also be seen as the ways that each personality type loses self-awareness. How deeply we are fixated on our specific focus of attention determines the degree to which we have lost connection with our own presence, with our own self:

Type Ones focus on what's wrong and needs fixing.

Type Twos focus on other peoples' needs and the desire to be appreciated.

Type Threes focus on tasks, roles, and results.

Type Fours focus on the new and different and what's missing—a sense that "best" is what is absent.

Type Fives focus on observing and understanding the world, and what others want from them.

Type Sixes focus on the bad news and threats, hazards, and difficulties.

Type Sevens focus on good news and a pleasant future, and the positive in all things.

Type Eights focus on taking charge, gaining power, and overcoming injustice.

Type Nines focus on other people's preferences, the inessential and unimportant.

AWARENESS OF THE OUR "SYSTEM"

The more aware we are of ourselves and others the more fulfilling our relationships will be. In my opinion, no tool is as accurate and comprehensive as the enneagram in helping us improve awareness on a broad, useful scale. Understanding how each of the nine types sees the world in different ways helps us see ourselves through other people's eyes and helps us understand others with compassion and clarity. Behaviors and attitudes that seemed foreign in the past now have context and make sense. Criticism lessens as people see that they are just as prone to the foibles of their styles as others are to theirs.

We have access to all the nine types, which I also call *strategies*. Most of us, however, don't see the other eight strategies as part of *our* system, at least not at first. It is only human nature to fixate on and use the parts of ourselves that we prefer and are comfortable with—no matter how ineffective it may be in different situations.

Our awareness grows as we realize that we are more than a personality type, more than a separate ego. We become more compassionate and more able to connect to others when we understand that we are much more *a system* than a separate conglomeration of parts. We are part of other larger systems that all fit together in an integrated whole. Because we are dependent upon each other, we are in some sense our family, team, department, company, state, country, and planet. When we operate from this perspective we act in ways that are life affirming and effective.

THE EFFECT OF STRESS

Behavior changes drastically when we are under stress. It can cause us to ignore, shame, or abuse people we love. Stress changes our behavior and seems to change our personality, and this is why people often confuse different personality types. For example, how can Jack be a Type Seven, the type that is usually happy-go-lucky and positive, when we experience him as stern, demanding, and critical? The answer is stress. How can Marie be a Type Two, the type that is normally caring and helpful, when we see her as pushy, uncaring, and manipulative? Stress again. In enneagram language we say that stress brings out the "low side" of our type, or that we take on the less resourceful aspects of a type we are connected to.

Stress makes us insecure and defensive or worse. Look at the list of behaviors below, adapted from the "Signs of Defensiveness" developed by William Schutz. You may recognize many characteristics caused by stress.

Aggression	Playing "poor me"
Loss of humor	Sarcasm
Taking offense	Blaming
Wanting to be right	Eccentricity
Wanting the last word	Being too nice
Flooding with information	"It's just the way I am."
Holding a grudge	Trivializing with humor
"I know that."	"Don't lecture me."
Jealousy	Inappropriate laughter

Stress negatively affects both our IQ and EQ. Success and happiness depend on our ability to use emotions to enhance our own emotional wellbeing as well as our positive relationships with others; however, stress is one of the biggest impediments to our expression of emotional intelligence. In *The Stress Effect,* Henry Thompson writes, "When stress increases, cognitive and emotional intelligence is compromised. Perception changes and in many cases becomes less accurate and more biased. This sets the stage for less effective appraisal, which changes motivation, and motivation changes action."

In the chapters that describe the emotional competencies of each of the types, this book describes two ways that the types appear: "Normally," and "Under Stress."

Normally

We don't always behave at our best; we are affected by our normal habits, though not necessarily in negative ways. Our habitual behaviors often serve us. The Nine who strives to be peaceful is often a pleasant and reassuring presence; the Three who strives to be outstanding often thrives in relationships and motivates people to achieve; and the Eight who strives to be powerful can often mobilize forces to meet tight deadlines and overcome obstacles. So it is fair to say that many of us behave adequately most of the time, and that our behavior is basically useful but not necessarily optimal. It is this *most of the time* that is described in the "Normally" paragraphs.

Under Stress

Descriptions of behavior "Under Stress," are examples of counterproductive behavior. As already noted, stress causes us to become mistrusting and defensive, and to unconsciously rely on ineffective and inappropriate strategies. When these strategies don't work, stress continues to build. Rather than try alternative ways to accomplish what we want, stress causes us to depend more and more on old habits, making us less effective and less connected.

Fear can bring out the worst in us and force us to see the world in limited ways. We tend to fall into defensive and risk adverse patterns. We tighten up and "hunker down" and clarity, creativity, and joy go out the window. Trust, on the other hand, allows us to build bonds with people, to delight at what life has to offer, and to love freely. Keep in mind that the portrayals of the types "Under Stress" in this book describe a wide variety of behaviors ranging from stressed to extremely stressed.

There is a third way that we show up—when we are aware—that is not included in the chapters that describe the emotional competencies of each of the types. These descriptions can be found in other sections of the book.

Aware

When we are at our best—unstressed, relaxed, focused, secure, and *aware*—we are less affected by our habitual, negative behavior. We are more flexible, responding naturally and appropriately to life's challenges. When we are aware, we behave with emotional intelligence and psychological maturity. Aware people are *balanced*. For example, the balanced Three is focused on striving to be outstanding while not being overly competitive. A balanced Three has integrated her ability to be at her individual best with the ability to be a team player and share in the success of the relationship or team. From an EQ perspective, an aware person, regardless of personality type, will use empathy when interacting with people, but will not lose sight of other EQ competencies such as confidence and conflict management when making decisions.

THE SIX PRACTICES

Several years ago I read Patrick Lencioni's *The Five Dysfunctions of a Team*. I realized that the elements in Lencioni's book were the perfect complement to the work I did with the enneagram and teams. *Awareness to Action Teams*, the name I've given to the combination of these elements, has made for a powerful workshop for work teams and groups. I realized that all of the team-related skills in *The Five Dysfunctions of a Team* also apply to personal, non-work related relationships. I turned the Five Dysfunctions into positive *practices,* added *Be Aware* to the list and *The Six Practices* were born. These form the foundation and behaviors required of any relationship:

- Be Aware
- Establish Trust
- Deal With Conflict
- Make a Commitment
- Be Accountable
- Achieve Mutual Goals

The Six Practices, emotional intelligence, and the enneagram come together to provide the book's major components.

READING THIS BOOK

If you are new to the enneagram, I suggest you complete The Enneagram Strategies Profile (ESP) to determine your enneagram type, which can be found and completed for free on my website: www.bobtallon.com. Then read all of Part One, which explains the terms used in the book, particularly the relationship between the "connecting points"—the two types that each type is linked with, which are called the Neglected and Support points. These are discussed further in Chapter One. The relationships between the Preferred, Neglected, and Support points are presented in charts in Chapter Three.

My first book, *Awareness to Action,* did not include the enneagram wings or the subtypes, but this book does. My discussion of these concepts is intentionally brief; my goal is to focus primarily on how they relate to connecting and building relationships. Exploring the wings and subtypes will further deepen your knowledge of your personality type.

A book such as this, which many will use as a reference guide, can't help but have some repetitions. For example, the sections called *Building Rapport* and the chapter called *How Can We Connect?* discuss similar information, but from different viewpoints. *Building Rapport* is written from a general point of view, that is, the advice applies to the type being addressed. *How Can We Connect?* draws on some of the same material, but is written from the point of view of a specific type; for example, a Type One giving advice to a Type Two, a Type Two giving advice to a Type Three, etc. Some repetitions appear in other parts as well, which I have left in for clarity and ease of reference.

I use the words personality, type, style, and strategy interchangeably throughout the book. The words awareness and mindfulness are also used interchangeably, with only a few variations, when noted. Terms such as best self, higher self, authentic self, and true self, while referenced only briefly, are also used interchangeably.

PART ONE: STRATEGIES

Part One focuses on the "working tools" of this book. Chapter One provides a brief overview of the enneagram strategies as well as descriptions of the strategies in the charts called Summary of (the specific type's) Strategy Relationships, for example Summary of Type One's Strategy Relationships. These charts use the terms "discomfort" and "distortion" to describe one of the primary ways each type behaves under stress. For more on this see The Neglected Strategy in Chapter One.

The concept of emotional intelligence (EQ) is described and the most important EQ competencies for relating to others are listed. Chapter Two discusses the ways that we can connect through the enneagram and EQ, specifically through enneagram strategy, enneagram wing, enneagram subtype, and EQ. This chapter goes into greater detail about the critical importance of EQ in connecting with people. Chapter Three is an in depth discussion of the nine strategies.

PART TWO: PRACTICES

Part Two introduces the *Six Practices* and the EQ competencies that are most important for achieving proficiency in each practice. Two common features in Part Two are called the *Wake-Up Call*—brief assessments and reflection exercises before each of the *Six Practices*—and *Take Action*—suggestions and challenges related to each of the practices. Chapter Four: Are We Aware Enough? addresses the EQ competency of self-awareness, and includes a section on Blind Spots, and the antidote for each of the blind spots called Turning Around the Blind Spot. Chapter Five: Can We Trust Each Other? discusses the EQ competency of trustworthiness and introduces how to build rapport with each type. Chapter Six: Can We Deal With Conflict? focuses on the EQ competencies of conflict management, empathy, and communication. Chapter Seven: Can We Make a Commitment? considers how the capacity for resiliency and adaptability affect our ability to make and keep commitments. Chapter Eight: Can We Be Accountable? explores achievement drive and self-control; a section called Changing Ineffective to Effective Behavior examines six major weaknesses of each type and how they can be turned into strengths. Chapter Nine: Can We Achieve Mutual Goals? looks at how the competencies of cooperation and optimism are critical for partnering with others to achieve mutual goals.

PART THREE: CONNECTIONS

Part Three focuses on specific ways to connect with each of the personality types. Chapter Ten: How Can We Connect? introduces the reference guide that spells out the types' similarities—which I call Connections—and differences—which I call Disconnects, and guidance to build rapport and connect with different personality types. This material is written from the perspective of each type in the relationship, and focuses on what gifts and strengths each type can offer the other. For example, in a relationship between a Type One and a Type Two, there are two sections: "Connecting With a One From a Two's Perspective," and "Connecting With a Two From a One's Perspective."

Appendix A: Framework for Creating Successful Connections is a graphic representation of the Six Practices and how awareness of each function precedes action. Although it is not represented in the diagram, the answer "yes" to each question implies that a preliminary step called "authenticity" (coined by myself and Mario Sikora) has been accomplished in order to move into action. Authenticity means that we have recognized and worked through conflicting commitments. We called this three-step flow from awareness to authenticity to action "The Awareness to Action Process." For a complete explanation of the process see *Awareness to Action*.

PURPOSE NOT PERSONALITY

The enneagram is a wonderful map of the human psyche. Maps are useful and the more accurate the map, the more helpful it is. However, we should never lose sight of the fact that the enneagram is not reality, but, like a good map, it points to reality and helps guide us to the real thing. There is some danger in learning our personality type. Some people, after this discovery, feel that they have "found" themselves. For example, we may hear the enneagram enthusiast say, "I'm a Nine. That's why I seek harmony." We need to be on guard against oversimplifying this very complex subject, and on guard against misidentifying ourselves as our personality type.

We are not our personality! Our enneagram type is a map, a description, an estimation of the motivations and behaviors of our particular style. So it is inaccurate to say, "I'm a Three, or an Eight." It is more accurate to say, "I act like an Eight," or "I'm most like a Three," or even, "My personality style is best represented by Type Four." In fact, the enneagram points to the ways we are *least* like our best, most effective self (what some people call their higher self, true self, or authentic self)—which could be seen as the integration of all of the strategies. Our best self is aware of all the strategies and uses them freely and appropriately as the situation demands. Our best self puts personality type aside and lets purpose, not personality, be the guide for action.

With awareness we can see that the other eight strategies are simply not our *preferred* strategy. With greater awareness we realize that the other strategies are really parts of us that we use less frequently, reject, or even disown. We restrict how we relate to people when we ignore these other parts. When the way we define ourselves becomes flexible and more comprehensive, it becomes *bigger*, emotionally, psychologically, and spiritually. When my definition of what my "Nine-ness" means expands to include healthy behaviors normally associated with other types, I'm more complete, and predictably, happier, more mature, and more effective in life and in relationships.

Richard Swartz' *Internal Family System (IFS)* is a psychotherapy that teaches that we do not have one personality, or one "I," but we consist of many "parts." Jay Earley, PhD writes in his IFS based book, *Self-Therapy*:

"You can think of parts of yourself as little people inside you. Each has its own perspective, beliefs, feelings, memories, and motivations. You may have heard of the 'inner critic' or the 'inner child,' the most famous of our parts. But these are simple concepts that only begin to touch on the richness and complexity of our inner life. Our inner family may include a lonely baby, a wise mentor, an angry child, a stern mother, a calm meditator, a magician, a happy animal, a closed-off protector, and so on."

George Gurdjiefff, the *Fourth Way* teacher and grandfather of the enneagram, taught something similar: "Man has no permanent and unchangeable 'I.' Every thought, every mood, every desire, every sensation says 'I'." Robert Assignoli, the developer of *Psychosynthesis* taught that we have "subpersonalities"—parts within our dominant personality. Hal and Sidra Stone, creators of *Voice Dialogue*, describe the parts as "voices" that we can hear, speak, and act from.

The enneagram reveals that we have three clearly identifiable strategies— one *preferred* strategy, which is our normal or default choice, one *support* strategy, that we fall back on when we are stressed, and sometimes when other strategies aren't appropriate, and one *neglected* strategy that we often ignore, but access when we are relaxed, feeling secure, and at our most confident. We've got three strategies right off the bat, and have access to more as we grow in emotional intelligence. Staunchly committing to maintaining or defending our personality, often expressed as "I gotta be me," is usually a sign of stubbornness, insecurity, and a lack of emotional intelligence. Emotional intelligence is at play when we know it is time to flex our style—to have the courage to break out of the restrictive box of our preferred strategy. Steve Chandler urges us to be flexible and creative, and to learn to reinvent ourselves:

"When I reinvent myself in the most exciting and beneficial way, I don't change from an inferior personality into a superior one. I change from a noun to a verb. I reinvent from static fascination with my past and its patterns into joyful action. My world changes from trying to improve myself to learning to leave myself behind. This false persona (the Greek word for mask) is something that went through its final edit in junior high school. It is not real. It is not you. To truly reinvent from noun to verb, you need to replace personality with purpose. Then you can be whomever you need to be based on what you are creating right now."

The enneagram is an invaluable tool to help us understand and relate to people when we are "normal" and "under stress." When we are "aware" we are at our best—physically relaxed and poised, mentally curious and alert, and emotionally simple and open; this is when we more easily access our completeness.

3 CLEAR STRATEGIES

PREFERRED - DEFAULT CHOICE

SUPPORT - FALL BACK W/ STRESS

NEGLECTED - OFTEN IGNORE - BUT WHEN
ACCESSED WHEN WE ARE
RELAX, FEELING SECURE - AT OUR
MOST CONFIDENT

Part One: Strategies

"There's something I know about you that you may or may not know about yourself. You have within you more resources of energy than have ever been tapped, more talent than has ever been exploited, more strength than has ever been tested, more to give than you have ever given."

JOHN GARDNER

1

An Overview of the Strategies and Emotional Intelligence

"There can be no knowledge without emotion. We may be aware of a truth, yet until we have felt its force, it is not ours. To the cognition of the brain must be added the experience of the soul."

Arnold Bennett

The enneagram is a model of nine personality types, or strategies, and describes how these strategies affect the way we maneuver in the world. Our strategy profoundly influences the way we think, feel, and behave and describes our strengths and weaknesses. We are familiar with each of the strategies and, ideally, use the appropriate strategy for the appropriate situation. However, we tend to over-rely on one strategy (our *Preferred Strategy*) no matter the situation, believing that this strategy is the solution to most of our challenges. This habit of preferring one strategy to deal with a variety of situations and people creates automatic, unconscious behavior—an "auto-pilot" characterized by narrow vision, limiting beliefs, and blind spots. The enneagram helps us see the value of including more flexible, effective actions and helps us gain freedom from the less resourceful aspects of our personality. Knowledge of our strategy and the strategies of people we interact with improves our ability to relate to people who are not like us.

The Nine Strategies

Here is a brief summary of the nine strategies with their representative personality type names and typical characteristics:

Strategy of Type One—Striving to be Perfect, *Perfectionists* are energetic, active people who seek to be flawless, proper, appropriate, and to feel that everything is right with them and the world. They try not to make mistakes or be less than perfect.

Strategy of Type Two—Striving to be Connected, *Helpers* are sensitive to the personal lives and feelings of others, and seek to be appreciated and united with others. They try not to be physically or emotionally detached.

Strategy of Type Three—Striving to be Outstanding, *Performers* are goal-oriented and driven to be successful; they are competitive and desire to be seen as valuable, accomplished, and top performers. They try not to be average or get lost in the crowd.

Strategy of Type Four—Striving to be Unique, *Individualists* are emotionally sensitive and seek meaning and value; they are original, independent, and yearn to be appreciated for their special and different qualities. They try not to be uninteresting or commonplace.

Strategy of Type Five—Striving to be Detached, *Observers* are reserved and analytical and seek information and objectivity; they try to understand why and how things work. They try not to be uninformed, emotional, or emotionally overwhelmed.

Strategy of Type Six—Striving to be Secure, *Guardians* are safety conscious, and seek to be part of a group, cause, or philosophy; they desire to be safe and secure. They try not to be unprepared or careless.

Strategy of Type Seven—Striving to be Excited, *Enthusiasts* are fun loving, optimistic, and energetic; they seek to be stimulated, adventurous, and humorous; they desire to live in a happy world filled with interesting options. They try not to be bored or boring.

Strategy of Type Eight—Striving to be Powerful, *Challengers* are strong, action-oriented, and willful; they try to influence people and make things happen; they desire to defend and protect their integrity. They try not to be vulnerable or to depend on others.

Strategy of Type Nine—Striving to be Peaceful, *Peacemakers* are easy-going, friendly, and unassuming; they try to build harmony and desire to live in a world that is established on unity and acceptance. They try not to seek attention or cause conflict.

The Preferred Strategy

The *Preferred Strategy* is the personality type that we prefer over the other eight. It is the strategy that we are most comfortable with, but it is not the only one we use, or should aspire to use. This strategy can also be considered our *default strategy* (or default point) because we rely on it, often unconsciously, when all else fails to meet our needs. Using it makes life feel safer and more comfortable.

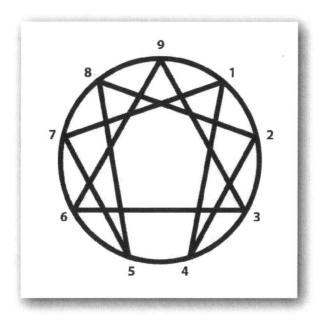

The Neglected Strategy

On the enneagram figure each point is connected to two other points. No matter what our personality type, we experience discomfort with the strategy found at one of the points connected to it. Because it's not our preferred strategy, that strategy doesn't feel right. This discomfort causes us to distort the true meaning of that strategy rather than see its usefulness. This discomfort and distortion causes us to "neglect" the strategy—feeling as if it is too risky to comfortably include in our normal behavior.

The discomfort occurs because the two strategies seem contradictory. For example, Helpers prefer the strategy of Striving to be Connected. They inaccurately perceive the strategy at one of the connecting points, Point Four, Striving to be Unique, as distant and inaccessible, and as an obstacle or contradiction to their desire to be connected. Helpers confuse being unique with being isolated, and will neglect that strategy and many of the behaviors associated with it. This doesn't mean that Helpers—or any of the other personality types—will *never* use their Neglected Strategy. However, we tend to under-use it, and the more we confuse its true meaning, our personality type distorts our application of it when we do use it.

Our Neglected Strategy can also be considered our *balance strategy* because using it in appropriate and mature ways balances our over reliance on our Preferred Strategy. In the example above, Helpers become more their own person, less dependent on others, and more focused on dealing with their personal needs when they use the Striving to be Unique behaviors of Point Four. Our ability to grow is greatly enhanced by our willingness to confront and correct our normal default to our Preferred Strategy and become more comfortable with our Neglected Strategy.

The Support Strategy

The other connecting point is called the *Support Strategy* because this strategy supports our Preferred Strategy or serves as an alternative response when the Preferred Strategy is not effective. The Support Strategy can enhance our effectiveness when we are at our best. For example, Aware Eights, the Challengers, use their Support Strategy, Striving to be Detached (found at Point Five) when they curtail immediate action and access information in order to make a more reasonable, effective response, thus supporting their desire to be powerful.

On the other hand, the Support Strategy can also be considered our *stress point* because we so often fall into its negative behaviors when we are under stress. For example, stressed Nines, the Peacemakers, may use their Support Strategy, Striving to be Secure, found at Point Six, in a negative way by becoming anxious, suspicious, or belligerent—all unproductive aspects of point Six—feeling that they must be overly guarded to maintain their safety.

EMOTIONAL INTELLIGENCE COMPETENCIES THAT ENHANCE RELATIONSHIPS

The terms "personality" and "emotional intelligence" are often used to incorrectly describe the same behaviors, so let's clear this up. In *The EQ Edge,* Steven Stein and Howard Book write,

"Personality is the concept most often confused with emotional intelligence, but differs in two important ways. First, like IQ, the traits that comprise our personalities are fixed. If we're by inclination honest, introverted, or loyal, we're unlikely to strike off in some new and unexpected direction. Psychologists call these traits "static," and term an individual's personality as a whole, "strategic" –another way of saying that it operates over the long haul…Emotional intelligence, however, is made up of short term, tactical, "dynamic" skills which can be brought into play as the situation warrants. Thus the individual building blocks of emotional intelligence—and its overall structure—can be improved by means of training, coaching, and experience."

An *emotional competency* is a specific skill based on emotional intelligence that makes us more effective. The competencies used in this book are grouped into two broad categories: personal competencies, and social competencies. They can be further separated into four narrower categories: Self-Awareness, Self-Management, Attunement to Others, and Relationship Building. The *personal competencies,* such as self-control and self-awareness, refer to our ability to manage and successfully use our emotions; the *social competencies*, such as communication and cooperation, refer to our ability to recognize and understand emotional states in others and to use this understanding to effectively interact with them.

There are many emotional competencies, such as achievement drive, leadership, and initiative that relate to functions other than connecting with people. The competencies we'll be focusing on for establishing and maintaining relationships are:

Self-Awareness: identifying one's thought processes, emotions, and skills
Self-Control: restraint exercised over one's impulses, emotions, or desires
Self-Confidence: confidence in one's powers and abilities
Adaptability: flexibility in handling change
Trustworthiness: maintaining standards of honesty and integrity
Optimism: expecting the best possible outcome

Resiliency: enduring in the face of obstacles

Achievement Drive: meeting or improving standards of excellence

Empathy: awareness of and participation in others'
feelings, ideas, and needs

Communication: listening openly and sending convincing messages

Cooperation: working with others toward shared goals

Conflict Management: negotiating and resolving disputes

2

Connecting–Let us Count the Ways

"We are tied together in the single garment of destiny, caught in an inescapable network of mutuality. And whatever affects one directly affects all indirectly. For some strange reason I can never be what I ought to be until you are what you ought to be. And you can never be what you ought to be until I am what I ought to be. This is the way God's universe is made; this is the way it is structured."

Martin Luther King

CONNECTING THROUGH ENNEAGRAM TYPE–THE STRATEGIES

We may think that people of similar type would get along, after all "birds of a feather flock together." Or do they? Do we choose mates that are like us, or do we need differences to create chemistry? When I first began teaching the enneagram, the questions I got the most were, "Who should I marry?" "Which type should I date?" and "Who would I get along with best?" Of course the answer is always, "Somebody emotionally healthy and mature!" Just because someone is your type doesn't mean you will see eye to eye. You may instead compete with each other, have power plays, or be jealous of each other, just like couples or groups of dissimilar types.

However, there does seem to be some agreement among enneagram practitioners about which types are attracted to each other. For example, detached, introverted Fives are often found with outgoing, nurturing Twos because Twos "do all the talking," allowing Fives to comfortably retreat inside. Proper, serious Ones often gravitate toward spontaneous, fun loving Sevens because Sevens help Ones lighten up and enjoy themselves. Careful, anxious Sixes can often be found with carefree, trusting Nines because Nines help Sixes relax and feel safe.

The developers of the website *9Types.com* conducted a study of 457 couples to determine marriage patterns between couples who knew their enneagram type. Here are some of their findings:

- Marriage patterns are not random. For example, of all female Eights in the study, 37% of them married male Nines, even though only 19% of all men in the study were Nines. There are a lot of such pairings that happen at far above chance levels.
- Men and women choose very different personalities for their mates. Male Nines with female Fours are common (16 couples), while male Fours with female Nines are extremely rare (two couples). Female Eights preferred male Nines, whereas Male Eights preferred female Twos and Sixes.
- The six most common type pairings are:
    - 18 pairs: male Eight, female Two
    - 16 pairs: male Nine, female Four
    - 15 pairs: male Six, female Two
    - 15 pairs: male Nine, female One
    - 14 pairs: male Five, female One
    - 14 pairs: male Six, female Nine

This study is intriguing, and creates great food for thought and discussion, but it is important to remember that lasting connections come from finding *emotionally healthy* individuals and groups regardless of type.

In *The Essential Enneagram* Lynette Sheppard writes, "The Enneagram personality system can be at its most powerful when applied to our relationships. True understanding begins when we can experience the worldview of others in our lives by feeling what reality feels like to them. By shifting our vantage point and by learning how our own personality perceives the world, we can begin to find ways of dramatically improving our relationships. Being in relationship with another personality type is like visiting another culture. In order to work and love well while in this culture, we need to learn the language and customs. In this way, we can begin to honor one another's unique differences and to celebrate our human diversity."

CONNECTING THROUGH ENNEAGRAM WINGS

Wings are the styles on either side of our enneagram type. For example, the wings of style One are Nine and Two; the wings of style Two are One and Three; the wings of style Three are Two and Four, and so forth. Wings flavor or create nuances that describe our specific style and give us flexibility. It is rare to find a person who is a "pure" type, that is, someone who is not influenced by the wings. We may have a lot in common with both of our wing styles or favor one over the other. A strong preference for one wing over the other will result in marked differences in personality type. For example, a Type Nine who favors his One wing will be more restrained and less aggressive that a Type Nine who favors his more assertive Eight wing.

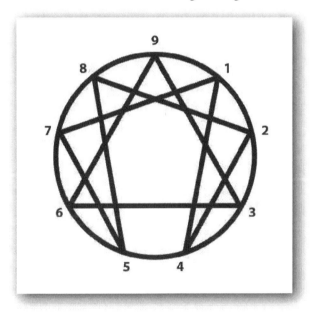

On the enneagram symbol, the types are laid out on a circle. Don Riso and Russ Hudson teach that it is helpful to think of the circle as a color wheel with the types blending together in color ranges. For example, we may have the red range from fire red through maroon to pink, all comprising the red family. This blending and movement between the types on either side of us means that we share and can understand the worldview of dissimilar types.

In *The Wisdom of the Enneagram,* Don Riso and Russ Hudson write:

"This way of looking at the types shows us that there is a continuum of human expression, just as there is a continuum on the color spectrum. There are no real divisions between the varieties of personality types, just as there are none between the colors of the rainbow. Individual differences are as unique as different shades, hues, and intensities of color. The nine points on the Enneagram are simply "family names" that we use to speak meaningfully about differences in personality, ways of speaking about main features without getting lost in details."

In *Nine Lenses on the World,* Gerry Wagner writes about paradigm shifts to neighboring styles (wings):

"...each core type actually represents the synthesis of its neighboring styles, so that, for example, Style One represents an attempt to resolve the issues of Style Nine and Style Two...Sometimes one wing style will offer a way out of a stuck point or compulsion related to the core paradigm, whereas the other wing may exaggerate an imbalance. For example, Fives who tend to seclude themselves through withdrawing into their private thoughts may discover that they can reconnect with their feelings and relationships by accessing the adaptive characteristics of their neighboring style Four...On the other hand, by adopting the cautious approach of their other neighbor, the Six...Fives may exacerbate their fears about their own adequacy, or their suspicions about others, drawing them deeper into the isolating labyrinth of their own thoughts instead of leading them out into contact with others."

From this example we can see that different types may be trying to resolve the same issues and can have a lot in common. For example, a Type Eight can have a dominant Seven wing as can a Type Six, so although these two have different core types (Preferred Strategies), they share a wing type, and may have similar interests and perspectives. While this book does not go into great detail about the wings of each type, it is helpful to recognize that there are many factors in play when people connect with others individually and in groups.

CONNECTING THROUGH ENNEAGRAM SUBTYPES

Subtypes are further variations of our enneagram type. They are based on three instincts that occupy much of our attention; they are called *self-preservation*—the focus on our needs for material supplies and sustenance such as food, clothes, shelter, and family relations; *social*—our instinct to fit in, to belong, to relate to people in groups, and in society in general; and *intimate*—the instinct that governs our sexuality, the vitality in our bodies, and our impulse to attract, bond with, and interact with our closest relationships.

We have all three of these instincts (and many more, of course) but we favor one over the other two. Having a favorite instinct gives us a pre-occupation and a distinct style. We often connect with people who have similar subtypes. For example, in my wife's family, her father, younger brother, and my wife are *self-preservation* subtypes. When they get together it doesn't take long before they're clustered together discussing favorite restaurants, foods, and "What's for dinner?" When that discussion wanes, they switch to money and clothes. I, on the other hand, am a *social* subtype, as are my mother-in-law and my wife's other brother. We grow weary of the *self-preservation* discussion quickly, preferring to talk about people, politics, history, religion, and "What's going on in the world?" The *intimate* subtypes are busy trying to create interest, and are wondering, "Am I being noticed?" so they can attract someone with whom they can forge a special bond.

Subtypes in relationships can be tricky; they can either balance or polarize the relationship. For example, if both partners are social subtypes, they may enjoy similar groups and social interests, but they may neglect self-preservation issues such as handling money, food shopping, and planning for the future. We often see different subtypes in relationships because they make a good team and balance things out.

Understanding the impact of subtypes can be a powerful way to connect with people. Determining our dominant subtype can be a challenge. Most people don't think in these terms and the instincts can be quite unconscious. I've described the three subtypes for each of the types as a starting point for investigation. I've adopted standard, often used names that indicate the subtype's focal point, such as Strength and Beauty for the Intimate Six, and Prestige for the Social Three.

CONNECTING THROUGH EMOTIONAL INTELLIGENCE

Emotional intelligence (EQ) is a major skill in connecting with people and establishing satisfying and lasting relationships. Building productive teams and achieving results together can't happen without EQ competencies such as cooperation, resiliency, trustworthiness, and communication. Without self-awareness, empathy, impulse control, and the ability to deal with conflict, it is impossible to relate in loving and caring ways with others. Luckily, emotional intelligence can be learned, and better still, emotional intelligence can increase as we get older. Cognitive intelligence (IQ) peeks at about age 17 and remains constant throughout adulthood, and may wane during old age. By contrast, current research studying neuroplasticity shows that emotional intelligence rises steadily throughout life, and can continue to grow well into the senior years. Emotional intelligence is the ability to:

- Identify our emotions and manage our responses to them. (For example, recognizing that we are angry with someone but not giving in to the temptation to escalate the conflict.)
- Identify the emotions of others and manage our responses to them. (For example, recognizing that someone is emotionally upset and taking the time to listen patiently and show appropriate empathy.)

What's important about emotional intelligence?

Improving emotional intelligence means improving all aspects of our life, at work and in our personal life, and in our individual and group relationships. In the book *The Millionaire Mind* by Thomas Stanley, 733 United States multi-millionaires were asked to rate the factors (out of 30) that were most responsible for their success. The top five were:

- Being honest with people
- Being well disciplined
- Getting along with people
- Having a supportive spouse
- Working harder than most people

All five factors are based on emotional intelligence. IQ was rated 21st out of 30 factors and only 20 percent of the millionaires endorsed it at all. Repeatedly, in all categories of jobs and in all kinds of organizations, studies show that *emotional intelligence* mattered *at least twice as much* as IQ. Improvement in emotional intelligence means improvement in effectiveness in connecting with everyone at work and in other spheres of life.

In *Emotional Intelligence 2.0* Travis Bradberry and Jean Greaves describe the advantages of mastering the skills of connecting:

"People who manage relationships well are able to see the benefit of connecting with many different people, even those they are not fond of. Solid relationships are something that should be sought and cherished. They are the result of how you understand people; how you treat them and the history you share.

"The weaker the connection you have with someone, the harder it is to get your point across. If you want people to listen, you have to practice relationship management and seek benefits from every relationship, especially the challenging ones. The difference between an interaction and a relationship is a matter of frequency. It's a product of the quality, depth, and time you spend interacting with another person."

Awareness of our similarities and attractions to other enneagram types, wings, and subtypes offer rich territory for finding ways to connect with the people we meet.

3

A Deeper Look at the Strategies

TYPE ONE--THE PERFECTIONIST: STRIVING TO BE PERFECT

"I believe that every right implies a responsibility; every opportunity an obligation; every possession a duty." **John D. Rockefeller, Jr.**

Perfectionists are striving to be perfect. They are idealists who desire to be good, correct, proper, logical, principled, self-controlled, reliable, and purposeful. They are serious, industrious, and conscientious. Ones are focused on rules, procedures, reforming and improving, and making sure that they are always doing the right thing; they want to make the world a better place. Perfectionists fear becoming defective, bad, irresponsible, immoral, incorrect, and dishonest. Stressed Perfectionists can be unbending, self-righteous, and critical, and focus more on avoiding mistakes than being good. Their fear of being flawed can hold them back from taking action.

SUBTYPES OF THE PERFECTIONIST

Intimate: Jealousy
Intimate Ones desire the perfect relationship. They want their partners to be 100 percent dedicated to them. They fantasize that this relationship is one-of-a-kind and that both parties share similar values and standards. Perfectionists

watch their partner's actions carefully and judge them on how committed their partner is to them and to the relationship. Stressed Ones are demanding and controlling and can verbally lash out with accusations of unfaithfulness for even innocent behavior. They fear that someone a bit more "perfect" may encroach on their territory. Their repressed anger is expressed as jealousy aimed at anyone who may jeopardize their perfect relationship. They are occasionally confused with Eights because both types share a heightened passion and an invasive anger.

Social: Inadaptability

Social Ones feel that they represent *the* correct social norms and values and that it is their job to pronounce them to the world. They are compelled to take a stand for what is right, to crusade for the correct cause, and to preach, teach, and moralize. Stressed Ones' behavior can become myopic and petty; their rigid social ideals, their tendency to see the world in black and white, and their literalism ("You said you'd meet me at one o'clock, not five minutes after!") can appear as criticism, anger and stubbornness. They may show their inflexibility and anger with complaining about "shoulds" and "should nots," or by exiting a "late" meeting in a dramatic display of indignity.

Self-Preservation: Worry

Self-Preservation Ones focus on their material well-being, and try to overcome anxiety with hard work. They worry about being "good enough" to survive, and focus on the perfect food, job, and shelter. They try to play it safe and obsess about making the right decisions about their health, job, and physical activity. They are concerned over making mistakes and being judged negatively, and that people won't approve of them, thus jeopardizing their ability to survive. Stressed Self-Preservation Ones can be workaholics, fearing that they won't measure up. They can be overly focused on hygiene, fitness, and nutrition. They are anxious or overly self-controlled and envious of others who seem to have it easier than they do. Their obsession about what could go wrong can make Self-Preservation Ones resemble Sixes.

WINGS OF THE PERFECTIONIST

The One With a Nine Wing
Ones who favor their Nine wing are discerning and philosophical. They have high standards and tend to see the world as a disorderly place that needs fixing. They maintain an ideal image of how things should be, but keep their distance, preferring a more withdrawn, cerebral approach to reforming things. True idealists, they dream about the perfect relationship and the utopian world. The influence of their Nine wing makes this style of One less energetic and less judgmental than the One with a Two wing. Less aware Ones with a Nine Wing can fall prey to procrastination when they put off doing important things fearing that they won't be done perfectly.

The One With a Two Wing
The Two wing makes Ones more concerned and caring about making things right. They are more extroverted and more energetic than the more idealistic One with the Nine wing. Both Ones and Twos believe they should be good, and this combination creates a concerned, warmer One—a person who wants to roll up her sleeves and make changes. This One is a crusader for what is just and right, and combines discernment, advocacy, and selfless action in the service of changing things for the better. Less aware Ones with a Two Wing can neglect their own needs in deference to the needs of others. When their hard work is not appreciated they can become hurt and disappointed, resulting in anger, resentment, and criticism toward the offending parties.

THE PERFECTIONIST'S EMOTIONAL INTELLIGENCE SUMMARY SCORECARD

The following list does not address all the competencies related to establishing and maintaining relationships. It includes only the most obvious strengths and challenges normally identified with Type One. Depending on emotional maturity, life experience, and particularly the Perfectionist's degree of stress, all of the items may not apply. Consider this list a starting point for personal inquiry.

Strengths	Challenges
Self-Control: restraint over one's impulses, emotions, or desires	*Self-Awareness:* identifying one's thought processes, emotions, and skills
Trustworthiness: maintaining standards of honesty and integrity	*Empathy:* awareness of and participation in other's feelings, ideas, and needs
Resiliency: capacity to endure in the face of obstacles	*Optimism:* ability to anticipate and expect the best possible outcome
Achievement Drive: meeting or improving standards of excellence	*Adaptability:* flexibility in handling change

THE PERFECTIONIST'S RELATIONSHIP DILEMMA

A Perfectionist's high standards, logic, precision, and goodness can be attractive. It is easy to be drawn to their high morals and ethics. They trigger the part in us that wants to do good, to follow the rules, get in shape, eat the right foods, etc. Our own "perfectionist" part keeps us in line, gets us to work on time, and puts us on the straight and narrow—and there is something very appealing there.

The dilemma is that Ones can focus on what is wrong in a relationship and what needs fixing. If Ones don't balance their desire to make the relationship perfect with acceptance and compassion, we may find their suggestions for improvement to be critical and judgmental. Their need for the highest quality may lose its luster and feel more like a never-ending drive for the unreachable goal. Under stress Perfectionists can be too serious, and can forget about having fun and enjoying the relationship and life in general. If Perfectionists don't temper their controlling and micromanaging with patience and openness, we may feel frustrated and put off. "She's perfect," may feel like "She's never satisfied."

WHAT PERFECTIONISTS HIDE FROM OTHERS

"I'm not as perfect as I appear to be." *Anger* and frustration cause Ones to resent having flaws and to try to hide them. They fear that if they are seen as less than perfect they will lose their voice of moral authority. Their internal story of "I must always be perfect" hides their deep fear of being corrupt or "bad."

THE GIFTS OF THE PERFECTIONIST

Ones bring precision to a relationship. They are methodical and can make clear, logical decisions about appropriate action and behavior.

Ones excel at setting and following rules. They are consistent, reliable, and rigorous.

Ones provide us with great examples of honesty, logic, and morality. They are wise and discerning people who inspire us to recognize injustices and attempt to fix them.

Aware Ones express the virtue of serenity. They allow themselves and others to be "works in progress," who need no judging, fixing, or tinkering. They accept situations just as they are, without trying to change, improve or control them.

At their best Ones embody the quality of clarity. They see reality as it is without prejudice and preconception. Aware Perfectionists embody the vision of goodness, fullness, impeccability, and purity, not in a moralistic way, but in the sense of the brilliance and clarity of pure, clear water. They see reality with great wisdom, as it truly is, as if to say, "I can see this clearly. I know what it is. I've got the whole picture."

Summary of The Perfectionist's Strategy Relationships

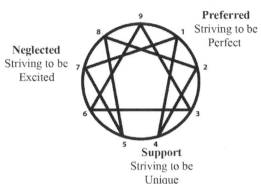

Preferred
Striving to be
Perfect

Neglected
Striving to be
Excited

Support
Striving to be
Unique

Preferred Strategy	*Neglected Strategy*	*Support Strategy*
Striving to be Perfect (1) *Aware* Ones at Point 1 prefer striving to be perfect in an open-minded way. They are moral, task-oriented, efficient, and "straight-laced." They are models of decorum, clear logic, and proper behavior. *Stressed* Ones at Point 1 distort "perfect" into "repressed" and can be rigid and critical of themselves and others. They are literalists and see things in black and white.	**Striving to be Excited (7)** *Aware* Ones at Point 7 balance perfection with excitement. They are accepting and open to new ideas, capable of showing enthusiasm, and having fun, often with a dry humor. *Stressed* Ones at Point 7 "neglect" this strategy, misinterpret it as *irresponsible*, and fear that if they have too much fun, they'll make mistakes and become corrupt. They resist change and spontaneity.	**Striving to be Unique (4)** *Aware* Ones at Point 4 use uniqueness to support their desire to be perfect. They stand alone, crusaders for correctness. They embrace the role of moral authority, willing to make a commitment for what they think is right. *Stressed* Ones at Point 4 try to force their unique view of correctness on others and feel alienated when others disagree. Rejected, they become angry and disenchanted.

TYPE TWO–THE HELPER: STRIVING TO BE CONNECTED

"The whole idea of compassion is based on a keen awareness of the interdependence of all these living beings, which are all part of one another, and all involved in one another."
Thomas Merton

Helpers are striving to be connected. They are generous, caring, and empathic. They focus on nurturing relationships, and helping people get what they want. They are friendly and outgoing, build rapport naturally, and quickly bond with others. They are sensitive and considerate and draw people to them. Stressed Twos overdo striving to be connected and may impose inappropriate "help" on others; they can fail to take care of their own needs and become emotionally dependent on others. They demand attention from others. Stressed Twos fear that if they are not closely connected to others they will become useless and isolated.

SUBTYPES OF THE HELPER

Intimate: Aggression/Seduction
Intimate Twos use their charm, flattery, and keen rapport-building ability to connect with select and often powerful people. They use body language, expressive tones and words in seductive, but not necessarily sexual ways. Intimate Twos can be aggressive in their pursuit of personal recognition. They have a strong need to be desired, approved of, and to find personal value through love. Both male and female Intimate Twos can have an obsessive desire to bond with an elusive partner. Male Intimate Twos use aggression to overcome obstacles to union, and female Intimate Twos use seduction to prove their desirability. Both genders seek to win the prize that will bring them the acceptance they yearn for. They can be confused with Eights because both types share the habit of "collecting conquests."

Social: Ambition
Social Twos seduce through achievement. They are drawn to powerful people and they market themselves well, through propaganda, flamboyance, or

"blowing their own horn." Acceptance is sought through both social approval and accomplishments. They are masters at empathizing and tuning into other people's needs to create an important, even indispensable role in a person's life, within a group or cause. Being connected with the "movers and shakers" is usually more important than being in charge or taking center stage. The Social Two's deep need to belong is combined with their ambition to fit into social hierarchies and to be seen as special and important in whatever group they set their sights on. They are the most aggressive Twos, and seduce through achievement, power, and influence. Social Twos can resemble Social Threes.

Self-Preservation: Privilege

Self-Preservation Twos take care of others so others will take care of them. They create comfortable, personable relationships with people, hoping to become someone's "favorite." Because they focus on supporting and nurturing others, Self-Preservation Twos can develop a sense of entitlement, or "me first," when it comes to getting their needs met. They often have a child-like quality—a desire to be Mommy's or Daddy's favorite—and can become co-dependent in their relationships. They see themselves as special, but can exhibit a false modesty, or even a martyr quality, insisting that others go before them, while secretly desiring to be asked to go to the front of the line. They may be confused with Fours because both types share a self-absorbed quality.

WINGS OF THE HELPER

The Two With a One Wing

Helpers who favor their One wing are serious and interested in alleviating suffering. The reforming quality of Type One combines with the Two's need to help and be of service. They are discerning and objective in their assessment of who needs help, and they resist playing favorites. They are stereotypical Good Samaritans who criticize themselves about not doing enough, and are often bothered by guilt. Both Twos with a One wing and Twos with a Three wing turn to others to feel good about themselves and can become dependent on people. Twos with a One wing follow the rules, avoid breaking emotional boundaries and focus on correcting wrongs and improving bad situations. Less aware Twos with a One Wing can be zealots, swept up by justice—helping the downtrodden and righting wrongs—while neglecting their own needs.

The Two With a Three Wing

This style of Helper is highly motivated to be successful, like a Three. They seek connection through personal relationship and use charm, warmth, and charisma to be noticed and loved. They are sociable, friendly, and take pleasure in hosting parties, facilitating meetings, and entertaining their favorite people. They are organized and goal oriented and can be workaholics. They are great team players and delegators without the need to do everything, especially the "dirty work." While they have their favorites and like to help others and be the "power behind the thrown," this Two learns to adapt and to function well with different people in different situations. Less aware Twos with a Three Wing desire to be seen with influential people and can become overly focused on "managing up"—selectively helping those who can help their career or advancement.

THE HELPER'S EMOTIONAL INTELLIGENCE SUMMARY SCORECARD

The following list does not address all the competencies related to establishing and maintaining relationships. It includes only the most obvious strengths and challenges typically identified with Type Two. Depending on emotional maturity, life experience, and particularly the Helper's degree of stress, all of the items may not apply. Consider this list a starting point for personal inquiry.

Strengths	Challenges
Empathy: awareness of and participation in other's feelings, ideas, and needs	*Self-Awareness:* ability to identify one's thought processes, emotions, and skills
Optimism: ability to anticipate and expect the best possible outcome	*Self-Control:* restraint over one's impulses, emotions, or desires
Cooperation: working with others toward shared goals	*Self-Confidence:* confidence in one's powers and abilities
Communication: listening openly and sending convincing messages	*Achievement Drive:* meeting or improving standards of excellence

THE HELPER'S RELATIONSHIP DILEMMA

A Helper's nurturing nature, generosity, and ability to anticipate what we need, (sometimes before we know it ourselves) can be very attractive. We feel cared for and paid attention to. Twos can make themselves indispensable to us. They trigger the part in us that wants to reach out and help people. Our own "connected" part keeps us in relationships, encourages us to pick up the phone and call a friend, to be empathic, and to consider the needs of others before our own—and there is something very appealing there.

The dilemma is that the Two's love and empathy may come with strings attached. We may find that something is expected for all this attention, and we are often clueless what that something is. Under stress Twos may expect us to anticipate *their* needs as well as they can read ours. You'll hear them say things like, "If you loved me, you'd know what I want," and "I shouldn't have to tell you." Often, of course, we don't need what they're giving because they're giving to get something *they* want. If Helpers don't balance their neediness and codependence with respect for our private space and independence, we may feel consumed by them. "He's so loving," can feel like "He's smothering me."

WHAT HELPERS HIDE FROM OTHERS

"I'm not as caring as I appear to be." *Pride* prevents Twos from overtly expressing their needs, so they must get their needs met indirectly. Twos believe that by appearing to be helpful, others will be helpful to them. It is as if they are doing good deeds for "good deed" vouchers that they can cash in later. Their internal story of "I must always be connected" hides their deep fear of being unloved.

THE GIFTS OF THE HELPER

Twos bring empathy to a relationship. Helpers are skilled at understanding what people need, and expressing empathy toward others. They are emotionally considerate, sensitive, and warm.

Twos excel at helping others thrive. Twos are supportive and are great second lieutenants who help others succeed.

Twos provide us with great examples of service, goodness, and caring. Helpers value people and inspire us to create an atmosphere of kindness and wellbeing.

Aware Twos express the virtue of humility. Helpers are humble, able to love others genuinely without the need for approval, praise, or the appreciation of others.

At their best Twos embody the quality of love. Helpers have the special ability to understand and express compassion and kindness towards others without the need to express love by flattering or forcing their affections. They don't see themselves as "special agents of love." Instead, they express a more inclusive attitude, as if to say, "Love is everywhere, and everyone is equally deserving of love."

Summary of The Helper's Strategy Relationships

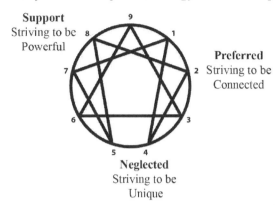

Support
Striving to be
Powerful

Preferred
Striving to be
Connected

Neglected
Striving to be
Unique

Preferred Strategy	*Neglected Strategy*	*Support Strategy*
Striving to be Connected (2)	**Striving to be Unique (4)**	**Striving to be Powerful (8)**
Aware Twos at Point 2 are selfless and caring. They help people meet their needs, and build rapport easily.	*Aware* Twos at Point 4 are willing and undaunted to stand alone, independent, and without the need to be noticed, acknowledged and admired by others.	*Aware* Twos at Point 8 use their influence and power with people to *make things happen*, which helps them stay connected.
Stressed Twos at Point 2 distort "connection" into "dependence," seek to be aligned with important people, have difficulty setting boundaries and may fail to take care of their own needs.	*Stressed* Twos at Point 4 "neglect" this strategy, misrepresent it as *isolation*, and fear that if they are too "different" they will lose their connection with people.	*Stressed* Twos at Point 8 can be aggressive, controlling, and manipulative, They may force people to take sides ("It's me or them."), and coerce people into behaving the way the Two thinks they should.

TYPE THREE–THE PERFORMER: STRIVING TO BE OUTSTANDING

"The value of achievement lies in the achieving." **Albert Einstein**

Performers are striving to be Outstanding. They are organized, competent, competitive, pragmatic, and make great efforts to be the best at whatever they try. They are goal-oriented, polished, politically astute, and place great value on productivity and presenting an image of high achievement. Threes are positive, influential, and charming. They adapt easily and challenge themselves to win. Stressed Threes overdo striving to be outstanding and seek attention. They may inflate their importance and accomplishments. They believe that "image is everything" and fear that if they are not obsessively working and marketing themselves they will become mediocre.

SUBTYPES OF THE PERFORMER

Intimate: Masculine/Feminine

Intimate Threes aspire to have, at least in Western culture, a "movie star" quality. They seek approval and recognition around gender identity and appeal. They create an image that is based on being the most attractive and desirable man or woman in the group. They compete with others about being the best "catch," and will shape themselves to become what they think is most appealing to their desired object. Image is key with this subtype, with a tendency to stay in a performer's role no matter what the environment or relationship. The male Intimate Three emphasizes his strength and masculinity, but his strength may be more based on *looking* strong and tough than actually being that way. Similarly, the female Intimate Three may confuse femininity with looking like the latest starlet, and wearing the most fashionable clothes and make-up. Ultimately, Intimate Threes see sex appeal as the key to being desired and accepted, and will take on the characteristics of the person they are trying to connect with. Intimate Threes are sometimes confused with Intimate Sixes.

Social: Prestige

Social Threes gain praise, admiration, and approval by having a prestigious social image. They focus on how they are perceived by their target group, and doing whatever is necessary to be seen in the right light. Their drive for acceptance and success is directed toward winning social approval and achieving status in social institutions. To that end, they strive to know the right people, live in the right neighborhood, and profess the values of the right groups—whether they are country clubs, volunteer organizations, church groups, or political parties. They strive to be the best and most admired in any group they belong to. Sometimes labeled chameleons, Social Threes can change their image and behavior to fit into whatever desired group they are with.

Self-Preservation: Security

Self-Preservation Threes seek security through money and a safe, reliable position. Classic workaholics, they believe that financial success is the surest way to security. And security can be a moving target for them. If a million dollars in the bank created a feeling of safety at age 30, they may need ten million at age 40. They present the image of success and are often seen as the person who "has it all together:" the most expensive house, the best car, the most attractive mate, and the fattest wallet. Second best won't do for Self-Preservation Threes; they have to have the best and the most. They compete for resources, constantly seeking approval for their accomplishments. Stressed Self-Preservation Threes may compete fiercely with their own peers and family members to be seen as the best.

WINGS OF THE PERFORMER

The Three With a Two Wing

Threes with a Two wing are more people oriented, more caring, fun loving, and generous than Threes with a Four wing. Their focus is not solely on work and professional achievement. They seek satisfaction in personal relationships, and in their public and private lives. They draw people to them with their charm, appeal, and attractiveness. These Threes are conscious of the image they project and how their desirability can help them achieve their goals. Extremely adaptable, they can take on different images to be successful in intimate and social settings. Less aware Threes with a Two Wing become overly adapted to the needs of others. They become more and more outwardly directed and lose their personal identity by pleasing people and becoming indispensable.

The Three With a Four Wing

These Threes are more introspective and they are interested in personal and professional development. Less prone to changing image and adapting themselves to others, they are serious minded and committed to excellence. They appreciate art, beauty, and fashion for its aesthetics and not simply for its ability to attract attention. They are dedicated people and can resemble Ones in their drive for excellence and being the best. These Threes gain self-esteem from their career achievements. They measure themselves by their professional rather than personal qualities, and by the success of their latest project. A less aware Three with a Four Wing combines feelings of uniqueness with superiority and can be overly sensitive to criticism or failure. They can become depressed and distant when they are not recognized for their achievements.

THE PERFORMER'S EMOTIONAL INTELLIGENCE SUMMARY SCORECARD

The following list does not address all the competencies related to establishing and maintaining relationships. It includes only the most obvious strengths and challenges typically identified with Type Three. Depending on emotional maturity, life experience, and particularly the Performer's degree of stress, all of the items may not apply. Consider this list a starting point for personal inquiry.

Strengths	Challenges
Self-Confidence: confidence in one's powers and abilities	*Cooperation:* working with others toward shared goals
Adaptability: flexibility in handling change	*Empathy:* awareness of and participation in other's feelings, ideas, and needs
Resiliency: capacity to endure in the face of obstacles	*Trustworthiness:* maintaining standards of honesty and integrity
Achievement Drive: meeting or improving standards of excellence	*Conflict Management:* negotiating and resolving disputes

THE PERFORMER'S RELATIONSHIP DILEMMA

A Performer's focus on achieving, competing to be the best, working hard, looking good, and being successful can make them very attractive. We can feel secure that the Three's ambition will help insure that the bills are paid and our future is on solid ground. Threes motivate us to set ambitious goals and to work hard to accomplish them. They trigger the part in us that wants to achieve and have our contributions noticed and rewarded. Our "outstanding" part keeps our nose to the grind stone and keeps us striving to do more with our gifts—and there is something very appealing there.

The dilemma is that Threes can put so much effort into creating the right image that they—and we—don't know who they really are. We may be happy at first with their dedication to work and their great image, but will grow weary of not being the priority in the relationship. Before long, we resent coming in a distant fourth after work, marketing, and networking. Stressed Threes avoid expressing feelings, viewing them as a hindrance to being productive. The relationship may have been a goal at one time for the Three, but now that the goal is achieved, it's on to the next goal. If Performers don't balance their constant goal-oriented behavior with relaxing and enjoying life and the relationship, we may feel we are always chasing them on *their* treadmill and always in their shadow. "He's such a success," may feel like "I hardly ever see him."

WHAT PERFORMERS HIDE FROM OTHERS

"I'm not as together as I appear to be." *Self-deception* causes Threes to present an "all together" image because anything less would not meet their need to be the best. They can't face the possibility that others would see them as unsuccessful or incapable. Their internal story of "I must always be outstanding" hides their deep fear of being worthless.

THE GIFTS OF THE PERFORMER

Threes bring achievement to the relationship. Performers are accomplished and seek success in everything they do.

Threes excel at being in the spotlight. Performers thrive on being noticed for their accomplishments and are naturally at ease in front of a group.

Threes provide us with great examples of effectiveness, motivation, and success. Performers are great mentors and motivators who inspire us to work for the good of people and to delight in another's success and accomplishments.

Aware Threes express the virtue of truthfulness. Performers present themselves honestly and openly, not overly concerned with the perfect image; they allow us to see them, warts and all.

At their best Threes embody the quality of value. Performers demonstrate their inherent worth independent of accomplishment, rank, or status, whose value does not depend on their latest success. Threes live without the need to impress, embellish, or gain the good opinion of others, as if to say, "My value, like everyone's value, is based on the simple fact of being human."

Summary of The Performer's Strategy Relationships

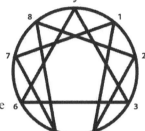

Support
Striving to be
Peaceful

Neglected
Striving to be
Secure

Preferred
Striving to be
Outstanding

Preferred Strategy	*Neglected Strategy*	*Support Strategy*
Striving to be Outstanding (3)	**Striving to be Secure (6)**	**Striving to be Peaceful (9)**
Aware Threes at Point 3 are organized, goal-oriented, accomplished, productive, and optimistic.	*Aware* Threes at Point 6 use achievement to ensure that they are contributing to the group and that their position and accomplishments create security.	*Aware* Threes at Point 9 are relaxed and demonstrate an air of calm competence, and the confident, polished persona of a professional.
Stressed Threes at Point 3 distort "outstanding" into "*attention-seeking*." They emphasize image over content, and want others to be aware of their accomplishments, possessions and attributes.	*Stressed* Threes at Point 6 "neglect" this strategy, misinterpret it as *mediocrity*, and fear that if they become too secure (comfortable) they will lose their drive to be outstanding.	*Stressed* Threes at Point 9 look to others for cues on how they should behave, and may act relaxed to disguise their anxiety over meeting challenges.

TYPE FOUR–THE INDIVIDUALIST: STRIVING TO BE UNIQUE

"To be oneself, simply oneself, is so amazing and utterly unique an experience that it's hard to convince oneself so singular a thing happens to everybody." **Simone de Beauvoir**

Individualists are striving to be unique. They are sensitive, intuitive, refined, and live in fresh and creative ways. They seek people and experiences that are elegant or unusual. They adhere to elite standards and seek emotional intensity. Individualists recognize the beauty in people and nature that is frequently missed by others. Stressed Fours overdo striving to be unique; they isolate themselves, and feel unappreciated and misunderstood. They can become emotionally volatile, angry, and overly dramatic. Stressed Individualists fear that if they don't put their own authentic stamp on their world their individuality will become stifled.

SUBTYPES OF THE INDIVIDUALIST

Intimate: Competition
Intimate Fours are competitive in all of their relationships, but especially their intimate ones. Competition is used to overcome a feeling of inner deficiency. They believe that love is scarce and must be fought for with members of their own sex. They try to persuade potential rivals and objects of their attention of their superiority and their willingness to fight for what is theirs. Envy, and even hatred, can play a part in their aggressive stance. Convinced that they should have what others have, they seek to eliminate threats to their success. Stressed Intimate Fours are intense, dramatic, and volatile. Their rivals' power or attractiveness is seen as a personal challenge and their self-worth increases or decreases in comparison with "the competition."

Social: Shame
Social Fours feel that the world has specific standards that they can't meet. Feelings of inadequacy and shame are provoked by social situations, with

envy directed toward other people's status or connections. They sense that they don't fit in—that something is fundamentally missing in them, so they may try hard to follow the rules, and can appear awkward and overly formal. Social Fours struggle to resolve their tension between individual authenticity and an acceptable social role. They experience shame about both desiring love and wanting the prestige of the social class. Stressed Social Fours feel deficient, often throwing negative barbs at themselves, such as "I'm stupid," "I'm ugly," and "I'm unlovable." Social Fours may depend on their membership in exclusive organizations to bolster their sense of deficiency and lack of confidence.

Self-Preservation: Dauntlessness

Self-Preservation Fours are willing to take great risks to achieve their dreams. They are less dependent and more self-contained than other Fours—less demanding of the world, they are demanding of themselves, determined to leap into new situations, or to pack up and move across the country when something more authentic appears elsewhere. Their tenaciousness and ambition can make them look a bit like Threes. Their behavior may appear reckless to others as though they are casting their fate to the wind, but to the Self-Preservation Four they are making the necessary sacrifices, often at great cost, to get what they feel they need to survive. They experience tension between wanting material security and feeling bored and detached from it all.

WINGS OF THE INDIVIDUALIST

The Four With a Three Wing

Fours with a Three Wing are creative and enterprising, productive and achievement oriented. They are more outgoing and talkative than other Fours and can be very ambitious. They desire to express their creative side in useable, socially accepted ways, and have a keen eye for what is practical, yet inspirational. These Fours are distinctive, with good taste and a dislike of anything mundane or off-putting. They seek recognition for their accomplishments and creations and are very conscious of their image and the opinions of others. They may have a flare for the extravagant, while still seeking refinement and sophistication. Less aware Fours with a Three Wing exhibit more image than substance and can be outrageous in appearance and more artificial than authentic.

The Four With a Five Wing
These Individualists are distinctively creative and tend to express themselves in unconventional ways. They combine emotional introspection with intellectual curiosity and rational objectivity. They are more introverted and restrained than Fours with a Three Wing and are at home in their imagination and fantasies. They enjoy the exotic and the esoteric. Whereas their Four counterparts create with an end product and a clear audience in mind, these Fours are more interested in the creative process itself and create more for themselves than for others. They see themselves as mysteries to be explored and analyzed. A bit "in the world but not of it," they can be minimalists, eccentrics, and bohemians. Less aware Fours with a Five Wing can over-analyze and over think things and retreat into an intellectual maze, more interested in fantasy than reality. They withdraw from people and relationships feeling misunderstood and "on the outside looking in."

THE INDIVIDUALIST'S EMOTIONAL INTELLIGENCE SUMMARY SCORECARD

The following list does not address all the competencies related to establishing and maintaining relationships. It includes only the most obvious strengths and challenges typically identified with Type Four. Depending on emotional maturity, life experience, and particularly the Individualist's degree of stress, all of the items may not apply. Consider this list a starting point for personal inquiry.

Strengths	Challenges
Self-Awareness: ability to identify one's thought processes, emotions, and skills	*Self-Confidence:* confidence in one's powers and abilities
Trustworthiness: maintaining standards of honesty and integrity	*Optimism:* ability to anticipate and expect the best possible outcome
Empathy: awareness of and participation in other's feelings, ideas, and needs	*Adaptability:* flexibility in handling change
Communication: listening openly and sending convincing messages	*Achievement Drive:* meeting or improving standards of excellence

THE INDIVIDUALIST'S RELATIONSHIP DILEMMA

An Individualist's sense of authenticity, appreciation of beauty, search for truth and meaning, and commitment to find that "one special person" can be attractive. They make us feel special when they relate to us with depth and genuine interest. They trigger the part in us that wants to be original, artistic, romantic, and open to life's more intense side. Our own "unique" part helps us see our authenticity, special gifts, and deeper, more emotional side—it encourages us to find the meaning and purpose of our life—and there is something very appealing there.

The dilemma is that Fours can focus on what is missing in life and in their relationship. They feel that what is close at hand is too mundane to make them feel complete, and fantasize that only something distant and exotic will satisfy their yearnings and solve their problems. Stressed Fours can become bored or depressed with the routine of ordinary life, believing that drama and intensity are barometers for an authentic life and relationship. Being in a relationship with a Four may be an emotional roller coaster ride—rejected when we get too close, then desired and wooed when we retreat. We may be originally drawn to the Four's depth and feeling but may grow weary of the intense emotionality. If Individualists don't balance their intensity with equanimity we may feel overwhelmed. "She's so romantic" can feel like "She's such a drama queen."

WHAT INDIVIDUALISTS HIDE FROM OTHERS

"I'm not as sensitive as I appear to be." *Envy* that other people are treated bett,er than they are leads Fours to cultivate an aura of emotional hypersensitivity, frustration and anger. They can become vindictive when they don't receive special treatment, believing that their expression of resentment is justified and will help compensate for the unfair way they have been treated. Their internal story of "I must always be unique" hides their deep fear of being ordinary, without a "real" identity.

THE GIFTS OF THE INDIVIDUALIST

Fours bring originality to a relationship. They see special qualities in themselves and others and create beauty and excellence without compromising quality.

Fours excel at appreciating and creating something different. Individualists love opportunities to express themselves, so they do well in relationships where they can add their own flare.

Fours provide us with great examples of authenticity, depth, and sensitivity. Individualists are imaginative, introspective people who inspire us to live life with depth, truth, and intensity.

Aware Fours express the virtue of equanimity. Individualists are mentally and emotionally calm, balanced and contented, and are evenly tempered in difficult times.

At their best Fours embody the quality of self-awareness. Individualists recognize their unique identity—filled with meaning, importance and originality. Aware Fours know that each person is a unique individual. They appreciate their own qualities and characteristics, without envy or comparison to others, as if to say, "I know and accept who I am and I trust that my gifts will serve me well."

Summary of The Individualist's Strategy Relationships

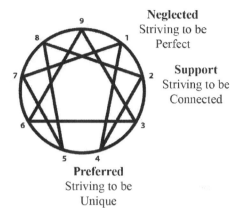

Neglected
Striving to be
Perfect

Support
Striving to be
Connected

Preferred
Striving to be
Unique

Preferred Strategy	*Neglected Strategy*	*Support Strategy*
Striving to be Unique (4)	**Striving to be Perfect (1)**	**Striving to be Connected (2)**
Aware Fours at Point 4 are inspirational, elegant, refined, creative, reflective, and sensitive.	*Aware* Fours at Point 1 are logical, insightful, intellectually precise, and objective observers.	*Aware* Fours at Point 2 understand others and build relationships with interesting, talented, and desirable people.
Stressed Fours at Point 4 distort "uniqueness" into "isolation," deal with the world by withdrawing, becoming melancholic, defiant, critical of themselves and others, and non-communicative.	*Stressed* Fours at Point 1 "neglect" this strategy, misinterpret it as *repression*, see rules as an obstacle to the expression of their uniqueness, and fear that their creativity will be stifled.	*Stressed* Fours at Point 2 may over-depend on approval from others and feel entitled; they can be demanding and possessive and hold unrealistic expectations for relationships.

TYPE FIVE–THE OBSERVER: STRIVING TO BE DETACHED

"To acquire knowledge, one must study; but to acquire wisdom, one must observe."
Marilyn vos Savant

Observers are striving to be detached. They are watchful, logical, analytical, self-sufficient, and reserved. They focus on problem solving, innovative ideas, and data gathering. Their mission is to make the world a more intelligent and enlightened place. Stressed Fives overdo striving to be detached and become distant, dry, and isolated from the expression of their emotions. They may act like "know-it-alls," as a way to defend themselves and dominate others with data. Stressed Fives fear that if they don't protect their privacy and resist the demands of others they will lose influence, confidence, and emotional control.

SUBTYPES OF THE OBSERVER

Intimate: Confidence
Intimate Fives don't see themselves as attractive and appealing and seek the one special person they feel confident enough to share their intimate moments and secrets with in order to overcome their inhibitions. Sex becomes a way to gain confidence more than an expression of love. Sharing insider information helps them feel safe and creates the foundation for forming a close relationship. They balance the tension of selecting someone whom they feel they can trust and connect with at a secretive level ("You're the only one I'd ever tell this to.") while still maintaining their autonomy. Intimate Fives can appear confident, and their assurance of their intellectual prowess may come off as arrogance.

Social: Totems
Social Fives want to be seen as a fount of knowledge. Extremely aware of the intellectual heroes of society, they yearn to be the next expert in the field, or to be the present expert's confidant. They hunger for knowledge and mastery of the totems—the symbols (diplomas, certificates, and degrees)—of the group they

wish to fit into. They see themselves as the interpreters, analyzers, and counselors of the group, creating a specialized niche that they own. They also *collect* the symbols of their specialty—such as books, stamps, wines, smoking pipes, CDs, etc., —giving them special power and position. Social Fives share their totems as a way of connecting with people, but this sharing of totems rather than themselves may obstruct their more intimate connection with people.

Self-Preservation: Refuge

Self-Preservation Fives seek a secure place where they can feel at home. They subscribe to the axiom that a "man's home is his castle," and they desire to retreat into its safety. Having enough to survive without reliance on the outside world can make them stockpile supplies, especially money. Their refuge can be a room in their home, an attic study, or a camper parked in the driveway. They can be shy, and distant, desiring to avoid social contact. Stressed Self-Preservation Fives may have a disdain for social contact and an inability to confront or deal with anger. They may have no special loyalty for a geographical locale, as long as they can go to their refuge—their own safe place that shelters them from the demands of the world.

WINGS OF THE OBSERVER

The Five With a Four Wing

These Fives combine passion with perception and have a creative way of thinking. They are curious about life and art and seek to create a unique, personal vision. More introspective and creative than the Five with a Six wing, they are less interested in science and drawn to varied expressions of creativity and art, especially their own versions of it. They can be actively engaged in life, preferring to act rather than observe from the sidelines. Mixing the imaginative and the dramatic with analysis and rationality, their interests often lean toward the surreal, the magical, and the spiritual. Less aware Fives with a Four Wing can struggle with intense feelings, can be loners, and have difficulty relating to others.

The Five With a Six Wing

Although normally more interested in ideas and theories than people, Fives with a Six Wing can be very committed to the important people in their lives. They can become interested in groups and causes and defend them with great passion. Fives are normally detached, but the healthy Six wing helps Fives have the courage to become engaged, and the faith to trust in themselves. They are more practical and more assertive than Fives with a Four Wing and are drawn to technical, business, and intellectual fields. Less aware Fives with a Six wing are suspicious about the intentions of people and fear that others will invade their space. They can lose faith, become less confident, and seek safety by withdrawing from contact and engagement. Fearing what others think, particularly authority figures, they avoid standing up for themselves.

THE OBSERVER'S EMOTIONAL INTELLIGENCE SUMMARY SCORECARD

The following list does not address all the competencies related to establishing and maintaining relationships. It includes only the most obvious strengths and challenges typically identified with Type Five. Depending on emotional maturity, life experience, and particularly the Observer's degree of stress, all of the items may not apply. Consider this list a starting point for personal inquiry.

Strengths	Challenges
Self-Control: restraint over one's impulses, emotions, or desires	*Communication:* listening openly and sending convincing messages
Trustworthiness: maintaining standards of honesty and integrity	*Conflict Management:* negotiating and resolving disputes
Resiliency: capacity to endure in the face of obstacles	*Cooperation:* working with others toward shared goals
Achievement Drive: meeting or improving standards of excellence	*Empathy:* awareness of and participation in others' feelings, ideas, and needs

THE OBSERVER'S RELATIONSHIP DILEMMA

An Observer's quiet stillness, keen observational skills, depth of knowledge, and problem solving skills can be attractive. They can be fascinating, fun companions who seem to have an endless supply of information and sage advice. They trigger the part in us that is introspective, quiet, insightful, and comfortable with our intuition. Our own "detached" part helps us observe the activities of life and make sense of our world and relationships with unemotional, logical discernment—and there is something appealing there.

The dilemma is that Fives often view what people want from them as demands. They measure how much emotional commitment they will be required to make. Questions about the relationship or how they feel can cause them anxiety. They have a great need for privacy; prefer observing over participating, and thinking over feeling. We originally may be drawn to their self-sufficiency, ability to remain detached during chaos, and their exceptional analytical skills. However, if Observers don't balance their intense desire for privacy (which may feel like secrecy) and their difficulty accessing and talking about feelings, with connection and openness, we may feel ignored or rejected. "She's so wise" may feel like "She's so distant."

WHAT OBSERVERS HIDE FROM OTHERS

"I'm not as smart as I appear to be." *Holding back* keeps Fives from sharing their emotional life with others; therefore they relate through their intellect. They find their source of strength in their intelligence and knowledge, using them to keep people from getting too close. Their internal story of "I must always be detached" hides their deep fear of being helpless, incapable, and out of control.

THE GIFTS OF THE OBSERVER

Fives bring insight to a relationship. Observers can analyze and synthesize their observations, and see what other don't. Observers are perceptive listeners who help others understand the meaning of their own experience.

Fives excel at figuring things out. Observers are experts in situations where they need to investigate, analyze, research, innovate, and solve complex problems.

Fives provide us with great examples of wisdom, understanding, and analysis. Observers are independent witnesses who inspire us to understand people and the world.

Aware Fives express the virtue of non-attachment. Observers gather just what is needed and nothing more, with discernment and objectivity.

At their best Fives embody the essential quality of intuition. Observers experience an inner knowing and guidance in a deeply embodied and experiential way—a wisdom that is complete, and requires no gathering of additional information or analysis—as if to say "I've got a 'gut' feeling about this. I know what to do and what is possible."

Summary of The Observer's Strategy Relationships

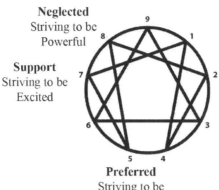

Neglected
Striving to be
Powerful

Support
Striving to be
Excited

Preferred
Striving to be
Detached

Preferred Strategy	*Neglected Strategy*	*Support Strategy*
Striving to be Detached (5)	**Striving to be Powerful (8)**	**Striving to be Excited (7)**
Aware Fives at Point 5 are curious, engaged, observant, logical, data driven, insightful, analytical, reserved, logical, and wise.	*Aware* Fives at Point 8 move their ideas into action, and can be interested in power, influence, and leadership positions.	*Aware* Fives at Point 7 eagerly dive into projects and enthusiastically engage in analysis with creativity and curiosity.
Stressed Fives at Point 5 distort "detached" into "remote," hold onto feelings and thoughts, preferring isolation to engagement. They may be distant, disengaged, and lack vitality.	*Stressed* Fives at Point 8 "neglect" this strategy, misinterpret it as *being uncontrolled,* and fear that if they don't restrain themselves they will become overwhelmed.	*Stressed* Fives at Point 7 can be distracted, forgetful, and manic if obsessed by intellectual pursuits; they can be unresponsive to normal expectations and social norms.

TYPE SIX–THE GUARDIAN: STRIVING TO BE SECURE

"Never let the fear of striking out get in your way." **Babe Ruth**

Guardians are striving to be secure. They are loyal, hospitable, energetic, cautious, and responsible. They find security in being part of something bigger than themselves, and are protective of the welfare of their relationships, family, and group. They respect and honor traditions and shared history. Socially charming and resilient, Guardians thrive on open communication and emotional transparency. Stressed Sixes overdo striving to be secure and become suspicious and distrustful. They fail to take the risks necessary for high performance and may settle for mediocrity. Stressed Guardians fear that if they relax their guard they will be vulnerable to danger.

SUBTYPES OF THE GUARDIAN

Intimate: Strength and Beauty

Intimate Sixes use strength and beauty as a way of overcoming fear and anxiety about their appeal. They are "counter-phobic" –people who don't run from fear but confront it head on with authority, willpower, physical strength, and bravery—even while still feeling fearful. The term "warrior" fits well here. Intimate Sixes also use intellectual prowess and a strong ideological or ethical stance as a show of strength—an "I can't be intimidated!" approach. Female Intimate Sixes may use their beauty to quell their fears, becoming sexually alluring and seductive. They are aggressive and can be abrasive, and believe that the best defense is a good offense. Both males and females surround themselves with strong and attractive partners, create beauty in their environment, and are often drawn to danger and intrigue. These Sixes are sometimes confused with Social Eights.

Social: Duty

Social Sixes calm their fear by following the rules and protocols of society, and especially the family, group, or philosophy they are most aligned with.

Understanding their own role, expectations, duties, and the criteria for acceptance are major concerns. Being dutiful to an authority figure, to someone who has more power and influence, means being accommodating and deferential. They follow the rules and the commands of the leader, not out of devotion and commitment, but out of fear. However, there is ambivalence about authority, and if authority figures prove unworthy, a Social Six's duty can turn to rebellion. The price that Social Sixes pay for crossing the leader and breaking the rules is the loss of the safety and protection of the group.

Self-Preservation: Warmth

Self-Preservation Sixes deal with fear by appearing harmless, warm and agreeable. They are non-threatening people who make themselves endearing as a way of ensuring their survival. Anxiety about being "left out in the cold" forces Self-Preservation Sixes to avoid ruffling feathers and to take few risks that may jeopardize their acceptance and security. They are trying to disarm a perceived threat, as if to say, "I'm not dangerous, so you don't have to be dangerous either." They may show their weaknesses and vulnerabilities to get others to protect them. This Six appears more anxious than the Intimate or Social Sixes. They are often confused with Twos, especially when flattering and complimenting people.

WINGS OF THE GUARDIAN

The Six With a Five Wing

The Six with a Five Wing is normally reserved and introverted. They are more serious and more private than other Sixes. They can be great problem solvers and analysts. Gifted with a highly developed ability to concentrate and focus on their inner world, these Sixes are more confident than their counterparts and more apt to express their opinions and beliefs. The Five wing helps them observe with objectivity and less reactivity and anxiety, and to trust their own observations, decisions, and skills. Less suspicious, and less prone to the belief that "it's a jungle out there," Sixes with a Five Wing can relax and let their guard down. Less aware Sixes with a Five Wing lose their courage and desire to engage in the world. Mistrust creeps in and they can become loners, observing suspiciously from afar. They may become secretive and find security in dogmas and belief systems, and aggressively blame others for their problems.

The Six With a Seven Wing
These Sixes are sociable, charming, and more extroverted than Sixes with a Five Wing. They are engaging and funny and can be optimistic and positive. Their thinking is much less concerned about survival and security and "in" groups and "out" groups. They can embrace variety and options and different possibilities. Aware Sixes With a Seven Wing are less serious, reactive, and guarded, and able to laugh at themselves, particularly their tendency to see conspiracies around every corner. Family and friend oriented, they are better able to trust and relax easily with a variety of people. Outgoing and upbeat, they like to keep things light, avoiding the heavier, more philosophical discussions of the Six with the Five Wing. Less aware Sixes with a Seven Wing can be distracted and anxious, and engage in diversions or making plans as a way to quell their anxiety. They can have difficulty starting things and making decisions, and they can be overly dependent on the advice and reassurance of others.

THE GUARDIAN'S EMOTIONAL INTELLIGENCE SUMMARY SCORECARD

The following list does not address all the competencies related to establishing and maintaining relationships. It includes only the most obvious strengths and challenges typically identified with Type Six. Depending on emotional maturity, life experience, and particularly the Guardian's degree of stress, all of the items may not apply. Consider this list a starting point for personal inquiry.

Strengths	Challenges
Cooperation: working with others toward shared goals	*Optimism:* ability to anticipate and expect the best possible outcome
Trustworthiness: maintaining standards of honesty and integrity	*Adaptability:* flexibility in handling change
Resiliency: capacity to endure in the face of obstacles	*Self-Confidence:* confidence in one's powers and abilities
Self-Control: restraint exercised over one's impulses, emotions, or desires	*Conflict Management:* negotiating and resolving disputes

THE GUARDIAN'S RELATIONSHIP DILEMMA

A Six's loyalty, commitment, reliability and support can be attractive. It is easy to be drawn to their warmth, friendliness, resilience, and keen observational skills. They trigger the part in us that wants to be attentive, aware, and vigilant. Our own "secure" part keeps us watching and questioning, connecting the dots, and inquiring about people and our environment. They model for us a way to find safety and community in the world—and there is something appealing there.

The dilemma is that Guardians can focus too much on what is threatening in the world, and what is problematic in the relationship. They plan for the worst so they won't be surprised or feel unprepared or unprotected. They want us to share their hyper vigilance and can become fearful, frustrated, and confrontational if we don't. Under stress, a Six's imagination and ability to sniff out weak arguments and hidden agendas can look like paranoia and mistrust. Their attention to worst-case scenarios can extend to the relationship, and they may hunt for clues to validate their suspicions, often ignoring evidence to the contrary. They can harbor an unspoken fear that we will leave the relationship. If Guardians don't balance their suspicion with trust and acceptance they can cause anxiety and second-guessing in the people around them. "He's so careful," may feel like, "He's so paranoid."

WHAT GUARDIANS HIDE FROM OTHERS

"I'm not as committed as I appear to be." *Fear* of experiencing the wrath of an internal or external authority figure drives Sixes to be responsible and loyal. This responsibility makes them appear to be committed to a given cause, while in reality their commitment is to their own security. Their internal story, "I must always be secure," hides their deep fear that the worst will happen and they will be left alone, unsafe, and unprotected.

THE GIFTS OF THE GUARDIAN

Sixes bring support to a relationship. Guardians are steadfast, dedicated, and accountable. They are hardworking, determined, and committed to the needs of others.

Sixes excel at anticipating problems. Guardians are great in the "Devil's Advocate" role where they can consider worst-case scenarios and plan for potential challenges.

Sixes provide us with great examples of vigilance, duty, and safety. Guardians demonstrate what it means to be prepared and faithful, and inspire us toward tireless stability and security.

Aware Sixes express the virtue of courage. Guardians are fearless and dedicated to guarding and defending themselves and their loved ones.

At their best Sixes embody the quality of faith. Guardians believe that they can make decisions and take actions confident that they can bounce back from hardships. They hold the conviction that they have an anchor, an inner support, without the need to mistrust themselves or to build an outside support system, as if to say "I believe in myself, even in the face of doubt."

Summary of The Guardian's Strategy Relationships

Neglected
Striving to be
Peaceful

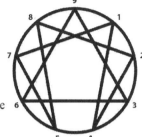

Preferred   **Support**
Striving to be   Striving to be
Secure   Outstanding

Preferred Strategy	*Neglected Strategy*	*Support Strategy*
Striving to be Secure (6)	**Striving to be Peaceful (9)**	**Striving to be Outstanding (3)**
Aware Sixes at Point 6 are vigilant, dutiful, careful, protective, consistent, and able to see through weak arguments and deceptive logic.	*Aware* Sixes at Point 9 use their skill at spotting and resolving potential problems to help them relax, feel safe, calm, and at peace. ("Work before play.")	*Aware* Sixes at Point 3 use being outstanding, accomplished, competitive, and productive to ensure their safety and security.
Stressed Sixes at Point 6 distort "security" into "mediocrity," avoid risks that can lead to achievement, can be fearful, suspicious, bureaucratic, and uncooperative.	*Stressed* Sixes at Point 9 "neglect" this strategy, misinterpret it as *passivity*, and fear that letting down their guard is irresponsible and leaves them vulnerable to unseen dangers.	*Stressed* Sixes at Point 3 may be overly competitive and boast about their achievements. They may also point out the shortcomings of others in order to gain security and ensure the safety of their position.

TYPE SEVEN—THE ENTHUSIAST: STRIVING TO BE EXCITED

"The real secret of success is enthusiasm. Yes, more than enthusiasm, I would say excitement. I like to see people get excited. When they get excited, they make a success of their lives." **Walter Chrysler**

Enthusiasts are striving to be excited. They are cheerful, upbeat, light-hearted, optimistic, joyful, and curious. They are inventive and entrepreneurial, and focus on options, possibilities and planning for the future. They are fun loving, like to talk, tell stories and keep people entertained. Under Stress, Sevens overdo striving to be excited and can become gluttonous, hyperactive, and manic. They may fail to complete things they have begun, become easily distracted, anxious, and act irresponsibly. Stressed Enthusiasts fear that if they don't stay active and fill their heads with enjoyable thoughts they may miss out on something exciting.

SUBTYPES OF THE ENTHUSIAST

Intimate: Suggestibility/Fascination
Intimate Sevens see infinite possibilities just around the corner. Impulsive and easily distracted, they crave the new and exotic. They are easily drawn to adventures, innovative ideas, and people, which can ignite a frenzy of planning and dreaming about their future. They are fascinated by novelty, intrigue, and newness. These Sevens may seek variety for variety's sake, and may have difficulty maintaining deep relationships. They have great imaginations and use their power of suggestion to influence others. Intimate Sevens can be confused with Fours because both types romanticize their relationships and project their fantasies onto their partners.

Social: Sacrifice
Social Sevens feel that their responsibilities and obligations to others should supersede their personal freedom. They achieve social acceptance by sacrificing themselves for the greater good of the group, family, or community. They are helpers and "do-gooders," willing to serve others to gain social recognition. This is similar to the Social Six's sense of duty and the One's idealism (creating

the "perfect" world). Social Sevens' sacrifices are in the service of a future that brings them the social standing that they believe they lack. Part of their planning invariably involves an idealized future when their obligations are satisfied and they can get on with fulfilling *their* dreams.

Self-Preservation: Like Minded People

Self-Preservation Sevens seek security in an extended family or a close-knit group of like-minded people. This circle of friends share common beliefs and interests and can be more important than their family of origin. These Sevens are earthy, fun loving, sensuous, and tender, and like to enjoy an abundant lifestyle. Optimistic and opportunistic, they are often good at business, and good at planning for a secure future. They enjoy fantasizing about fun projects and adventure, and sharing good ideas and good times with their nuclear and extended family. Drawn to a good time, Self-Preservation Sevens like to eat, drink, and be merry.

WINGS OF THE ENTHUSIAST

The Seven With a Six Wing

The Six wing helps Sevens focus on goals and activities in a responsible way. While Sevens are normally looking for options, excitement, and fun, Sevens with a Six Wing are more settled and less hyperactive; they are influenced by the Six's sense of loyalty and can commit to a trusted person or group. They are productive and supportive and enjoy life. These Sevens seem to have a lucky rabbit's foot in their pocket because things come easily to them. They seek variety, and people are drawn to their positive energy and playfulness. Less aware Sevens with a Six Wing appear anxious and fidgety, at times pacing and fussing. They doubt themselves and can resort to over planning and fast-talking as a substitute for following through on promises.

The Seven With an Eight Wing

These Sevens go for the gusto with joy and assertiveness. The Eight wing grounds them in the real world and helps them access their own power. The adventurous nature of the Seven combines with the ruggedness and strength of the Eight to create a fun-loving entrepreneur. They are driven to get all they can out of life. They are practical, determined, and willful. Sevens with an Eight Wing are less anxious and hyperactive than other Sevens. They don't see the world through rose-colored glasses as other Sevens; the Eight wing brings objectivity and directness to their perspective, and they have the strength and toughness to see the world as it is. Less aware Sevens with an Eight Wing are blunt and pushy. They demand what they want, and their normal playfulness about wanting more becomes self absorbed, demanding, and aggressive.

THE ENTHUSIAST'S EMOTIONAL INTELLIGENCE SUMMARY SCORECARD

The following list doesn't address all the competencies related to establishing and maintaining relationships. It includes only the most obvious strengths and challenges typically identified with Type Seven. Depending on emotional maturity, life experience, and particularly the Enthusiast's degree of stress, all of the items may not apply. Consider this list a starting point for personal inquiry.

Strengths	Challenges
Optimism: ability to anticipate and expect the best possible outcome	*Self-Control:* restraint exercised over one's impulses, emotions, or desires
Adaptability: flexibility in handling change	*Trustworthiness:* maintaining standards of honesty and integrity
Communication: listening openly and sending convincing messages	*Conflict Management:* negotiating and resolving disputes
Achievement Drive: meeting or improving standards of excellence	*Self-Awareness:* identifying one's thought processes, emotions, and skills

THE ENTHUSIAST'S RELATIONSHIP DILEMMA

An Enthusiast's positivity, joy, and delight in living can be attractive. It is easy to be drawn to their lightheartedness and enthusiasm. They trigger the part in us that wants to have fun, to be spontaneous, forget about our troubles, and act with abandon. Our own "excited" part keeps us positive, cheerful, adventurous, and young at heart—and there is something very appealing there.

The dilemma is that Sevens may obsess about avoiding what is unpleasant or uncomfortable. They focus on an idealized future where their options are open, and where there is little pain or emotional discomfort. While we may first be drawn to their passion for fun and adventure, life with a Seven can grow tiresome when they resist acknowledging difficulties or pain. A stressed Seven is an "eternal escapist," who will unrealistically seek greener pastures when the going gets tough. They may struggle committing to one person, and can become anxious and hyperactive. If Sevens don't balance their excitement with facing reality and being truthful, we can find their optimism unrealistic. "He's so much fun," can turn into "He's so distracted."

WHAT ENTHUSIASTS HIDE FROM OTHERS

"I'm not as happy as I appear to be." *Gluttony* causes Sevens to use their charm and vivaciousness to ensure that they will always have enough, or more than enough, of the good things in life. They struggle to maintain a facade of happiness and fun when in reality they feel anxiety and sadness like everyone else. Their internal story of, "I must always be excited," hides their deep fear of being deprived or trapped in pain.

THE GIFTS OF THE ENTHUSIAST

Sevens bring enthusiasm to a relationship. Enthusiasts experience delight in the ordinary things in life. Their good cheer and humor help lift us up and encourage us to focus on the positive.

Sevens excel at energizing people. Enthusiasts are great at creating energy around a concept, product, cause, etc. They have the ability to wake us up, get us to think out of the box, and begin something new.

Sevens provide us with great examples of spontaneity, stimulation, and optimism. Enthusiasts are adventurous, resourceful people who inspire us to make the most of each situation.

Aware Sevens express the virtue of sobriety. Enthusiasts accept life as it is moment-by-moment and day-by-day without dissatisfaction or the need to seek more.

At their best Sevens embody the quality of joy. Enthusiasts express simple happiness, delight and appreciation, and a sense of warmth in the heart. They are contented without the need to plan or create excitement, as if to say, "I appreciate the simple wonder of life, people, and the world. I'm satisfied with what is right here and now. Less can be more."

Summary of The Enthusist's Strategy Relationships

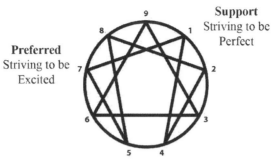

Support
Striving to be
Perfect

Preferred
Striving to be
Excited

Neglected
Striving to be
Detached

Preferred Strategy	*Neglected Strategy*	*Support Strategy*
Striving to be Excited (7)	**Striving to be Detached (5)**	**Striving to be Perfect (1)**
Aware Sevens at Point 7 are light hearted, focused on possibilities, upbeat, engaging, optimistic, intellectually curious, entertaining, and enthusiastic.	*Aware* Sevens at Point 5 are curious, focused on important details, impassioned, and capable of rigorous, intellectual pursuits.	*Aware* Sevens at Point 1 are responsible, charming and engaging in a controlled way. They can be the perfect facilitator or host.
Stressed Sevens at Point 7 distort "excited" into "irresponsible," become distracted and gluttonous, and make rash decisions without thinking through the consequences	*Stressed* Sevens at Point 5 "neglect" this strategy, misinterpret it as *remoteness*; they seek variety in thought and experience, and fear that if they are not in the center of activity they will become bored, or feel deprived.	*Stressed* Sevens at Point 1 become demanding and critical, expecting people to see things their way. They are fearful that others will prevent them from having fun and being satisfied.

TYPE EIGHT–THE CHALLENGER: STRIVING TO BE POWERFUL

"Most powerful is he who has himself in his own power." **Seneca**

Challengers are striving to be powerful. They are assertive, decisive, strong, independent, and confident. They are action-oriented self-starters who like to be in charge. They focus on getting things done and overcoming obstacles. Challengers are direct, protective, defensive, and eagerly stand up for their rights. Stressed Eights overdo striving to be powerful and do what it takes to get their needs met, including breaking the rules or norms that might get in their way. They imagine non-existent obstacles and enemies and their behavior can become uncontrolled and aggressive. Stressed Eights fear that if they are too connected to people they will be dependent on them, and become weak or vulnerable.

SUBTYPES OF THE CHALLENGER

Intimate: Possession
Intimate Eights try to possess and control their mates, their friends, children, and their environment. They like to "go for the gusto," to be on top, and to live life passionately. They test other's loyalty and trustworthiness in order to assess with whom they feel safe. They seek total commitment from others. They can be emotional, angry, hysterical, and boastful. Stressed Intimate Eights can seem like tyrannical dictators and can use humiliation and bullying to get their way. Giving in to another's wishes is very difficult for stressed Intimate Eights, and they do so only when they feel they are in control of the situation and the people involved.

Social: Friendship
Social Eights resolve their fear of not belonging by finding a "buddy." They seek loyalty and trust by bonding with someone in their same group. This bond also applies to social groups and causes, and Social Eights find safety in fraternities, teams, gangs, associations, and organizations. Mutual protection

of and loyalty to friends and groups who have a common agenda and set of values takes precedence over personal needs and feelings. Social Eights seek survival through alliance, and they overcome a sense of powerlessness by belonging to a group, and if possible, by being its leader. Protection is passionately emphasized, and "having each other's back," can substitute for intimacy or vulnerability. They may be confused with Intimate (counter-phobic) Sixes.

Self-Preservation: Satisfaction

Self-Preservation Eights are the most reserved and the least aggressive of the Eights. They emphasize being in control and avoiding vulnerability and re-maining fixated on what they feel will bring the satisfaction of their needs. The lustful excesses and aggressiveness of the other Eight subtypes are chan-neled into survival and material security. They monitor what they and others spend or consume, ever mindful of preserving resources. Like survivalists who see the world as a hostile place, they have a great desire for privacy, and are fiercely protective of friends and family; they establish and protect their envi-ronment and may stockpile resources.

WINGS OF THE CHALLENGER

The Eight With a Seven Wing

These Eights are independent, sharp minded, charismatic, and practical. The Eight's power and passion combine with the Seven's optimism result-ing in an Eight with a positive, forceful desire for fun. The Seven wing brings planning and a more strategic, inclusive view to the Eight's bias for action and exclusivity. The Seven's lightheartedness tempers the Eight's intensity and directness. Eights with a Seven Wing are social, talkative, big planners with big goals, who aren't afraid to take risks. They make friends easily and can get people to work with them and support their ideas. Less aware Eights with a Seven Wing can be impulsive and impatient. They can aggressively pursue fun and pleasure with little regard for the feelings of others.

The Eight With a Nine Wing

Eights with a Nine Wing are the "teddy bears" of the Enneagram; they are warm, friendly, protective, and not easily ruffled. More family oriented, less aggressive, and generally warmer than other Eights, they inspire followers and can make generous, caring leaders. These Eights are grounded and somewhat risk averse; they see the value in stability, harmony, and consensus. They are open to the ideas of others; they don't always have to have things their way, and they know how to cooperate for the good of others. Less aware Eights with a Nine Wing can "hunker down" like Nines and be homebodies. They want to be left alone in their private domain and take on a "don't hassle me" attitude, while stubbornly daring people to disturb their repose. Once aggravated they can seek revenge in an outburst worthy of any Eight, then quickly settle down.

THE CHALLENGER'S EMOTIONAL INTELLIGENCE SUMMARY SCORECARD

The following list does not address all the competencies related to establishing and maintaining relationships. It includes only the most obvious strengths and challenges typically identified with Type Eight. Depending on emotional maturity, life experience, and particularly the Challenger's degree of stress, all of the items may not apply. Consider this list a starting point for personal inquiry.

Strengths	Challenges
Self-Confidence: confidence in one's powers and abilities	*Empathy:* awareness of and participation in other's feelings, ideas, and needs
Resiliency: capacity to endure in the face of obstacles	*Self-Control:* restraint over one's impulses, emotions, or desires
Trustworthiness: maintaining standards of honesty and integrity	*Communication:* listening openly and sending convincing messages
Achievement Drive: meeting or improving standards of excellence	*Cooperation:* working with others toward shared goals

THE CHALLENGER'S RELATIONSHIP DILEMMA

A Challenger's strength, decisiveness, energy, and passion for living can be attractive. It is easy to be drawn to their "larger than life" persona, their desire to take care of others and their dedication to fairness. They trigger the part in us that wants to be in charge of our life, to "take the bull by the horns," and look out for the underdog. Our own "powerful" part keeps us pushing forward with rigor and dedication, keeps us focused on protecting ourselves, our loved ones, and our interests—and there is something very appealing there.

The dilemma is that a Challenger's attention is often focused on being harmed or controlled by others, so they try to be the most decisive, dominant, and controlling one in a relationship. Stressed Challengers are uncomfortable with emotions, and have a hard time showing vulnerability in a relationship. If Eights don't balance their assertiveness with compassion, cooperation, and understanding, their protectiveness can be overwhelming and feel like bullying. "He's so protective" can feel like, "He's a control freak."

WHAT CHALLENGERS HIDE FROM OTHERS

"I'm not as powerful or in control as I appear to be." *Lust* causes Eights to seek power, or at least the appearance of power. They believe that they need to be in charge, and if they are not respected and have control over others they won't be able to exert their will and have an impact on people. Their internal story, "I must always be powerful," hides their deep fear of being harmed and controlled by others.

THE GIFTS OF THE CHALLENGER

Eights bring passion to a relationship. Challengers are robust and forceful. They bring confidence, determination, and an adrenaline-like "turned-on" quality to whatever they try.

Eights excel at overcoming obstacles. Challengers bring tremendous initiative, drive, and a "never-say-die" attitude to challenges—and they thrive when the going gets tough. They welcome a good fight, competition and tests to their strength and resolve.

Eights provide us with great examples of justice, leadership, and independence. They are tenacious, forceful people who inspire us to take care of our own needs without burdening others.

Aware Eights express the virtue of innocence. Challengers feel that the world is a safe place and that there is no reason to believe anyone would harm them, and that they have no reason to harm others.

At their best Eights embody the quality of vitality. Challengers express vibrancy, strength, and aliveness—a sense of initiative, boldness and the ability to take action. Aware Eights believe that life unfolds appropriately in everyone without the need to control, dominate, or force anything, as if to say, "The capacity to be alive and to act is natural and shared by all."

Summary of The Challenger's Strategy Relationships

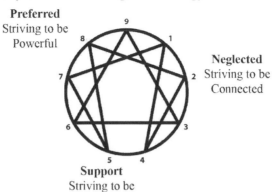

Preferred
Striving to be
Powerful

Neglected
Striving to be
Connected

Support
Striving to be
Detatched

Preferred Strategy	*Neglected Strategy*	*Support Strategy*
Striving to be Powerful (8)	**Striving to be Connected (2)**	**Striving to be Detached (5)**
Aware Eights at Point 8 are self-starters. They are confident, decisive, strong-willed, independent, and competitive. *Stressed* Eights at Point 8 distort "powerful" into "uncontrolled," and are aggressive, forceful, domineering, and angry. They may not adhere to rules, and can be impulsive and disruptive.	*Aware* Eights at Point 2 are warm, caring, sensitive, and protective. They are helpful and nurture deep and lasting relationships. *Stressed* Eights at Point 2 "neglect" this strategy, and misinterpret it as *dependence.* They fear that if they get too close to others they'll be seen as vulnerable, weak, and won't be able to take the lead and make decisions.	*Aware* Eights at Point 5 are informed, critical thinkers able to objectively make difficult decisions. *Stressed* Eights at Point 5 can become withdrawn, moody, and insensitive to another's needs. They may use knowledge to overpower people, and withhold information as a way to punish and control others. They angrily disengage from contact.

TYPE NINE–THE PEACEMAKER: STRIVING TO BE PEACEFUL

"Without inner peace, it is impossible to have world peace." **The Dalai Lama**

Peacemakers are striving to be peaceful. They are patient, calm, low key, pleasant, and unpretentious. They are diplomatic, disarming, and focus on maintaining inner harmony by minimizing their own needs and concentrating on the needs of others. Nines get along easily with most people and tolerate most everyone's point of view. Easy-going, affable, and charming, Peacemakers are unflappable and stable; they avoid conflict through patient mediation. Stressed Nines overdo striving to be peaceful and can become passive, stubborn, and inert, relying on others to make decisions and to act for them. Stressed Peacemakers fear that if they place too much importance on themselves they will be seen as "center stagers," overbearing, and obtrusive.

SUBTYPES OF THE PEACEMAKER

Intimate: Union

Intimate Nines have a true "seeker" quality, a deep longing to unite with another person, nature, or something bigger than them. They give up their personal boundaries and minimize their uniqueness as a way of merging with others in order to find happiness. They seek union with an undemanding other who will care for them. The most easy-going of the Nines, they can appear to be bothered by nothing, even people taking advantage of them. Intimate Nines live vicariously through others, and lose contact with their own identity. They hope that the love of another will help them feel noticed and valuable, and help them regain their lost sense of identity.

Social: Participation

Social Nines are the gregarious, friendly Nines. They merge, not with one person, but with the style and agenda of their friends and social groups. They join organizations but may not commit completely, often preferring to participate from the sidelines. They can be energized by group affiliation yet resist being controlled or absorbed by the group. Social Nines can walk the line between selfless contribution and half-hearted participation, drifting into pleasant, yet superficial contact with others. At heart, they question whether they really fit in social situations and whether they are welcome or not, so they imitate the behavior of others in an attempt to be accepted.

Self-Preservation: Appetite

Self-Preservation Nines merge with *fluff*—the non-essential stuff that doesn't satisfy their real needs. They have an appetite for food and a variety of possessions and stimulation. They use food, drink, shopping, partying, TV, relaxing and involvement in meaningless activities to numb them from unconscious anger and to "manage" conflict. Consumption and overindulging helps them satisfy superficial desires while avoiding essential needs such as personal, financial, and spiritual growth. Self-Preservation Nines surround themselves with creature comforts, relaxing routines, and simple pleasures. Choosing not to set the world on fire, they prefer to scale back involvement, minimize effort, and establish easy, manageable goals.

WINGS OF THE PEACEMAKER

The Nine With an Eight Wing

These Nines are gregarious and social. They can remain relatively unaffected by the uncertainties and storms of life. The Nine's urge to merge with others is balanced by the Eight's independence and need for space and autonomy. This allows Nines with an Eight Wing to guiltlessly possess their own power, confidence and authority. They can be their own people and provide for others with confidence and strength. The influence of the Eight wing helps Nines to be more proactive and to make things happen rather than adopt the accepting, surrendering behavior of other Nines. They can assert themselves without fear of offending others or being too dominant or showy. Less aware Nines with an Eight Wing are stubborn and defensive. They can have explosive tempers, surprising to themselves and others, as if blowing the top off of years of suppressed anger.

The Nine With a One Wing

Nines with a One Wing are moral, imaginative, philosophical, and spiritual. They can be dreamers with a magical, shamanistic bent. Idealistic, friendly and reassuring, they are good counselors, coaches, and therapists. Relaxed and caring but interested in making the world a better place, these Nines are less action oriented than Nines with an Eight Wing. The One influence adds order and purpose that motivates these Nines to seek improvement and self-development—to make things happen in their lives rather than let things be. They yearn for excellence and transcendence. Less aware Nines with a One Wing repress their frustration and anger. They can go numb, ignore their feelings, and express themselves passive aggressively or through expressions of resentment. They can become mired in meaningless, inconsequential "busy work," while ignoring the essential activities that would nurture their lives.

THE PEACEMAKER'S EMOTIONAL INTELLIGENCE SUMMARY SCORECARD

The following list does not address all the competencies related to establishing and maintaining relationships. It includes only the most obvious strengths and challenges typically identified with Type Nine. Depending on emotional maturity, life experience, and particularly the Peacemaker's degree of stress, all of the items may not apply. Consider this list a starting point for personal inquiry.

Strengths	Challenges
Trustworthiness: maintaining standards of honesty and integrity	*Adaptability:* flexibility in handling change
Cooperation: working with others toward shared goals	*Self-Confidence:* confidence in one's powers and abilities
Optimism: ability to anticipate and expect the best possible outcome	*Self-Awareness:* ability to identify one's thought processes, emotions, and skills
Empathy: awareness of and participation in others' feelings, ideas, and needs	*Conflict Management:* negotiating and resolving disputes

THE PEACEMAKER'S RELATIONSHIP DILEMMA

A Peacemaker's open, relaxed, pleasant, and unassuming nature can be attractive. It's easy to be drawn to their positive outlook. They trigger the part in us that wants to cooperate, forgive others, feel at peace with the world, and live in harmony with everyone. Our own "peaceful" part helps us accept people just as they are, allows us to see another's point of view, and makes us easy to get along with—and there is something very appealing there.

The dilemma is that Nines can be indecisive, vague, and noncommittal in an attempt to not "rock the boat" in a relationship. We may feel loved and accepted by them but also irritated when we don't know where they stand, when they seem to float through life as if half asleep, seemingly indifferent to themselves and the relationship. Stressed Nines can lose touch with their own energy and aliveness and become detached and depressed. If Nines don't balance their "peace, love, and harmony" attitude with assertiveness, decisiveness, and action, they can fall into a pattern of living through others—accepting other's decisions and choices while sacrificing their own. "She's so easy going," can feel like "She's so complacent."

WHAT PEACEMAKERS HIDE FROM OTHERS

"I'm not as agreeable as I appear to be." *Indifference* keeps Nines from voicing their disagreement. They take the easy way out and avoid discussion rather than disagree. They hide their own desires, fearing that others will dislike them if they make too many demands or if their needs are in conflict with those of others. Their internal story of, "I must always be peaceful," hides their deep fear of loss and abandonment.

THE GIFTS OF THE PEACEMAKER

Nines bring balance to a relationship. Peacemakers stay stable and solid during life's ups and downs. They have the resilience to deal with events that others find stressful. They can weigh the good and the bad dispassionately and see the benefits in different perspectives.

Nines excel at helping people feel comfortable. Peacemakers are unassuming, likeable, and responsible, and make others feel included and accepted. Their patience helps people relax.

Nines provide us with great examples of calm, acceptance, and tolerance. Peacemakers are open-minded, unpretentious people who inspire us to establish peace and harmony with others and ourselves.

Aware Nines express the virtue of action. Peacemakers are fully engaged in their lives and embrace reality wholeheartedly without being distracted by non-essential activities. They are decisive and committed to their own best interests.

At their best Nines embody the quality of unity. Peacemakers sense that everything is connected—that although we are separate entities, at the most fundamental level, everything is united. Aware Peacemakers don't deny their personal needs, or retreat from conflict, as if to say, "I don't have to hide my gifts or be 'less than' to achieve harmony and feel at peace."

Summary of The Peacemaker's Strategy Relationships

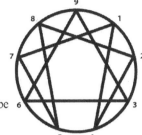

Preferred
Striving to be
Peaceful

Support
Striving to be
Secure

Neglected
Striving to be
Outstanding

Preferred Strategy	*Neglected Strategy*	*Support Strategy*
Striving to be Peaceful (9) *Aware* Nines at Point 9 are composed, relaxed, kind, pleasant, creative, disarming and non-confrontational.	**Striving to be Outstanding (3)** *Aware* Nines at Point 3 are confident, energetic, engaged, practical, ambitious, and goal-oriented.	**Striving to be Secure (6)** *Aware* Nines at Point 6 are protective and able to create an environment where others feel safe, acknowledged, and included.
Stressed Nines at Point 9 distort "peacefulness" into "passivity," and avoid things that disturb their inner calm; they often resist taking action, and overlook threats to their well-being, security, or success.	*Stressed* Nines at Point 3 "neglect" this strategy, and misinterpret it as *attention seeking.* They avoid behavior that draws attention to their value and accomplishments, which in turn undermines their ability to stand out.	*Stressed* Nines at Point 6 succumb to anxiety and avoid taking chances or making changes. They ignore situations that will disturb their sense of harmony. Anxiety can make them withdraw from contact.

Part Two: Practicing

"Make a decision today to take possession of the most powerful weapon in the battle against a sad life. That weapon is called 'practice.'"

STEVE CHANDLER

4

Are We Aware Enough?

"We ought to have the humility to admit that we do not know all about ourselves, that we are not experts at running our own lives"

Thomas Merton

Awareness is the most important emotional competency. It is where any real action must originate and where any relationship begins. Most of us think we are aware but in reality we could all do with a wake up call, something that could shake us out of our unawareness and autopilot. Awareness shows us that when we are not mindful of what we are seeing, hearing, and doing, it is as if it does not exist for us. If our child, employee, or partner comes to talk with us and we are distracted, we both go away feeling dissatisfied and hungry for connection and intimacy. The more mindful we are the more we understand interactions and events around us, and more profoundly, the more we are in touch with our personal values and what drives our behavior. Awareness is a basic survival skill, a basic business skill, and the foundation of all successful relationships.

Being aware means minimizing our tendency to linger in the past, replaying past offences, hurts, and mistakes (or successes, for that matter). It means liberating ourselves from our old baggage. The ability to observe and reflect on what is happening and to use that information to communicate and make decisions is one of the most valuable life skills we can have. In *Conscious Business* Fred Kofman writes:

"To live consciously means to be open to perceiving the world around us, to understand our circumstances, and to decide how to respond to them in ways that honor our needs, values and goals…. We not only perceive the external world, we can also bear witness to our internal world. We can pose questions like, 'Why am I thinking what I am thinking?' 'Do I have sound reasons for my conclusions?' …Not only do we experience self-awareness, we also recognize 'other-awareness.' I'm talking about something more subtle than perceiving other people from an external perspective. We know that beyond people's observable behavior, they are conscious, choosing their actions based on their reasoning. We can ask, 'What leads you to think what you are thinking?' 'Do you have evidence for your conclusions?' 'Why is this issue important to you?'"

Competencies and skills involved in being aware are Self-Awareness, and Seeing and Overcoming Blind Spots.

WAKE UP CALL: HOW CAN INNER AND OTHER AWARENESS IMPROVE RELATIONSHIPS?

In his book, *Focus, The Hidden Driver of Excellence*, Daniel Goleman describes three primary kinds of focus: *Inner, Other, and Outer.*

Inner focus refers to self-awareness and self-management: how well we know the values that guide our behavior, and our strengths and limitations. This focus helps us handle negative emotions and stay positive so that we can reach our goals and bounce back from setbacks.

Other focus describes how well we tune into people; understand how people perceive things, how they feel, and what we can do to help them be their best. This focus is essential for motivating people, persuasion and influence, negotiation and conflict management, and teamwork and collaboration.

Outer focus has to do with how well we can perceive the large, global forces that create our world, like how a new technology will affect a market, whose opinion matters most for a decision, or how global warming will affect us. *Outer* awareness allows us to anticipate what's coming.

For our purposes, we'll focus only on Goleman's *Inner* and *Other* focus. From an *Inner* focus perspective, think of any relationship you have been in, or are in now—it could be with a person at work or in your personal life. Now ask yourself how aware you are of *your* thoughts, feelings and behavior toward this person. Do you behave in a habitual, "automatic" way? What are the effects of being aware or not aware of this person?

Next, from an *Other* focus, consider how aware you are of *this person's* desires, motivations, thoughts, feelings, and actions. Do you take for granted he or she has similar desires or is motivated by similar things as you? Have you ever asked what motivates this person? Are you sensitive to this person's feelings? Do you ask how he or she is feeling? What is the impact of being aware and unaware of this person?

SELF-AWARENESS: BEING AWARE OF THOUGHTS, EMOTIONS, AND SKILLS

Self-awareness involves observing ourselves objectively and dispassionately. This is difficult indeed. Many of us begin our journey toward self-awareness through gaining feedback from others. When people we trust tell us what they see from their perspective, our eyes can open, and we can begin to wake up to reality. People skilled in Self-Awareness:

- Know their strengths and weaknesses.
- Have a realistic view of their values and contributions.
- Can identify and understand their feelings.
- Are aware of the effect of their behavior on others.
- Know which emotions they are experiencing and why.
- See the links between their feelings and their thoughts and actions.
- Recognize how their feelings affect their interactions with others.

The following section describes how each type expresses self-awareness by identifying their thoughts, emotions, and skills.

Type One: Perfectionists

Normally: Perfectionists are better able to identify their thoughts and skills than their emotions. They focus on how reasonable and logical their thinking process is. Ones may consider emotions as less important than thinking, and at times, as illogical and distracting. They often confuse anger with frustration and anxiety.

Under Stress: Perfectionists become overly critical of their abilities because they evaluate themselves by unrealistically high standards. Ones become increasingly angry but tend to feel shame and guilt about it and deny it. Denial is a reflection of how unaware stressed Ones can be of their emotions, especially anger.

Type Two: Helpers

Normally: Helpers focus on their emotions more than their thoughts and skills. Because they see themselves as compassionate and nurturing, Twos find it difficult to identify and admit to certain negative emotions. They focus a lot of their awareness on others, and judge themselves on how helpful they are to people.

Under Stress: Twos turn their attention almost exclusively to others; they lose autonomy, and their self-awareness decreases. They dramatize their emotions and overreact to events and people. They can become jealous, feel victimized and fail to see how this behavior undermines their ability to help others.

Type Three: Performers

Normally: Performers are more aware of their skills and thoughts than their emotions. They avoid emotions that hinder their productivity, such as sadness, shame, and guilt, and are often unsure of what they are feeling, and consider instead what they *should* be feeling. Performers look for clues from others as to the appropriate feeling or expression.

Under Stress: Threes overestimate and overstate their skills in an attempt to create a successful image. Overwork, stress, and burnout cause them to lose contact with their emotions and to be less aware of how to think, feel, and behave.

Type Four: Individualists

Normally: Individualists are extremely self-aware regarding their thoughts and emotions and can discern subtle variations in their feelings. They occasionally doubt their self-awareness when they feel that people aren't appreciating them; they may wonder "Don't they see what I see?"

Under Stress: Fours become overwhelmed by their emotions or by emotionally charged events. They lose perspective and objectivity and overdramatize their emotions or become paralyzed in an attempt to intensify their feelings. Stress causes them to inflate their abilities or lose confidence in their skills.

Type Five: Observers

Normally: Observers are very aware of their thoughts but downplay or ignore their emotions. They identify with their intellect and see themselves as thinkers rather than feelers. They hold onto feelings, preferring not to share them. They are somewhat uncomfortable with the skills needed for action, and are usually acutely aware of the anxiety they feel in groups.

Under Stress: Fives get lost in their thoughts, becoming even more out of touch with their emotions. Their feelings, particularly anger and frustration, can emerge unpredictably and uncontrollably, diminishing their clarity of thinking and behaving. They may either become arrogant or detached.

Type Six: Guardians

Normally: Guardians are very aware of their thoughts, emotions, and skills. They observe how they fit into the group and try to make sure they are in alignment with authority figures. Guardians, however, don't trust their own thoughts, feelings, or actions, and they doubt their decisions and reactions. This doubt makes them seem to be less aware than they actually are.

Under Stress: Guardians' ability to identify their thoughts, feelings, or skills is negatively affected by their anxiety. Under pressure Sixes can be quite confused about what they really think or feel. They stay busy in an effort to quell their mounting anxieties, further reducing their self-awareness.

Type Seven: Enthusiasts

Normally: Enthusiasts are aware of what brings them happiness but struggle identifying their feelings. They ignore feelings that will make them unhappy or uncomfortable. Sevens spend lots of time planning an exciting future but are often out of touch with their present experiences and emotions. Enthusiasts are better at identifying their skills.

Under Stress: Enthusiasts often overestimate their skills and abilities. They avoid unpleasant, boring thoughts by entertaining happy thought after happy thought. Stressed Sevens become hyperactive, seeking overstimulation—lots of talking, joking, and pacing—as a way to reduce their anxiety.

Type Eight: Challengers

Normally: Challengers are very aware of their skills, fairly aware of their thoughts, but poor at identifying their emotional states. They see things through a *like and dislike* lens—and they like power and control. Eights avoid introspection and like to keep things simple. They are poor at identifying the emotional impact they have on people.

Under Stress: Eights lose the ability to evaluate their thinking and act without awareness of the impact of their actions. They categorize people as either friend or foe and behave impulsively and often insensitively. They have an inflated view of their importance and overestimate their skills.

Type Nine: Peacemakers

Normally: Peacemakers focus more on others than on themselves. Their awareness is "out there" on the concerns of others and the events of the day. They are slow to recognize their own good qualities, and quick to point out their own flaws. They are more in tune with their feelings and thoughts and downplay their skills, often in a self-effacing manner.

Under Stress: Nines are unaware of their anger and work hard to ignore it. They undervalue or deny their skills and abilities. They're not aware of their positive impact, self-worth, and the respect and love that people have for them. Anxiety causes them to function on autopilot, living life from the sidelines.

TO IMPROVE IN SELF-AWARENESS:

- Observe yourself. Be mindful of your thoughts, feelings and actions.
- Establish a meditation practice. Daily meditation strengthens your "inner observer" enabling you to be more mindful.
- Be aware of your triggers and hot buttons and the length of time between being "set off" by a trigger and your reaction to it. Practice shortening the length of time between a stimulus and your reaction.
- Ask for feedback about your behavior, and listen with openness and with the goal of learning something new and useful about yourself. Ask for clarification and for examples. Make sure you thank anyone who is willing to give you feedback. Good feedback is priceless.
- Gain a clear, objective view of your values and contributions; don't over or under estimate them.
- Become conscious of the effect of your behavior by asking what impact your verbal, written, and nonverbal actions have on people. Ask people how your behavior makes them feel.
- Ask yourself which emotions you are feeling and why—for example, "Why am I feeling anxiety? What event caused it? How am I reacting to it?"
- Recognize how your emotions affect your behavior both negatively and positively. For example, does feeling frustrated cause you to make negative, irrational decisions? Does feeling angry move you to take decisive action?

- Discover your "blind spots" through feedback. Explore how your thinking process and your internal filters, biases, and preferences affect your thoughts, emotions, and behavior.

SEEING AND OVERCOMING BLIND SPOTS

The author Anais Nin threw light on the concept of blind spots with her often repeated quote, "We do not see the world the way it is; we see it the way we are." A psychological blind spot is a term first coined by Joseph Luft and Harry Ingham in 1955 as part of their Johari Window, a cognitive psychological tool to help people better understand their interpersonal communication.

As this concept relates to this book, psychological blind spots are things we can't see or don't want to see about ourselves; they may also be behaviors we distort in order for us to ignore or deny them. Of course, what we can't see about ourselves affects what we can see or not see about others. Our personality's strategy, when unknown or unaccepted, can be considered one of the largest blind spots we have. Our strategy serves as a bias that confirms and supports our conviction that we behave a certain way, and rejects things that contradict it. When we are blind to certain things, we must rely on others to help us see our true behavior. That's what feedback is all about.

Blind Spots and Feedback

Blind spots can also be things we *imagine* to be true of ourselves but that others don't see. When others tell us what they see by giving feedback in a supportive, responsible way, we have a better chance of hearing and accepting it; in that way we are able to test the reality of who we are and are able to make necessary changes. When we reciprocate by giving feedback to others, we can establish honest, practical, and powerful relationships.

The most easily accepted and most useful feedback is when we ask for it, rather than when someone gives it to us unrequested. So, *ask for feedback frequently and regularly.* A direct, honest phrase such as, "I'm interested in how you think I'm doing," or "I'd like to hear your opinion about..." is adequate. When you feel compelled to *offer* feedback, ask permission first. Feedback is more easily accepted when it is given with another's permission. Simply say, "I've noticed something. Are you open to hear some feedback?" Let people say yes or no.

Feedback is a powerful way to become more self-aware, to uncover your blind spots, to test your perception of reality, to appreciate how people really see you, and to stay on course in your relationships. Of course we all have more than one blind spot, and we all have many ways of improving in self-awareness. What follows are descriptions of typical blind spots of each of the nine types and ways of turning a blind spot from a weakness to a strength, described under Turning Around the Blind Spot.

Perfectionists: Striving to be Perfect
Blind Spot
Criticism. Perfectionists judge and criticize in an attempt to make things right. They believe that they know how things should be and feel that they have an obligation to fix the flaws in themselves and others. They feel that their correcting is helpful coaching, and that they are only trying to guide people to make improvements and move in the right direction. They are often shocked when others interpret their comments as criticism. Ones rarely see that their attempts to reform things are fueled by their anger that people aren't perfect— or at least the way they want them to be.

Turning Around the Blind Spot
Acceptance. Perfectionists need to relax, to be open and tolerant. By accepting other points of view Ones begin to make emotional contact with people and to get to know people more intimately. Ones should make efforts to be less skeptical, more joyful, friendly and personal. They should also not be so hard on themselves. As awareness grows, Ones may begin to realize what all the great mystics have taught: "All is well, all is well. Though everything is a mess, all is well." Without self-awareness, without waking up, Ones never feel satisfied with things. Instead, they are living a "frustration dream" that always needs fixing.

Helpers: Striving to be Connected
Blind Spot
Demandingness. Helpers demand that their needs be met. They exert pressure on others and feel entitled to special treatment because they believe they are so caring and attentive to others. Stressed Helpers use their "give to get" tactic as a way of manipulating people. Twos want to get what they want without having to ask for it—their "If you loved me you'd know my needs" philosophy. Stressed Helpers, who feel they do so much for others, harbor resentment that others don't do enough for them and that they never get what *they* want. "When will it be my turn?" is often their unspoken plea.

Turning Around the Blind Spot
Humility. Twos need to accept that they have desires just like everyone else, that they are not better or more evolved than others because they are helpers. Helpers fail to see that their pride is showing when they take the stance of "I don't have needs, but you do." They should ask for what they want rather than expect others to read their minds and give them special treatment. Helpers grow when they honestly express what they need, and offer constructive feedback.

Performers: Striving to be Outstanding
Blind Spot
Inauthenticity. Threes see no benefit in showing anything less than their best side. Because they focus on the positive and the best aspects of themselves, Performers may fall into the habit of deceiving themselves and sometimes others. They are practical and results driven, and look for the best solution and the most effective action even if it involves "fudging" the truth. Performers are blind to what others see as deceitful; they may see their deceit as reframing, spinning, or putting their best foot forward. Stressed Threes hide their imperfections or "human" qualities, fearing to be seen as ordinary. They can seem mysterious and can be hard to get to know.

Turning Around the Blind Spot
Authenticity. Performers need to be honest with themselves about how they often do anything in order to impress people, such as over promising, name

dropping, and misrepresenting themselves and their capabilities. Performers grow when they begin to see who they are behind the polished, manicured image. Authenticity for Performers means getting in touch with their feelings, rather than adopting the opinions and standards of the person or social group they are trying to impress. Performers grow when they learn to be spontaneous and honest and less rehearsed in their interactions with others.

Individualists: Striving to be Unique
Blind Spot
Self-Absorption. Individualists dive deeply into their own inner life with its rich array of challenges and often ignore or minimize the problems of others. They find their own lives more interesting than other people's lives. Because they feel they have been singled out and mistreated by life, stressed Individualists think the focus should be on them and their problems. A stressed Four's self-absorption can come across as aloofness—a distaste and dismissal for what they consider ordinary or mundane—preferring their own rich fantasy world to the real world.

Turning Around the Blind Spot
Focus on Others. Fours need to become more interested in the feelings, thoughts, and needs of others. By shifting focus to others (rather than their own internal state) they can tap into their innate intuition and sensitivity to others. Focusing on others means seeing the relationship from the other person's perspective. Being appreciative of what other people are dealing with and how others contribute to the relationship are ways for Individualists to develop greater self-awareness and to nurture their relationships.

Observers: Striving to be Detached
Blind Spot
Intellectual Arrogance. Fives think about, collect and categorize information. They spend much of their time studying and forming opinions about life, and figuring out what makes things work. They can isolate themselves from others, seek internal stimulation, and give the impression that their solitude is preferred to engagement with people. Stressed Fives often think that other

people are less knowledgeable and insightful and even stupid and dull. Less aware Observers come off as "know-it-alls"—believing they are never wrong and never without the facts.

Turning Around the Blind Spot
Generosity. Fives need to be generous both intellectually and emotionally. Observers should be open, accepting, and appreciative of the intellect and feelings of others. They grow when they see the human side of people, see what others have to offer in their own unique way, and appreciate people for attributes other than their intelligence and knowledge. Fives make an emotional connection with people by sharing their feelings.

Guardians: Striving to be Secure
Blind Spot
Complaining. Guardians don't trust their own decisions and the thinking process they use to make them. They are skeptical and suspicious and feel compelled to test themselves and others. They complain to see if people agree or disagree with them as a way of finding where people stand. You may hear them say something like, "I'm not so sure about the new boss" and then pause. They see this as "just sharing," but their comments often have a negative doom and gloom quality that can be off putting. Stressed Sixes fail to see that by complaining they rely on others to verify their opinions rather than trust in their own experience and insights.

Turning Around the Blind Spot
Trusting. Sixes need to trust themselves and others. They need to take responsibility for their own actions and believe that their own inner guidance can be trusted. Guardians can build confidence in their ability to perform and accomplish on their own by taking more "leaps of faith." They grow when they stop blaming others, the environment, etc., and believe that their own skills and intelligence are enough. Allowing themselves to fail—and seeing that it will not be the end of the world—helps Sixes open to their basic trust and innate courage.

Enthusiasts: Striving to be Excited
Blind Spot

Distractibility. Sevens stay distracted from unpleasant thoughts, feelings, and experiences. By not focusing on any one thing for too long, and by planning on what fun thing they can make happen next, Enthusiasts avoid the possibility of something becoming unpleasant or boring. Because stressed Sevens move from thought to thought so quickly, often without linking them together coherently, others may feel that they are thoughtless and unconcerned about others. Their distractibility may manifest itself in feigned forgetfulness, not fulfilling promises, and a lack of commitment and accountability. They may excuse themselves with the weary expression, "I was just going to do that, but I've been so busy."

Turning Around the Blind Spot

Commitment. Sevens should focus on the people and events in front of them. They need to be patient with ordinary tasks and deal with unpleasant issues rather than ignore them or redefine them as something less threatening or less unpleasant than they are. Sevens do well when they plan in a balanced and realistic way, that is, when they consider the dull and routine things that they have committed to, and when they find joy in the simple things. Sevens grow when they keep their promises and focus on *completing* tasks rather than simply talking about them.

Challengers: Striving to be Powerful
Blind Spot

Abusiveness. Challengers see the world as hostile and believe that the best way to survive is to be tough, always on guard, assertive, and aggressive. They consider their "straight talk and tough love" as protective and intelligent, whereas others see it as abusive. Although Challengers claim that they are trying to help weaker, defenseless people by being "brutally honest," they are often avoiding any weakness and incompetence they fear seeing in themselves. Another way this blind spot shows itself is the stressed Eight's unawareness of the impact of their behavior. People on the receiving end of their abusiveness feel hurt and disrespected, but the Challenger will often express surprise by the reaction, with a comment such as, "What are you so upset about?"

Turning Around the Blind Spot

Sensitivity. Eights should be more tactful and gentle in the way they talk and behave with people. They need to consider how others may interpret their interactions with them and then temper their directness with sensitivity. Challengers grow when they see that their sarcasm, toughness, and "don't take this personally," attitude can be hurtful to people. Empathy, compassion, patience, and self-sacrifice—although foreign to less-aware Challengers—are the keys to expressing sensitivity. Practicing empathy and applying the Golden Rule are ways that Eights can connect more compassionately and effectively.

Peacemakers: Striving to be Peaceful
Blind Spot

Passive-Aggressiveness. Stressed Peacemakers often express peace and harmony by keeping their opinions to themselves and ignoring their desires. Because it's not OK to be aggressive if you are striving to be Peaceful, Nines seek satisfaction by being passive-aggressive. For example, they may procrastinate, be "forgetful," stubborn, late for meetings, or make promises that they don't keep. Stressed Nines can be blind to the anger and aggressiveness in their behavior; their passiveness can mask an indifference to their own needs, desires, and passion for living. Their attitude of "I'm not that important" can announce to others that the relationship is not that important either.

Turning Around the Blind Spot

Assertiveness. Nines should be assertive and state what they want and need clearly and unapologetically. They need to take action rather than fantasize that things will take care of themselves. Nines should defend against people taking advantage of their easy going, overly trusting nature. They grow when they regularly perform reality checks and are honest about procrastination, denial that problems exist, and stubbornness. For Peacemakers assertiveness comes when they value themselves, and when they see that their presence and contributions matter just as much as anyone's. For Nines assertiveness means taking action on their own behalf.

TAKE ACTION ON AWARENESS

Our goal is to practice being more aware of our *Inner* focus—of *our* thoughts, feelings, and actions, and more aware of our *Other* focus—more conscious of *another's* thoughts, feelings, and actions. The tried and true method of developing *Inner* awareness is through a mindfulness practice such as seated meditation: Start by sitting for five or 10 minutes; simply sit upright and focus your attention on your breath. Pay attention to the breath coming in and out of your nostrils as you count to ten. Count "one" on the in breath, "two" on the out breath, "three" on the in breath, and so forth. That's it. You will invariably have thoughts and feelings that interrupt your counting; simply notice them and go back to counting, beginning at one.

This practice trains your mindfulness muscles. It is deceptively simple, but it is not easy. Thoughts will come and go; just stay with your breath. Begin to lengthen the amount of time you sit until you get to 20 or 30 minutes. Then begin to count your breath at other times, for example, waiting in line at the grocery store, or while you are driving to work. See this as *practice*, the same as a musician plays scales, or a tennis player hits backhands. You will become increasingly more aware of your own presence, and of your thoughts and feelings as you continue to practice. This basic ability to stay focused and mindful will have benefits in all areas of your life, resulting in a greater ability to be prepared, and an easier recovery from setbacks.

Regarding *Other* focus, the same muscles being developed in mindfulness meditation—both seated and randomly during your day—will help you sustain curiosity, ask deeper questions, and be more compassionate towards others. Begin to observe people, really watch them, and inquire into what they are doing and why they are doing it. Ask questions about them and listen.

Ask for feedback about your awareness of others, such as, "Am I listening better?" Research suggests that mindfulness increases self-awareness, empathic concern for others, and the ability to listen better.

5

Can We Trust Each Other?

"I don't need a certain number of friends, just a number of friends I can be certain of."

Alice Walker

While awareness is the cornerstone of connecting with people, trustworthiness runs a close second. Whether the relationship we are trying to establish is personal or work related, without trust we can't move further. When we are trustworthy people can rely on us. We can be counted on to do what we say we will do. If we make commitments, we follow through on them. A relationship founded on trust is characterized by emotional openness and comfort in revealing our weaknesses, fears, and mistakes. If we believe another is trustworthy, we feel safe asking for help and are comfortable giving and receiving feedback. We will give each other the benefit of the doubt when misunderstandings or conflicts arise. Competencies and skills involved in establishing and maintaining trust are Trustworthiness and Building Rapport.

WAKE UP CALL: ARE YOU TRUSTING, SUSPICIOUS, OR BOTH?

There's an old Arab teaching story that addresses a healthy balance between trust and skepticism that ends with the axiom: "Trust your neighbor, but always tether your camel." The following exercise asks you to consider how balanced you are regarding trust. Blind trust is just as damaging to a relationship as doubt, mistrust, and suspicion. The ability to trust depends on past experience, childhood messages, and a variety of factors. Personality plays a major role in trust. For example, Peacemakers, who prefer to disarm people with kindness, usually trust people without much question. They give others the benefit of the doubt, and like to see the best in others, even strangers. Guardians, on the other hand, have a healthy skepticism, and feel that people need to prove themselves before they deserve to be trusted. They often have a selective inner circle of friends and allies who have passed their test of trustworthiness.

Consider where you fall on the Trust Scale below. What impact does being either too trusting or too suspicious have on your relationships? What do you need to do to get closer to the middle of the scale—the balanced ideal—where you are open and willing to trust people, but careful enough not to be taken advantage of? What part does your personality strategy play in this style? What childhood messages, personal beliefs, or cultural norms determine where you fall on the Trust Scale?

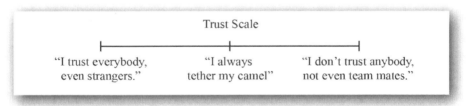

TRUSTWORTHINESS: MAINTAINING STANDARDS OF HONESTY AND INTEGRITY

Being trustworthy means in part that our words are aligned with our intentions. We maintain a level of transparency that lets others feel secure about who we are and what they can expect from us. Being trustworthy doesn't mean we will never let others down, but that we will offer and accept apologies and move on without holding a grudge or rehashing mistakes or hurts. It is an attitude and a way of behaving that honors the trust placed in us. People skilled in Trustworthiness:

- Are open and share personal information.
- Are vulnerable and make a commitment.
- Are consistently honest, ethical, and moral.
- Understand the difference between "spinning" yarns and being totally honest.
- Readily admit to their mistakes.
- Ask for and accept feedback.
- Confront unethical behavior in others.

The following section describes how each type establishes trust by maintaining standards of honesty and integrity.

Type One: Perfectionists
Normally: Perfectionists shine in this competency. They are reliable and often perform to higher standards than others. They don't make promises lightly, and they commit to their word and expect others to do the same. Perfectionists try to be fair in their assessments of others, and don't play favorites. They take great pride in being trustworthy.

Under Stress: Ones become rigidly Puritanical in enforcing laws and procedures, even when exceptions are clearly justified. Driven to appear flawless, stressed Ones deny rather than admit when they're wrong or dishonest. Very stressed Ones may exempt themselves from the rules but demand that others follow them.

Type Two: Helpers
Normally: Twos are honest about their desire to help and connect. However, they often practice a subtle form of dishonesty by flattering and fawning over people in order to be liked. They are masters at saying what they think people want to hear.

Under Stress: Helpers increase compliments to gain love and appreciation. They can deceive themselves, unaware that they "help" others as a way of manipulating them to gain approval. Stressed Twos struggle with keeping secrets, and create bonds with some people by gossiping about others.

Type Three: Performers
Normally: Performers are trustworthy and ethical. Some Threes, however, struggle with this competency because they are so focused on creating a successful image that they create an unrealistic one. Performers may exaggerate their value, mention names of influential "friends" whom they really don't know, or downplay mistakes in an effort to look good.

Under Stress: Threes can be deceptive; they become obsessively competitive, take credit for a colleague's contributions or misrepresent themselves or sabotage a competitor in an effort to win at all cost. Valuing image over reality, they create an unrealistic persona that is beyond credibility.

Type Four: Individualists
Normally: Fours set high standards of honesty and integrity and live their lives with refinement. Because their inner life is turbulent, Individualists look for things that are reliable and controllable. Trustworthiness is one of these areas—keeping their word makes them feel grounded and secure.

Under Stress: Fours can have a Jekyll-and-Hyde relationship with trustworthiness. Poor impulse control can cause them to disobey the rules, or to change the rules at their own discretion. At the same time, stressed Fours tend to place high expectations for integrity on others and react angrily when they are not met.

Type Five: Observers
Normally: Observers do well in this competency. They rely on accurate facts for their security and have an inner sense of veracity and logic that makes it difficult for them to be deceptive. However, Fives feel more secure when not revealing themselves, so they can deceive through omission by withholding what they're thinking or feeling.

Under Stress: Fives can be ""honest to a fault" especially when angry. As purveyors of "just the facts," they have no motive to lie, and will let the chips fall where they may. Their other approach is to become increasingly nonresponsive, not allowing others to get a glimpse of their real thoughts and feelings.

Type Six: Guardians

Normally: Guardians do well in this competency. Honesty and integrity mean consistency and certainty—what Sixes seek. They demonstrate their worth and loyalty through their strong work ethic. They are assertive and committed in their pursuit of honesty and integrity.

Under Stress: Stress makes Guardians more rigid about fulfilling their commitments, but no less honest. They may become argumentative and defensive and project their flaws onto others. This is a form of dishonesty because it puts the focus onto others, sometimes undeservedly.

Type Seven: Enthusiasts

Normally: Sevens tire of always being upbeat, and part of them desires down time and opportunities to relax. Because they prefer to keep this side hidden from others they can appear to have a secret life. This hiding may make them appear untrustworthy to others, although no deceit is intended.

Under Stress: Sevens tell "little white lies." They exaggerate and forget to include unpleasant details. As stress increases, Enthusiasts will be deceptive if necessary to avoid being confronted with mistakes, or to avoid their problems.

Type Eight: Challengers

Normally: Eights are straight shooters and verbalize exactly what they are thinking, with little concern for offending others. They value integrity, fairness, and justice, have high expectations of others and hold themselves to high standards as well.

Under Stress: When Challengers feel they have been wronged they do whatever it takes to even the score, even if it means being deceitful and fighting unfairly. Highly stressed Eights focus exclusively on their needs, ignore integrity, and act on simple self-interest.

Type Nine: Peacemakers

Normally: Nines score high in this area. Dishonesty makes it difficult for them to maintain their sense of well-being. They are also very trusting of others, choosing to see the best in people. Peacemakers find it easy to connect, and difficult to hurt and deceive people.

Under Stress: Nines lie through omission by not stating what they really believe or want. They agree to things to avoid disappointing people, but their actions and inaction undermine agreements. In an effort to fit in and feel liked, they commit to things and take on roles that they really disagree with.

TO IMPROVE IN TRUSTWORTHINESS:

- Behave ethically and consistently, be true to your own values, and confront any unethical behavior.
- Practice openness and simplicity. If you make a mistake, admit to it, share solutions, and ask for help.
- Don't make commitments you can't keep. Make realistic time and resource estimates.
- Don't misrepresent your experience or expertise. Be honest about what you can and can't do.
- Ask yourself which relationships in your life and work require more trust. Inquire into what's missing in your relationships. Be aware of how fragile trust is—that it takes time to build and can be lost in a moment.
- Follow through on all the truthful and valuable feedback you hear about yourself. People trust us when we heed their advice.

BUILDING RAPPORT

Each of the nine types has different fears and strategies to overcome those fears. When we help people feel safe and able to achieve their goals, they will more readily trust us; they will want to be aligned with us and with what we offer. There are general ways to build trust with each of the nine types; these involve helping them satisfy their preferred strategy. For example, when we help Threes feel accomplished, outstanding, and valuable, they will trust us and want to work with us; for Eights we will focus on helping them feel powerful, in control, and able to take action.

There are more subtle and refined ways to build trust. These involve *building rapport*— through questioning, listening, sharing, acknowledging, and establishing common ground.

Building Rapport With Perfectionists

- Help Ones to be proper, correct, and well prepared. Ensure that they will not feel judged or criticized, that they can feel safe and supported in striving for perfection and achieving quality.
- Ones make decisions by comparing things with the ideal. Show how what you offer is the ideal or a close approximation of it.
- Perfectionists want things to be logical and to make sense. They will not trust whimsical ideas and spontaneous approaches. Give them facts that they can analyze, debate, and ponder before expecting them to agree—and don't push for a quick answer.
- Emphasize the quality and reliability of your ideas—and emphasize *your* quality, fairness, reliability, competence, and commitment to value.
- Be detail oriented and speak in an orderly, precise manner. Proceed step by step to help Ones follow your logic.
- Perfectionists will trust you only if you can prove the accuracy of your statements. They want proof not opinions. They apply the same rigor to themselves.

Building Rapport With Helpers

- Help Twos to be connected to people, of service to others, and to feel genuinely appreciated for their good will, big heart, and people skills.

- Emphasize how you or your idea can benefit people and how it will bring people together. Emphasize how you will be personally involved with people throughout any interaction.
- Listen with empathy and be sympathetic to their needs. Small talk and getting to know them personally are powerful ways to influence Twos. Facts may be wasted on Helpers if you have not taken the time to break the ice and be friendly.
- Helpers are more people than task oriented; they respond to being needed, so let them know how they can be of help in some way. Maintain steady eye contact, smile, and be friendly.
- Make sure you tell Twos that you acknowledge the time they are giving you and that you appreciate their trust in you. Acknowledge that you notice the great influence they have on the people in their lives.
- Be aware that Helpers like to have power and influence, so tell them how your relationship and contributions will put them in a position to make things happen more effectively.

Building Rapport With Performers

- Help Threes to feel outstanding, noticed, productive, and appreciated for their contributions and accomplishments.
- Emphasize your relationship's usefulness, profitability, marketability (if appropriate), and ability to make the Three more visible.
- Get to the point. Keep the small talk to a minimum and be sure your communication is practical. Clearly explain your objective and how it can help Performers achieve their goals.
- Emphasize actions steps and results. Appeal to productivity, practicality, and getting the job done.
- Don't belabor details. Emphasize the bottom line. Performers want to make a quick decision, make things happen and move on to the next opportunity. Let them know their return on investment.
- Be enthusiastic, positive, and direct—and compliment their successes. Performers respond to praise for what they have accomplished.

Building Rapport With Individualists

- Help Fours to feel unique, appreciated, and emotionally connected.
- When presenting your thoughts to Individualists respect their space, office, and environment. They try to create just the right mood of sensitivity and elegance. You can be sure that objects in their office have been arranged for a specific impact. Don't move anything! Compliment them on their good taste and how interesting their space is.
- Give Fours a chance to process your ideas. They like to compare different concepts and make a feeling-based, intuitive decision. They have a sense of what is missing, what is best, what is workable for them. Gallup polls and social status will not influence them as much as their own taste and judgment. Respect their insight.
- Individualists are generally, but not always, more people than task focused. Aware Fours are good listeners and are sensitive to the needs of others.
- Communicate with creativity, depth, and with a difference—and try to arouse their imagination. Individualists enjoy getting excited about a compelling idea. Use symbols, stories, and metaphors that have an emotional, even dramatic impact—these will have greater appeal than raw data.
- Fours can be intense, and they appreciate intensity in others. Being emotionally open and vulnerable with Fours allows them to be themselves and to express their real feelings.

Building Rapport With Observers

- Help Fives to feel comfortable, unpressured, competent, informed, insightful, and assured that their contributions will be heard and their personal space respected.
- Let Observers know about the thought and research that went into your ideas. Fives are not so much status and label conscious as they are performance conscious.

- You may be able to establish trust based on the numbers alone. Too much passion can scare off Observers.
- Help Observers sort through the facts to see the big picture. They can become enamored with details. Walk them through examples and scenarios rather than tell them what to do or think. Be logical and sequential.
- Fives will feel that they can make a better decision if they have the freedom to do so, especially if they can be relieved of the pressure of deadlines, people, and tight schedules. Help Fives to decide by supplying the facts, the logic behind your recommendation, and then give them time. Let them sleep on it.
- Don't get too personal. Asking too many personal questions can be a turn off for Observers. Don't stray from the agenda, and deliver the facts with little emotion.

Building Rapport With Guardians

- Help Sixes to feel secure, responsible, and assured that involvement is safe for them and the group.
- Let Sixes know what's in it for you, and for your group. They're suspicious. If you don't profess any self-interest they may not trust you.
- Sixes are intellectually curious and want the facts, and they don't make decisions based solely on emotions. They are also strong team players and want to know other people's positions before deciding. Don't be in a hurry for a decision.
- Be serious about their concerns. Guardians want assurances. Answer any and all objections with facts and describe the steps you would take to solve any problems. You won't allay their worries and misgivings with statements such as, "Oh, don't worry about that," or "We'll cross that bridge when we get to it." Sixes want to be convinced with factual evidence and your guarantee. "Doubting Thomas" wants to be shown.

- Resist the temptation to sugar coat, exaggerate, reframe, or conceal things about the relationship. Sixes can detect con men a mile away and are ever fearful of being taken advantage of.
- Summarize what you've agreed to, the risks involved, any contingency plans, guarantees, etc., and profess your allegiance and desire to be a part of the team.

Building Rapport With Enthusiasts

- Help Sevens to feel excited, happy, satisfied, and assured that they will have freedom to pursue other options if desired.
- Appeal to the Enthusiast's sense of adventure. Emphasize the fun part, the interesting and the positive. Down play the routine and the mundane aspects of your relationship, service or product. If you can handle the grunt work for them (the boring paperwork and details), they will listen attentively.
- Let Sevens lay out their dreams and visions. Allow them to get excited about what they want, and help them see how that dream can be accomplished.
- Present as many options as you can. Let Sevens know that they will have ample opportunity to decide, to revisit, to brainstorm, experiment, and to change their mind. Sevens like to be involved in design and planning more than implementation. Focus on creating the big picture, and down play the hard work.
- Be creative. Enthusiasts love to be entertained and dazzled. They are entertainers and appreciate your effort at thinking outside the box, being innovative, and making people laugh. Sevens believe that nothing, including work, should be boring.
- Sevens like to be inspired, to make an impact, and to help people. Appeal to their desire to inspire, educate, motivate, or positively change the lives of those who interact with them.

Building Rapport With Challengers

- Help Eights feel powerful, in control, autonomous, and assured that they can take action and that their ideas will be considered and hopefully implemented.
- Challengers see themselves as decision-makers. Never tell them what they can't do. In most cases they're not overly concerned about the opinions of others because they know deep down they will make their own decision.
- Eights can be impulsive and can easily make decisions in the heat of battle. They believe that it is better to make a decision, even if it is the wrong one, than to be indecisive. They prefer to go by their instincts, and although they gather data, intuition drives their actions.
- Forego small talk and warm-ups and get to the point. Eights have little tolerance for unrealistic optimism. They want to know what they are in store for, what could possibly go wrong, etc. Avoid coming back later and telling an Eight, "Oh I forgot to tell you…"
- Be confident and stick to your guns. Challengers will automatically challenge your convictions. Demonstrating how strongly you feel by holding your ground will reassure Eights more than giving in to their challenges.
- Debate and friendly argument are ways Challengers learn about people. "Can you stand the heat?" "Can you deliver?" Eights are not subtle and they want to know what you can do for them; they learn this through verbal jousting, questioning, and testing.

Building Rapport With Peacemakers

- Help Nines to feel peaceful, composed, unhurried, unworried, and confident that their contributions will be considered and valued without much debate.
- Emphasize the ease of operation, reliability, and the "no hassle" quality of your relationship. Peacemakers want things to run smoothly and without conflicts. Appeal to their need to feel safe and supported.

- State your recommendation or preference. Nines like to hear what other people would do. They like information from those around them to help them find their own preferences because they often struggle with knowing what they want.
- Peacemakers are more people than task focused, and they prefer to make decisions by consensus. They like to share the credit and to have as many people as possible involved in important decisions.
- Silence doesn't mean that a Nine is in agreement with you. Nines are often noncommittal and unsure. Anxiety over decisions may cause them to put off coming to an agreement. Provide reminders. Summarize what you have discussed, and set clear objectives with dates and deadlines.
- Peacemakers can become overwhelmed by large projects. Approach large projects by breaking them into smaller components. Be clear about expectations and the Nine's role.

TAKE ACTION ON BUILDING TRUST

Share Information

- Offer to share one or two insights you have gained about your style based on what you know about your personality type. Ask a partner or teammate to do the same.

Ask For Feedback

- Select people you will ask for feedback and decide what you will ask about. Request that they focus their comments on you (not them), and follow these ground rules:
  1. Let go of the past.
  2. Tell the truth.
  3. Be supportive and helpful—not cynical and negative.
  4. Focus on improving, not judging.
  5. Suggest what actions you can take to be a better partner in the relationship.

6

Can We Deal with Conflict?

"Conflict magnifies and illuminates who we are. It seizes and startles you into seeing what makes you uncomfortable. It pushes your boundaries—intellectual, emotional, and physical. Conflict, if treated properly, offers the chance to change your mind altogether."

Kathy Cramer, Ph.D.

Conflict is a normal, healthy part of a relationship. Although many people think that disagreements and conflicts are negative and to be avoided, they are opportunities to learn more about each other and to deepen the connection. It's unrealistic to think that two or more people will agree on everything. Being open to conflict is a way to disagree and challenge each other's ideas in a healthy way. Conflict helps us find answers and make better decisions together. Conflict can trigger strong emotions, signaling a deep, personal need—usually a need to feel trusted, safe, respected, and valued—and often a need for greater connection.

Conflict is a gold mine for those who can see. In *Change the Way You See Everything Through Asset-Based Thinking*, Kathy Cramer, Ph.D. writes: "When faced with conflict, explore the possibilities that opposing forces can both be true simultaneously. Taking this perspective immediately dissolves animosity and piques curiosity. You find yourself wondering, 'What's their truth? Where is the value of their side?' When you finally give up the belief that yours is the only truth, it changes the game forever. Now you're in a position to see what new truth you can create together." Competencies and skills involved in dealing with conflict are Conflict Management, Empathy, and Communication.

WAKE UP CALL: WHAT'S YOUR CONFLICT TOLERANCE?

If we find ourselves in a relationship without occasional conflict we should question if: (1) we are being honest with each other, (2) we feel comfortable enough to express differences, and (3) we trust each other enough to disagree. If a relationship is always perfect perhaps differences are being ignored and not resolved. Purposefully causing conflict is just as damaging as ignoring issues we disagree with. Various expressions are used to describe how to deal with conflict, such as "Know when to hold 'em, and know when to fold 'em." Another favorite is "pick your battles." How much conflict can you tolerate? What do you consider to be productive and non-productive? Consider where you fall on the Conflict Tolerance Scale below.

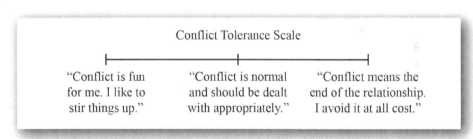

Conflict Tolerance Scale

"Conflict is fun for me. I like to stir things up."   "Conflict is normal and should be dealt with appropriately."   "Conflict means the end of the relationship. I avoid it at all cost."

CONFLICT MANAGEMENT: NEGOTIATING AND RESOLVING DISPUTES

Dealing with conflict draws on a variety of emotional competencies including empathy and communication, as well as the ability to make others feel valued through questioning, listening, sharing, and acknowledging. People skilled in Conflict Management:

- Manage people who don't agree with them with awareness and diplomacy.
- Foster open discussion, acceptance, and feedback.
- Anticipate potential conflicts, discuss them openly, and help resolve them.
- Practice give and take, and don't always have to win.
- Can appreciate and question other perspectives with objectivity.
- Are willing to accept small, incremental wins without the need for a "slam dunk."

The following section describes how each of the nine types deals with conflict.

Type One: Perfectionists

Normally: Perfectionists are logical and dispassionate, and don't dwell much on problems once they've been resolved. Ones see things in black and white, disregard emotions and rely on logic in negotiating and resolving conflict. Their logic is geared to making their point rather than to listening to the logical arguments of others.

Under Stress: Ones become rigid, stubborn and unwilling to hear what others say, especially on moral or ethical issues. They get angry and demand that others see their point of view. As tension mounts, Perfectionists struggle to remain unemotional and either become angry or disengage, giving others "the silent treatment."

Type Two: Helpers

Normally: Helpers work hard not to be embroiled in disputes, but if they do get involved, they might cooperate to a fault, giving in to please others. However, Twos have another side that is assertive and willing to take a stand. Helpers are good at resolving third-party disputes and bringing people together.

Under Stress: Helpers are stubborn, resist compromise and project their agenda and motives onto others—accusing others of usurping control, selfishness, and manipulation. Unaware Twos can be volatile and aggressive.

Type Three: Performers

Normally: Performers see conflict as a barrier to accomplishing tasks and a waste of time. They avoid emotional disputes whenever possible in the interest of efficiency and productivity. Threes manage conflicts unemotionally, allowing the accomplishment of goals to determine the actions to take to resolve issues.

Under Stress: Performers see only winning, and are combative, arrogant, and evasive. They avoid public, complicated confrontations, choosing instead to play politics, and cut back room deals to get people on their side.

Type Four: Individualists

Normally: Individualists have a paradoxical approach to dealing with disagreements. They willingly explore emotional conflict, and their empathy helps them see other perspectives. Their shyness, however, makes them reluctant to be too self-revealing. Their need to fully process their feelings makes it difficult for Fours to take action in difficult situations, and they may seem stubborn and aloof.

Under Stress: Individualists are combative, refuse to listen and compromise, preferring to retreat and sulk. They are rigid and critical, ignore their own shortcomings, and accuse others of being at fault. Increased tension causes Individualists to become more hostile, more withdrawn, and self-pitying, seeing themselves as misunderstood victims.

Type Five: Observers

Normally: Fives are unemotional and detached about conflict and are uncomfortable with the emotional reactions and volatility found in arguing, so they avoid it. Others may interpret an Observer's lack of emotional response as a sign of arrogance, disinterest or unwillingness to work towards an agreement.

Under Stress: Fives avoid conflict. Conflict is emotionally overwhelming to stressed Fives and they withdraw intellectually and physically, often leaving the room to find emotional safety.

Type Six: Guardians

Normally: Guardians often overreact to conflict, becoming fearful or aggressive. They misinterpret minor conflict as a huge threat. Because connection with the group is so important, Guardians may see disagreement as a personal attack, rather than as simple debate and discussion. They focus on the worst and miss the more hopeful aspects and growth potential that conflict can provide.

Under Stress: Guardians are overcome with fear and think that certain people are against them. Tension causes Sixes to cluster people into "in" and "out" groups and view those who disagree with them as enemies. In these situations there is no compromise, and defeating the opposing force is the only option.

Type Seven: Enthusiasts

Normally: Enthusiasts avoid conflict as long as possible, believing that it thrusts them into unpleasantness and negative thinking. If they can't avoid dealing with a dispute, they'll delegate it to someone else or get both sides focused on positive outcomes. Enthusiasts think that problems will resolve themselves if they can focus on possibilities.

Under Stress: Sevens ignore the source of the conflict by retreating. If they don't get satisfaction they become combative and insist that their needs be met regardless of the cost to others. Unaware Enthusiasts have trouble understanding why others are bothered by their behavior.

Type Eight: Challengers

Normally: Challengers enjoy some degree of conflict. They state their perspective assertively and confidently and often look for a challenge to overcome. They believe that their desires are more important than others' and make demands rather than requests. They may act too quickly, failing to consider others' feelings or viewpoint.

Under Stress: Challengers are drawn to conflict, believing that potential enemies are everywhere. Because they often demonize their opponent, they may have no desire to make peace. They try to resolve conflict by force rather than negotiation and are only satisfied when the other side gives in.

Type Nine: Peacemakers

Normally: Peacemakers try to avoid conflict. However, if conflict causes Nines great internal disharmony or threatens their autonomy, they will argue to reestablish their sense of inner peace. Nines make effective mediators for third-party conflicts, are supportive, and make all sides feel heard and appreciated. However, they may neglect expressing themselves out of fear of offending others.

Under Stress: Peacemakers can behave passively or aggressively—passively by ignoring or fleeing from conflict and adopting an attitude of magical thinking: "If I ignore it, it'll go away."—or aggressively by stubbornly refusing to give an inch.

TO IMPROVE IN CONFLICT MANAGEMENT

- Use self-awareness and self-control to consciously and logically choose what to say and do.
- Be empathic toward others, but emphasize logic and reason.
- Deliberately look at issues from different perspectives. Be aware if you are reluctant or unable to understand the viewpoint of others. This reaction is an important warning signal, because it will be impossible to resolve conflict if you cannot, at least partially, understand another point of view.
- Encourage open discussion and feedback and consider alternative solutions instead of going with the first option that presents itself. Be creative and imaginative.
- Our disagreements with people are often based on one of two things: data (the facts), and our judgments (our opinions, biases, history, etc.). Try to be aware of the difference between the data and your judgments, and focus on the data.
- Set aside 15 minutes a day for problem solving. Get away from your normal activities and think about how you interact with others and how you make decisions. Ask yourself if your decisions are driven by emotion or reason.

EMPATHY: BEING AWARE OF AND PARTICIPATING IN OTHERS' FEELINGS, IDEAS, AND NEEDS

Being empathetic requires two fundamental skills: the ability to feel what another feels and the ability to effectively communicate. Empathy means: (1) we are willing to be vulnerable, to get in touch with our own sensitivity and allow ourselves to imagine what it would be like to be in another's situation; (2) we are moved to understand what has happened, why it has happened and how we can help; (3) we feel a need to communicate compassion and understanding and to share our human experience with another.

The first step in improving our ability to be empathic is to *become aware of how empathic we are.* What are our barriers and tendencies in communicating kindness and understanding? What are our fears in letting ourselves be open to the suffering of others? What is our capacity to forgive people, to offer help, and to enrich our connection? People skilled in Empathy:

- Are interested in and attentive to people—watching, wondering, and allowing themselves to be affected by others.
- Care what happens to people and are sensitive to the feelings and needs of others.
- Understand the difference between expressions of emotions and "drama."
- Respect and tolerate ideas and opinions that they don't agree with.

The following section describes how well each type deals with conflict by being aware of and participating in others' feelings, ideas, and needs.

Type One: Perfectionists

Normally: Perfectionists are not highly attuned to the emotional states of others, and focus more on logic and practicality. They have difficulty empathizing with ideas that are in conflict with their own. When Ones see people's needs as correct or lawful, they are good at agreeing with and meeting them.

Under Stress: Ones struggle with empathy. They are more self-critical and project their judgments onto other people—criticizing people for their shortcomings and emotional needs. Perfectionists expect people to be logical and serious and to avoid frivolity and emotionality.

Type Two: Helpers

Normally: Helpers excel in empathy. They naturally sense the needs of others and anticipate what support is needed. Twos put their gifts to use and are often found in helping professions such as medicine, teaching, human resources, and social work.

Under Stress: Twos demand that their needs be met first. They are manipulative and pretend to be empathic when they are trying to take care of themselves. Pressure causes stressed Twos to aggressively demand attention, to be applauded and cared for.

Type Three: Performers

Normally: Threes struggle with empathy because their attention is on accomplishing tasks rather than feeling compassion. They regard feelings as distractions from being focused and effective, and become frustrated when people let emotions stop them from achieving goals.

Under Stress: Performers increasingly ignore their emotions and their empathy diminishes. They are uncomfortable around emotional people and are confused about how to react; they depend on others for guidance on how they should feel and what they should say or do.

Type Four: Individualists

Normally: Individualists are very empathic. Fours feel their own pain, anxiety, and sorrow acutely, and can understand and sympathize with others. They enjoy discussing feelings and are deeply caring and nurturing.

Under Stress: Individualists are self-absorbed and struggle to feel empathy for others. They are rigid in their views and demand that others acknowledge their suffering. Angry and envious, stressed Fours minimize others' problems, feeling that their own pain and disappointment outweigh that of others.

Type Five: Observers

Normally: Observers have difficulty showing empathy and relate more through thinking and sharing information. Fives are shy and uncomfortable talking about their feelings; they struggle trying to relate to the emotional issues of others.

Under Stress: Observers experience increased discomfort being exposed to emotional people. They avoid these situations if possible and under increased tension they flee from or deny others' emotions, shutting out the world rather than participating in it.

Type Six: Guardians

Normally: Guardians are aware of and responsive to other people, and are attuned to what others are thinking and feeling. They meet people's needs and are friendly and dependable. Sixes are keen observers and seek to understand people; this helps them anticipate the behavior of others and to judge whether they can be trusted.

Under Stress: As anxiety increases, Guardians become suspicious and more concerned about their needs than the needs of others. Increased tension makes Sixes paranoid and less willing to participate in others' feelings, ideas and needs.

Type Seven: Enthusiasts

Normally: Enthusiasts are quick to share in someone's joy, excitement, and enthusiasm. They are happy for the good fortune of others and desire the best for everyone. They are also aware of a person's less joyful feelings but choose not to dwell on them. Sevens prefer to ignore their own negative feelings and avoid people they regard as negative.

Under Stress: Enthusiasts may appear to be out of touch with their feelings when they fend off their unhappiness and the unhappiness of others; they can seem insensitive when they ignore the distress and anxiety of others. Their behavior leaves little room for being aware of or participating in the feelings, ideas, and needs of others.

Type Eight: Challengers

Normally: Challengers struggle in this area. They seem unaware of the feelings of others. They're uncomfortable with their own emotional needs and those of others and prefer to downplay them. Because they feel strongly that people should take care of themselves, Eights don't feel a strong need to emotionally comfort others.

Under Stress: Challengers regard emotional needs as weaknesses and feel self-contempt for having them. They project their own contempt onto others. The discomfort of seeing another's sensitivity or need for emotional comfort causes stressed Eights to ridicule or punish them for being weak.

Type Nine: Peacemakers

Normally: Nines are empathic and can easily identify with people's needs, discomforts and hurts. Peacemakers have a strong desire to connect. They do this naturally and are energized by the lives and interests of others. Being compassionate toward people makes them feel good about themselves.

Under Stress: Peacemakers ignore or reject what disturbs their inner peace. They become angry or frustrated when forced to deal with the unpleasantness of someone's negative emotions, needs, or ideas.

TO IMPROVE IN EMPATHY:

- Practice being open and sensitive to the feelings, ideas, and needs of others. Listen closely for emotional cues, and ask about the well-being of others. A simple, "How are you doing?" is a powerful way to connect. Never take it for granted, people notice when we ask, and when we don't, because it sends the message that we care.
- Give people the benefit of the doubt; assume that they are operating with good, positive motives. Focus on the positive—confront issues, not people—and allow people to save face.
- Look for a person's gifts. Acknowledge them and make them feel valuable.

- Respect and tolerate perspectives and opinions that you may not agree with.
- Consistently try to understand the way other people feel. Ask how you can serve: "What is one thing I can do to help strengthen this relationship?"
- Get rid of sarcasm. Retain your sense of humor while avoiding nit picking and subtle insults. If you offend people, apologize.
- Feel empathy for yourself. Forgive yourself for not being perfect, and offer your forgiveness to others as a gift.

COMMUNICATION: LISTENING OPENLY AND SENDING CONVINCING MESSAGES

Along with conflict management and empathy, effective communication is the third emotional competency required to deal with conflict. Understanding is a goal in any communication process. Understanding at a basic level is easily achieved, but a deeper understanding that can resolve conflict requires focus and hard work. This involves overcoming barriers to communication, being able to express ourselves effectively, and active listening. People skilled in Communication:

- Use emotions, tone of voice, and nonverbal communication to convey their message.
- Encourage open dialogue and accept bad news without defensiveness, and good news with graciousness and gratitude.
- Listen openly without interrupting. Don't assume that others are good listeners.
- Greet people by name.
- Communicate clearly and convincingly.
- Ask relevant questions.

The following section describes how well each type communicates through listening openly and sending convincing messages

Type One: Perfectionists

Normally: Perfectionists struggle with listening without judgment. They have a strong desire to offer their opinion or advice. Ones send rational, thorough, and earnest messages rather than passionate and inspiring ones. They instill trust by focusing on logic and correctness.

Under Stress: Perfectionists listen through judgmental ears and send messages laced with advice and criticism. Their communication is influenced by their rigidly held opinions rather than the facts, and their listeners may feel unheard and invalidated. Perfectionists often resort to guilt or an appeal to a higher moral authority to be convincing.

Type Two: Helpers

Normally: Helpers do well in this area. They are good listeners and respond positively. They focus on others more than themselves and enthusiastically share personal details about their lives. They are supportive, have good interpersonal skills, and have a strong desire to connect with people.

Under Stress: Twos are dramatic, emotional, and aggressive. They are less interested in listening, communicating, or helping others and become focused on their own needs. Stressed Helpers dominate interactions and offer little space for others to talk.

Type Three: Performers

Normally: Threes listen well, but with an agenda: to find common ground in order to create beneficial relationships that will help Performers achieve *their* goals. They listen for important facts such as names, titles, and relationships. Threes are charming and make people feel valuable. They are better at sending than listening to messages.

Under Stress: Performers boast about their successes to people they regard as important and influential, so they focus more on bosses and less on peers and subordinates. As pressure to be the best increases, stressed Performers over sell themselves and their accomplishments, make promises they can't keep, and send messages that sound too good to be true.

Type Four: Individualists

Normally: Individualists are good listeners who are emotionally available and eager to discuss problems. They like intensity and drama, dislike small talk, and may lose interest if discussions are mundane or tedious. They are passionate, inspiring, and convincing when discussing their interests.

Under Stress: Individualists are self-absorbed; they bemoan their problems, bad luck, and how unfair the world is toward them. Envy is a common theme and they like to point out people's flaws. Stressed Fours are hypersensitive to criticism and may "shoot the messenger."

Type Five: Observers

Normally: Observers are quiet and struggle initiating conversations in social settings, preferring to listen. They are more comfortable talking in one-on-one conversations. They communicate factually and with great insight, and express excitement when talking about their interests. They can be overly abstract and focused on obscure data, and they avoid showing their feelings.

Under Stress: Observers show off their intellect and command of the facts. They may talk down to people whom they believe are not as intelligent as they are. The more stressed they are the less they share their feelings, becoming increasingly disinterested and detached. Stressed Fives may become silent and disengaged in large groups.

Type Six: Guardians

Normally: Guardians are excellent communicators. They are outgoing, engaging, and curious, and make people feel important and appreciated. Sixes are intelligent listeners and troubleshooters and they evaluate ideas for their strengths and flaws. They send well considered, convincing messages.

Under Stress: Mistrust and anxiety prevent Guardians from sharing as much as they could. They listen with suspicion and bias. They question the speaker's ideas and focus on their own counter arguments. Increased tension causes Sixes to see only the negative and become mired in pessimism.

Type Seven: Enthusiasts

Normally: Enthusiasts are entertaining and love to tell stories. They are convincing speakers who can build excitement. They may prefer talking to listening, struggle waiting for their turn to speak, and may interrupt out of impatience. Sevens like to keep conversations fast paced and upbeat.

Under Stress: Enthusiasts are self-centered, and dominate the conversation. If a message doesn't fit their agenda, stressed Sevens reject it. They prefer talking about future plans and fantasies. Increased pressure causes Sevens to listen less and speak at a faster pace. Their hyperactivity and impatience can leave people overwhelmed.

Type Eight: Challengers

Normally: Challengers excel at sending convincing messages, and are average listeners. Confident that they know the truth, they only partially listen, or listen in order to challenge the speaker. They are impatient and interrupt to state their case. Eights convince with power, excitement, and confidence, and can drown out other people's ideas by passionately expressing their own.

Under Stress: Challengers become loud, demanding, and abusive. They give commands and make demands rather than engage in dialogue. As tension mounts stressed Eights stop listening to other viewpoints, convinced that their ideas are the only ones worth hearing.

Type Nine: Peacemakers

Normally: Peacemakers are good listeners and express interest in the views of others. They are convincing communicators, instilling a sense of trust and comfort in the listener. However, they can give the impression that they're interested when in fact they aren't; they are simply being polite, while consumed in their own thoughts, or eavesdropping on other conversations.

Under Stress: Peacemakers listen poorly; they resist hearing or delivering unsettling news. They protect the group—and themselves—by sugarcoating and procrastinating. Their messages are incomplete, vague, and lack details. With increased stress, they are argumentative, trying to get others to agree with them in an effort to create consensus.

TO IMPROVE IN COMMUNICATION:

- Be curious, and don't assume that you've been understood. Ask, "What questions do you have?"
- Listen without interrupting. What are the words, the tone, and the nonverbal message conveying? Was the message congruent? In other words, did the words match the tone and the nonverbal message?
- Summarize, or ask someone to summarize what was said or agreed to.
- Test your accuracy and understanding by paraphrasing discussions.
- Try to see the entire picture. Be aware of your blind spots and biases.
- Attempt to keep people as informed as possible. Ask yourself: Am I withholding information that others need? Do I allow time to address questions and problems? Do I give people only the information *I* think they need, or do I allow *them* to determine what they need?
- Acknowledge another's feelings. A statement such as "I can see that you feel strongly about this…" helps people believe that they are really being listened to.

TAKE ACTION ON DEALING WITH CONFLICT

In his book, *What Got You Here Won't Get You There*, Marshall Goldsmith gives sound relationship advice to leaders trying to take their leadership skills to the next level. Much of his advice is simple, tested, and reliable, such as the following:

Forgive People and Move On

- Who do you need to forgive?
- What events do you need to let go of?
- Stop judging; begin helping.
- Be aware that you may be interpreting something as conflict when it is a difference in personality style.
- Follow "The Golden Rule."

- Trust that dropping your grievances will benefit the relationship and the team.
- Let go of the past. Focus on moving forward.

Admit Your Mistakes and Apologize

- Ask yourself if a conflict is based on *your* behavior.
- During disagreements be open to see when you are wrong and admit when you are.
- Apologizing creates closure, which lets you move forward. Everybody makes mistakes; brave people admit them.
- Keep it simple: "I'm sorry. I'll do better."

7

Can We Make and Keep Commitments?

"Whatever you can do or dream you can, begin it. Boldness has genius, power and magic in it. Begin it now."

Johann Goethe

After determining that we can trust each other and deal effectively with conflict, the next question to ask is whether we can make and keep mutual commitments. When we are truly connected in a productive and caring relationship, we will commit to a goal and remain committed until the goal is accomplished. Making a commitment is easy when we are in agreement and when things are going smoothly. The real test of commitment is when misunderstandings arise, actions go off course, and we begin to question the relationship. Competencies and skills involved in making and keeping commitments are Resiliency and Adaptability.

WAKE UP CALL: HOW DO WE KNOW WE'RE COMMITTED?

Commitment means that we've made a promise, and no matter what happens, we won't waver. A commitment has certainty and passion. It has power and vision. When obstacles appear they don't deter us because the thing we're committed to is what matters the most, above all else. One of the memorable scenes in the movie "Star Wars" shows an exasperated Yoda saying enigmatically to Luke Skywalker, "Always with you it's what *cannot* be done! Hear you nothing that I say? You must unlearn what you have learned." Luke replies reluctantly and with very little confidence, "All right. I'll give it a try," to which Yoda famously declares, "No! Try not. Do. Or do not. There is no try."

We often say what Luke Skywalker said: "I'll give it a try." But "I'll try" is no indication of a commitment, no matter how sincerely and impassioned we declare it. How do we know when we, or someone else is committed? Author Steve Chandler believes that our *actions*, not our words, indicate commitment. He tells the story of an employee, let's call him Jack, who is in St. Louis, asking his teammate, Harry, if he'll meet him in Philadelphia for an important meeting.

"I'll try," says Harry.

"That's not very convincing," says Jack.

"Oh, you know I'll be there," says Harry.

"That's not much better," says Jack.

"I promise," says Harry "I'm making a commitment to be there."

"I'm still not convinced," says Jack. "I want a *real* commitment. Then I'll feel confident that you'll be there."

"A real commitment? What would that be?" asks Harry.

"Show me a plane ticket and a hotel reservation in Philadelphia," says Jack. "Then I'll know you're committed."

It's easy to make promises. But words are simply words if they are not backed up by action. Is this a pattern of yours? How often do you assume that you will fulfill your commitment only to fail to deliver?

How can you *take action* regarding your commitments? What one or two actions can you take that will "lock in" your commitments, hold your feet to the fire, and provide negative consequences if you fail to keep your promise?

RESILIENCY: ENDURING IN THE FACE OF OBSTACLES

Resiliency and endurance are essential skills for keeping commitments. Can we remain dedicated when we are stressed, unsure of the relationship or the goal, or when the grass looks greener on the other side of the fence? Can we remain focused when things get boring and tedious, or when we feel out of control, or unsafe? When we make a commitment we establish buy-in around important decisions even when people initially disagree. People skilled in Resiliency:

- Stay the course when the going gets tough.
- React to pressure with hardiness, curiosity, and rigor.
- Can tolerate another's discomfort.
- Know how to deal with upsetting problems and can see difficult people as a challenge rather than a threat.
- Know when they are reaching their stress threshold.
- Recover rapidly from tension and upset.

The following section describes how each type expresses resiliency and endurance in the face of obstacles.

Type Ones: Perfectionists

Normally: Perfectionists use obstacles to verify their belief that the world is imperfect, that part of being good involves working hard when we have a challenge. Ones are pessimistic, expect roadblocks, and are prepared for them. They endure and function well during challenges. If they believe in the cause or relationship, obstacles will often increase a Perfectionist's commitment.

Under Stress: Perfectionists express resilience negatively by digging in their heels and staying the course. They act like martyrs, and believe that life is a chore and not meant to be enjoyed. Ones view their stubbornness as righteousness. They confuse being judgmental and placing blame with problem solving.

Type Two: Helpers

Normally: Helpers see obstacles as chances to help those in need, so they can do well in this competency. They focus on people in trouble, but they may have difficulty dealing with their own problems. They struggle with asking for help and resent having to do so. They prefer that help be offered voluntarily.

Under Stress: Helpers refuse to ask for help when they need it most. They expect special treatment, and for people to be at their beck and call. Stressed Helpers may perceive their personal troubles as a good chance for others to repay them for all that the Helper has done for them.

Type Three: Performers
Normally: Performers have a high capacity to overcome obstacles. They relentlessly pursue their objectives and use them as fuel for their competitive fire. They have confidence in themselves and their ability to accomplish goals, and take pride in proclaiming what they have achieved against the odds.

Under Stress: Performers aren't interested in working on projects or relationships that don't bring success, recognition, or advancement. In such cases they prefer to delegate the heavy lifting to others and may disengage from the project or relationship.

Type Four: Individualists
Normally: Although Individualists probably won't admit that they like problems, they may find solace in obstacles, because obstacles verify their belief that life is unfair to them and that they must work harder to function than most people. They withdraw from people and seek solitude to process their troubles and recharge themselves.

Under Stress: Fours bemoan their fate, over-dramatize their situation and resist taking action to overcome obstacles. As stress increases Individualists feel more and more victimized, and may disengage or seek help from a perceived rescuer.

Type Five: Observers
Normally: Observers do well in this category if they can stand back, think logically, and gain clarity and supporting data while not getting emotionally affected. They enjoy good, intellectual challenges, but avoid emotional ones.

Under Stress: Observers struggle with resiliency if they don't have the opportunity to detach and give themselves time to analyze the problem. When forced to face problems under pressure Fives retreat from people, feel anxious, and obsessively over analyze.

Type Six: Guardians

Normally: Guardians do well here because they anticipate problems and how to handle them. They prepare for the worst so they are seldom caught off guard. Sixes draw on their emotional strength, logic, and strong network of friends and family to help remain strong and resilient.

Under Stress: Guardians see obstacles as insurmountable catastrophes. Tension causes them to become frantic and over reactive, and to imagine challenges that don't exist. Stressed Sixes focus on the worst rather than best outcomes and are paralyzed by fear rather than mobilized to act.

Type Seven: Enthusiasts

Normally: Enthusiasts have an optimistic point of view toward challenges if they see them as exciting. They can shift focus from the negative to the positive and work toward resolution. Sevens are creative and skilled at brainstorming possibilities; they rebound from adversity quickly.

Under Stress: Optimism works in reverse when Enthusiasts underestimate the work required to solve problems, and they have little taste for long, drawn-out challenges. They're frustrated by roadblocks and may quit prematurely. Stressed Sevens blame others for their bad luck and overlook their own role in creating obstacles.

Type Eight: Challengers

Normally: Challengers do well with handling obstacles. They see obstacles as a way to test their will power and resiliency. For Eights, winning a challenge reassures them of their power and control. Eights take pride in enduring difficulties more than other types.

Under Stress: Challengers over react and can "use a sledgehammer to kill a fly." Complaining about obstacles and exaggerating their hardships energizes them. The more intense their troubles, the more aggressive Eights become—reacting rashly, even brutally, to defeat the competition.

Type Nine: Peacemakers

Normally: Peacemakers react fairly well to problems. They are positive and believe that things will work out for the best in the long run. Nines go with the flow and accept obstacles as part of life. They prefer to look at the big picture, downplay challenges, and convey this perspective and optimism to others.

Under Stress: Peacemakers ignore obstacles and refuse to experience their impact. They wait for things to resolve on their own. As threats grow Nines lose their calm perspective and feel overwhelmed. Increased tension results in anger and fear, and feelings of being trapped; Stressed Nines become shut down and resigned to the status quo.

TO IMPROVE IN RESILIENCY:

- Learn something from your mistakes. When you attempt something and fail, ask yourself what you have learned, rather than criticize yourself or blame someone else. Discovering the value in your mistakes will make you smarter, more productive, and happier.
- Deal with upsetting problems with balance and appropriateness, without over or under reacting, and recover rapidly from stress.
- Don't put off dealing with problems; get involved with them when they are happening. Waiting for stressful situations to pass may work occasionally, but is usually not the best strategy.
- See the difference between failure, which is part of life, and labeling yourself a failure. Take control of your self-talk: change statements such as "I always," or "I never" to "This time," or "Occasionally." Change critical statements such as "I'm a jerk," to truthful ones like "I made a mistake this time." Take responsibility only for your own actions.

ADAPTABILITY: FLEXIBILITY IN HANDLING CHANGE

Adaptability tests our ability to handle multiple requests and frequent changes and demands. It enables us to stay committed when original agreements, goals, and plans change. Change happens more rapidly than ever before; it is inevitable and is to be expected. Being adaptable in order to keep commitments is an important measure of the strength of a relationship. We will see many variations in how the nine types perceive and react to change, especially when the pressure is on. People skilled in Adaptability:

- Are open, curious, and creative in finding ways to adapt to changing circumstances.
- When given enough evidence, can change their opinions and behavior.
- Are flexible in the way they perceive and interpret circumstances and people.

The following section describes how skilled each type is in being adaptable to handling change.

Type One: Perfectionists

Normally: Perfectionists have difficulty making changes if their morals, standards, and values are questioned, which they see as unchangeable. They can appear uncooperative and pessimistic if they feel they are being asked to compromise in these areas. On the other hand, Ones are on a quest to improve themselves and their world, so they are often trying to change something.

Under Stress: Perfectionists are committed more and more to maintaining the status quo, where a rigid adherence to the rules and regulations are sacrosanct. They can become dogmatic and resist change out of fear of making mistakes. They become increasingly stubborn and mistrust others' judgments and decisions about making changes.

Type Two: Helpers

Normally: Helpers embrace change when they see it as an opportunity to rescue or help people, and when the change will bring people closer together. If the change requires them to make personal sacrifices and can impress important people, Twos will be assertive, compassionate, and enthusiastically involved.

Under Stress: If Helpers feel unappreciated for their sacrifices, their anger and resentment grows. They express their anger at not being seen as helpful and important. They seek the support and protection of key people who can protect them from the fallout of change and help bolster their self-esteem.

Type Three: Performers
Normally: Performers shine in this area. Threes use their ability to make quick changes as a way of meeting challenges and accomplishing goals. They subscribe to "the end justifies the means," and consider changes as ways to rise to the occasion and show their commitment to being the best.

Under Stress: Performers are adaptable, sometimes to a fault. They abandon their own point of view if it means being successful and making the correct impression. They are overly political and appeasing and do or say what is necessary to win people over to their side.

Type Four: Individualists
Normally: Individualists welcome a change that allows them more freedom to express themselves. They value autonomy and dislike being restricted by arbitrary rules. They can make change for change sake—if it's *their* change. Fours resist change when it affects their creativity or personal expression.

Under Stress: Individualists take change personally, as if it were created to make their lives miserable. As stress increases, Fours can use change as an excuse to rebel—to express anger toward people who have not appreciated them; they respond by being moody, brooding, and passive-aggressive.

Type Five: Observers
Normally: Observers are good at handling change if it allows them to learn more and/or improve things. They hold few imposed "sacred cows," such as policies, rules, and social norms. However, they greatly value their personal patterns as comforting and supportive. Having their own processes and routines helps them to spend time doing the things they find meaningful and necessary.

Under Stress: Observers can be condescending and arrogant. They reject change and those who suggest it. They use stubbornness, the "silent treatment," and passive-aggressiveness to express their disapproval. Fives will wait out the opposition rather than behave aggressively. Their commitment will wane more and more if they think the changes are stupid or ill conceived.

Type Six: Guardians
Normally: Guardians adjust to change fairly well if someone they trust initiates it. However, change causes anxiety for less-aware Sixes who feel threatened and fearful that they won't have adequate support to manage the change. They favor tradition, routine, and what is familiar, and mistrust the unfamiliar and unpredictable. They feel they can't trust what they don't know, and can't commit to what they don't trust.

Under Stress: Guardians mistrust changes in general. They see danger that may not be there and are suspicious by nature. They may become unbending and combative and can panic or become overwhelmed by anxiety. They seek security in routine, and their commitment will be to the past, the old ways, people, and systems.

Type Seven: Enthusiasts
Normally: Change excites Enthusiasts. They see change as positive and necessary and embrace it as an opportunity to expand their horizons. Sevens are open to suggestions and will commit to ideas that they can become excited about. They excel at initiating things and are great change agents.

Under Stress: Sevens dislike changes if they feel that their options will be limited. They may lose interest and commitment if things become tedious, boring, or too difficult. They initiate their own change, break arrangements, promises, or relationships. Also, under increased stress Sevens refuse to change while demanding that others do so.

Type Eight: Challengers
Normally: Challengers are suspicious of change not made by them. They become angry and stubborn if change is imposed on them. Initiating change, however, strengthens their sense of control. They are valuable instruments of change, and they mobilize people to support new ideas and plans.

Under Stress: Challengers are confrontational when change is forced on them. They find it much easier to commit to their ideas than to someone else's. They defend their ideas stubbornly, proclaiming, "My way is the only way." They are disruptive, defiant and may undermine change that they disagree with.

Type Nine: Peacemakers

Normally: Peacemakers struggle with committing to change that pushes them out of their steady and comfortable environment. They may promise to make changes, but if they aren't completely in agreement, Nines may resist complying by slowing down, procrastinating, and agreeing outwardly while resisting inwardly. However, once Nines accept the change, they are able to adapt and commit.

Under Stress: Peacemakers dig in for the long haul. If change requires effort that is emotionally difficult, stressed Nines may become angry, stubborn, and argumentative. They blame others for not being open-minded and not seeing their point of view. Stressed Nines may stubbornly refuse to make changes that may benefit them just to make a point, and to prove that they have backbone.

TO IMPROVE IN ADAPTABILITY:

- Be open to changing your opinion when given new, convincing data. Become a change agent when change is necessary and when it solves problems.
- Appreciate adaptability as a valuable skill—realize that the more able you are to change, the more successful you will be in any relationship.
- Adapt your reactions and behaviors to fit the situation and the person. Resist seeing everyone through your "tunnel vision" lens. *One size does not fit all.*
- Expect that your work environment and personal relationships are dynamic and chaotic, and may involve conflict—and remember that conflict is not necessarily a bad thing.

- Count to ten. If you encounter changing priorities, get more information before you react. Processing and internalizing the change will make it easier to accept.

TAKE ACTION ON MAKING AND KEEPING COMMITMENTS

Stop Making Excuses and Blaming Others

- Consider areas where you fail to keep commitments with people. See how blaming others and making excuses allows this to continue.
- Where do you procrastinate? Where do you do what's more interesting? Where do you avoid doing what's unpleasant?

Drop the Non-committed "Victim of Circumstance" Language

- "I'll do my best," "I'll try," "If I get to it," and "I've been meaning to do that," are examples of weak, vague, non-committed language.

Take Committed "Owner of My Own Destiny" Action

- "By 4 PM this Friday," "I've cleared my calendar," "I bought the ring," are examples of strong, clear, committed language.

8

Can We Be Accountable?

"Our chief want in life is to find someone who will make us do what we can."

Ralph Waldo Emerson

Being accountable means that we will do what we say we will do; it means honoring commitments, and holding others and ourselves accountable for decisions and promises. Being accountable involves being open to feedback about our actions. When we're accountable we accept input, questions, and encouragement from others to help us stay or get back on track. For example, we may question what thought process we went through, what excuses we made, what options we chose that caused us to be out of accountability, and if this is a pattern in our life.

People and groups that hold each other accountable make sure that poor performers are held responsible and feel pressure to improve. They point out potential problems early, ensure that people are answerable to the same standards, and avoid bureaucracy, hierarchy, and reluctance to address issues. Specific emotional competencies and skills that address accountability are Achievement Drive, Self-Control, and Changing Ineffective Behavior.

WAKE UP CALL: ARE WE CLEAR AND ACCOUNTABLE?

The ManKind Project is a non-profit, educational organization, with the stated purpose to "support men in leading meaningful lives of integrity, accountability, responsibility, and emotional intelligence." It helps men discover and live personal missions of service in the world. After their initial "New Warrior" training, men meet regularly to support each other in accomplishing their missions and to grow as men. These meetings follow a well-defined structure of four rounds. One part is called the "Warrior Round," when each man is asked to reflect on how faithful he has been to his personal mission and how well he has kept his agreements to the men in his group and to the people in his life—if he is, in fact, "clear and accountable." Each man takes his turn in stating if he is accountable or if he is "out of accountability." If he has not been accountable, he has the opportunity to state the situation and be guided through the following questions:

"What was your commitment?"

"What choice did you make rather than keep your commitment?"

"What was the impact of your choice on you?"

"What may have been the impact on others?"

"Is this a pattern in your life?"

"What message did your actions send to others?"

"Is that the message you intended to send?"

"If not, what new commitment can you make now?"

A warrior, whether man or woman, young or old, is accountable to commitments made. Of course we all make mistakes and fail, and this simple process helps us come back into alignment with our commitments, to renew them, and to learn from our mistakes. It is important to see that the process leaves no room for excuses, and makes us focus on our *choices and the impact they have had on others and us.*

The next time you find yourself out of accountability, step into your "Warrior" and give this Q and A process a try.

ACHIEVEMENT DRIVE: MEETING OR IMPROVING STANDARDS OF EXCELLENCE

What are we accountable for in a relationship? Whether a work team or a personal friendship, we will invariably have mutual goals that we want to accomplish in order to make the relationship viable, interesting, and worthwhile. Achievement drive is not simply about accomplishing tasks and then checking them off our To-Do List. It's more about improving our previously established standards, and consistently doing more than just the minimum. And the power of being in a workable relationship involves encouraging our partners and teammates to help us accomplish our goals by holding us accountable. People who are skilled in Achievement Drive:

- Desire to do their best, are competitive and ambitious.
- Establish stretch goals and work hard to accomplish them.
- Avoid playing it safe, and take appropriate risks.
- Ask for feedback and use it to improve.

Type One: Perfectionists

Normally: A passing grade is not good enough for Perfectionists so they do well in this competency. Their drive to succeed is a way to prove their value and to gain rewards and recognition. Excellence, especially flawless performance, is an indicator of perfection, capability, and constant improvement for Ones.

Under Stress: Perfectionists respond by working longer hours and making greater efforts. Fear of making a mistake makes stressed Ones cautious and hesitant. They move from trying to improve themselves to trying to improve others, and blame others for hindering their progress.

Type Two: Helpers

Normally: Helpers pursue excellence, but they don't have the kind of achievement drive that is normally associated with high-performers. They want to gain the respect and appreciation of people—especially powerful and/or influential people. They are motivated more by establishing and maintaining relationships than by raw ambition. Helpers pride themselves in being pleasing and accountable to others.

Under Stress: Helpers feel unappreciated and insist on recognition. Increased pressure causes them to inflate their importance and contributions. If stressed Twos don't get the acknowledgment they feel they deserve, they become rebellious and demanding.

Type Three: Performers

Normally: Performers excel in this competency. They are goal setters who want to be the best and to be acknowledged as such. They thrive on competition and breaking records. Being a winner brings Performers the approval and validation that they crave.

Under Stress: Performers become obsessive in a desire to achieve more. If they're not exceeding standards, they may exaggerate their achievements. They may disparage the competition and others whom they feel threaten their success.

Type Four: Individualists

Normally: Individualists are uninterested in excellence if it is connected with ordinary, (and what Fours consider) meaningless standards. They are committed if the standards involve their personal expression, and their sense of elegance and aesthetics. They are true to themselves and more accountable to their own vision than that of others.

Under Stress: Individualists lose interest in attaining excellence and are pessimistic that they can. They withdraw rather than try to improve things. With increased stress, Fours become fatalistic and unwilling to lower their standards in order to achieve excellence in the "mundane" world.

Type Five: Observers

Normally: Observers are normally not that interested in standard measures of excellence. Their interest lies in proving the excellence of their knowledge. They prefer to pursue their own intellectual curiosities and to find answers to problems that others miss. Outside pressure holds little sway and they are accountable to themselves more than others.

Under Stress: Observers are contended to live in their own world. They feel that their interests and skills are not appreciated and not often rewarded. Stressed Fives will pursue their real interests on their own; they may behave more and more like hermits, isolating themselves from society's definition of achievement.

Type Six: Guardians

Normally: Guardians do very well in this area. They pride themselves in being loyal and feel secure when they meet group standards. They strive to be responsible and to contribute to the welfare of their family, their relationships, and their team. Being watchful and making steady improvements helps Guardians gain approval from their peers and gain the security they crave.

Under Stress: Guardians push harder to do better, but pressure to perform and to be accountable increases their anxiety. They criticize themselves for not achieving more and/or blame others for getting in their way. If being excellent makes them too visible or a target for criticism, stressed Sixes scale down their activity, preferring the safety of conformity and fitting in.

Type Seven: Enthusiasts

Normally: Enthusiasts enjoy competition and the satisfaction of doing something well. They set challenges for themselves as a way of making life more interesting. They are more intrigued by the thrill of engagement than the end result itself, and are driven more by personal satisfaction than being accountable to someone else's standards or expectations.

Under Stress: Enthusiasts have difficulty if achieving excellence is boring to them. When the excitement wanes, Sevens lose interest. Under increased pressure they become rigid, critical, and demanding. As obstacles increase, Sevens fear failure and avoid being held accountable. They may create a reason, such as being too busy, for changing course.

Type Eight: Challengers

Normally: Challengers see standards as opportunities to test their excellence. Breaking records and being Number One energizes them. They challenge others by creating higher standards for people to achieve. They are less concerned about being accountable to established standards than to their own, believing "I hold myself accountable to no man."

Under Stress: Challengers lose the meaning and context of standards—norms and rules that hold people together and make them accountable—and use standards as ways to dominate: "I can outperform anyone!" They may take on the role of the "Maverick," and push themselves and others to test their worth, by holding people accountable to *their* (the Eight's) standards rather than established ones.

Type Nine: Peacemakers

Normally: Peacemakers are uncertain about excellence. They have a great, but unspoken, desire to do big things but feel that if they are too visible they'll be seen as boastful and unlikeable. Nines find creative ways to improve on how things are done while still staying within a comfortable range. They hate to let people down and can be overly accountable to people, often sacrificing their wants for the wants of others.

Under Stress: Peacemakers lack high self-esteem and confidence that they have the drive and energy for excellence. Highly stressed Nines struggle to meet standards, demean themselves, and question why others would value their contributions. Highly stressed Nines undermine their accountability and resign themselves to mediocrity.

TO IMPROVE IN ACHIEVEMENT DRIVE:

- Be a lifetime learner. Seek to master new skills, new technologies, and better ways to interact with people.
- Accept standards as valuable ways to be accountable and hold others accountable.

- Set challenging goals and work aggressively toward accomplishing them.
- Ask for help, mentoring, and coaching. Work with others to make decisions and agreements that people can aspire to.
- Monitor your performance as it relates to standards. Does it meet the criteria for exceptional performance? Can you do better?
- Measure yourself against external standards (the competition) and internal standards (your personal goals and values) and strive toward excellence in both.
- Respectfully challenge the status quo. Constantly ask why things are done the way they are currently being done.

SELF-CONTROL: CONTROLLING OUR IMPULSES, EMOTIONS, OR DESIRES

Self-control helps us get what we want and avoid what we don't want. Also referred to as self-regulation, self-control is key in enabling us to function in a relationship and be accountable to others. It involves using our heads and our hearts—as Eleanor Roosevelt so aptly put it: "To handle yourself, use your head; to handle others, use your heart." Some personality types have too much control—they hold back their energy and repress their desires—while other types see expressing themselves, no matter how exuberantly, as a sign of strength and confidence. Joseph Campbell took a moderate approach to self-control: "How to get rid of ego as dictator and turn it into messenger and servant and scout, to be in your service, is the trick." People skilled in Self-Control:

- Have power over their urges, and restrain from acting on disruptive impulses and emotions.
- Act with patience and manage their nervousness and anxiety.
- Concentrate and think clearly under stress.
- Maintain control and poise around hostile or disruptive people.
- Are responsible for their actions and don't blame others for their own mistakes.

Type One: Perfectionists

Normally: Perfectionists take great pride in controlling their impulses, desires and emotions and they excel in this competency. They are disciplined, vigilant, and enthusiastic about following and upholding rules of good conduct. Accountability and integrity are focal points for Perfectionists and they are dependable, hardworking, sober, and discerning.

Under Stress: Perfectionists overdo trying to control things, especially emotions. They become austere and passionless and miss the more sensitive side of relationships. Perfectionism trumps spontaneity, creativity, and fun. Stress causes Ones to over-control others by being demanding, impatient, and critical; they impose their need for improvement onto others.

Type Two: Helpers

Normally: Helpers can control their desires and urges but tend to express their emotions freely and abundantly in an effort to build rapport with others. They prefer to be more physical, spontaneous, and playful than most people. They regard routines and rules as impediments to creativity and freedom. Helpers may offer unrequested help and advice in their honest effort to be nurturing.

Under Stress: Stress can cause Helpers to disregard being accountable and feel that "rules are meant to be broken" if it is done in the service of connecting with people or satisfying an emotional need. They may disregard the budget, overspend, over eat, and overindulge in general.

Type Three: Performers

Normally: Performers see impulse control as a necessary skill to their success, so they do well here. They present an "all together" image to the world, and can delay gratification in order to reach their goals. They do all the right things—dieting, bodybuilding, socializing with the right people—to create a specific image. Threes resist the bad habits that would mean a loss of control and a failure to accomplish their objectives.

Under Stress: Performers who feel they may fail, be unrecognized, or passed over are driven to compete vigorously, if not desperately, in their desire to win. Extreme stress may cause them to resort to counterproductive, overly competitive behavior, such as being deceptive and cutting corners.

Type Four: Individualists

Normally: Individualists can present a contradiction around controlling impulses, emotions, and desires. They are private people and can be inhibited, and dread revealing too much of themselves. Therefore, their behavior is usually proper and refined. The contradiction lies in the uninhibited, rebellious side that Individualists often display. They rebel against being too regulated and too accountable to society's standards. Fours feel that they can only be authentic if they occasionally give in to their impulses.

Under Stress: Individualists find relief from stress by over indulging. Fours love intensity, and stress can make them excessively intense. They have difficulty controlling their emotions and become overly dramatic, replacing their normally proper, refined behavior with expressions of anger, rule breaking, and rebelliousness.

Type Five: Observers

Normally: Observers control their impulses, emotions, and desires very well. They are naturally reserved and detached from their emotions, particularly negative expressions. They are happy to remain low key, and to act with restraint. They have an inner focus, and are able to stay with projects for long periods without being distracted by their impulses or feelings.

Under Stress: Anger can cause Observers to become more autonomous—real loners—and to ignore accountability or rules that they feel don't apply to them. Stressed Fives experience little guilt over pursuing their own impulses rather than focusing on the task at hand. For them, their triggered hostility and frustration at the "intrusive" world legitimize acting out.

Type Six: Guardians

Normally: Guardians score high in this area. They use control as a way to create a stable, secure environment and state of mind. Accountability is paramount to a Guardian's peace of mind. They see self-control as a way to express how responsible and dependable they are. Prepared for danger, Sixes are often most in control in times of crisis. Emergencies help banish doubt and indecision and inform them of the correct action to take.

Under Stress: Guardians become inflexible, believing that survival means remaining in control and allowing no deviation from plans. However, increased tension causes less-aware Guardians to become fearful and ineffective. They may imagine the worst, become combative, or succumb to anxiety, making it difficult for them to remain accountable.

Type Seven: Enthusiasts

Normally: Aware Enthusiasts see how impulse control can help them be accountable to others, and they can be dedicated and perfectionistic. However, many Sevens struggle with containing their impulses. They express joy and excitement freely, and see restraint as an impediment to experiencing all of life. Control seems like the opposite of spontaneity and satisfaction. However, once committed, Enthusiasts use mental focus and hard work as a way to stay on track.

Under Stress: Enthusiasts can overindulge in whatever they do, believing that "if some is good, more is better." They are excited more by ideas, fantasies, future projects or relationships than actual accomplishments, and they may toss promises and accountability out the window if sidetracked by a strong impulse or novel alternative.

Type Eight: Challengers

Normally: Challengers see value in controlling their desires, impulses, or emotions if it is in the service of accomplishing their desires. They feel most accountable to themselves and feel that their instincts and judgments are better than most people's and should be followed. Delaying action causes anxiety for Eights so they tend to follow their first impulse, and avoid behavior that would leave them feeling vulnerable.

Under Stress: Challengers feel accountable only to their own needs and desires. They respond immediately and often aggressively toward stressors, and struggle to control their anger, often disregarding peoples' feelings. Stressed Eights may regard restraint as procrastination, indecisiveness, or weakness.

Type Nine: Peacemakers

Normally: Peacemakers use controlling their impulses as a way of being at peace. They avoid conflict by downplaying their own needs and desires, and feel that expressing emotions or demanding attention could displease people. They desire to build steady, predictable, and comfortable relationships. Nines are restrained in pursuing their own desires and impulses and believe that others should do the same.

Under Stress: Peacemakers don't control their impulse towards inertia, procrastination, and forgetfulness. They give in to wasting time with nonessential activities, rather than doing important work. Under increased stress, Peacemakers become stubborn, passive aggressive, and nonproductive.

TO IMPROVE IN SELF-CONTROL:

- Focus on your breath. Simply being aware of your breath can bring you back to your body and a sense of being in the present. Keep breathing. Count to ten, relax, and manage your nervousness and anxiety. Remember, "This too shall pass." Be patient. Whether your impulse is fight, flight, or freeze, take a moment to think through your actions.

- Be open to change and personal growth, which only comes from a willingness to tolerate discomfort and stress—whether this means resisting the urge to withdraw or the drive to attack—learn to tolerate the tension.

- Be aware of procrastination. Prioritize what needs to be done and identify what's important and urgent. Don't allow yourself to be distracted from working on your most important activities.

- Recognize when you are under stress. What situations, thoughts, people, and emotions trigger stress? Do your best to manage them or avoid them completely.
- Don't try to change anyone but yourself. Handle hostile or disruptive people without escalating the hostility.

Changing Ineffective to Effective Behavior

Perfectionists

Ineffective	Effective
Refuse to recognize your mistakes, defending instead the "correctness" of your opinions; perceive suggestions from others as criticisms.	Accept that your position is not always correct or the best solution. Take responsibility for your mistakes, and stay open to other people's opinions.
Become impatient and critical of your self and others, refuse to settle for only "perfection," as defined by you; being unable to let go of your position.	Remain patient and non-critical of yourself and others, accept established standards that may not meet your sense of "perfection."
Place work above personal needs, relationships, physical and emotional health; evaluate yourself and others solely on merit.	Balance work and personal needs, take time to relax and have fun; appreciate the value of emotional intelligence, political connections, charm, etc.
Resent people who do not follow the rules, as you perceive them; stay stuck in literalism and fundamentalism regarding rules and standards.	Give people the respect and space to follow the rules and to work their own way; be open-minded and respect other perspectives.
Act too seriously, avoid spontaneity, don't express personal feelings or concern for others, thus coming off as impersonal and distant.	Make an effort to be light-hearted and spontaneous, to have fun, to connect emotionally with people, and to express yourself on a personal level.
Get caught in time binds from being bogged down in details and the belief that things are never good enough; not able to see life's gray areas.	Meet deadlines and develop a healthy balance between details and the broader picture; learn what "good enough" means; appreciate life's gray areas.

Changing Ineffective to Effective Behavior

Helpers

Ineffective	Effective
Refuse to recognize your needs; be indirect or evasive about expressing what you want; focus too much on the needs of other people.	State your needs honestly and openly, recognize that your needs are legitimate; accept help from people without guilt or discomfort.
Coerce people to like you; respond with anger, sadness, or jealousy when people don't acknowledge you in the way you desire.	Allow relationships to grow naturally, accept normal praise, and the fact that people may not respond as emotionally as you.
Play favorites; judge some people as more worthy of your attention because of their connection to you rather than their merits.	Treat people objectively, regardless of their closeness to you or their power or influence or your assessment of their desirability.
Flatter people excessively; avoid giving negative feedback, hoping they will return your positive attention and praise you.	Present feedback honestly and without "sugar coating"; offer useful information rather than complimenting or flattering.
Increasingly seek more intimate relationships with people. Ask inappropriate personal questions and give unsolicited advice.	Respect the boundaries of people. Ask if they want feedback before giving it. Ask what people need from you before acting or advising.
Resist taking a visible leadership role, preferring to lead from behind by "advising." Use "connections" rather than data to influence people.	Take a clear, visible leadership role when appropriate; express yourself factually, with logic, precision and without manipulation.

Changing Ineffective to Effective Behavior

Performers

Ineffective	Effective
Being "all business" with people, disregarding human needs and feelings in an attempt to out perform and exceed expectations.	Express interest in people, not as a means to an end; value the importance of human needs and feelings in accomplishing tasks.
Project an unrealistic image that is self-promotional: "name dropping," boastful, and inflated, while omitting facts to look good.	Present yourself honestly without exaggeration, as a true reflection of your personal accomplishments, relationships, and experiences.
Compete excessively even with co-workers and friends, obsessed with success, even if it means risking the relationship or team goals.	Balance individual needs with relationship and team needs, cooperate with others, motivate people, and help people meet goals.
Take on more than you can do, make promises you can't keep, give the impression that you can do anything, to impress others.	Accurately access how much work you can accomplish, how much help you will need from others, and be honest about it with others.
Cut corners on quality, reframe original commitments in your favor, and communicate dishonestly to avoid appearing "average."	Honor commitments to the letter; be thorough, completely committed to quality, and deliver exactly what you promise.
Never slow down, believe you need to "keep swimming or drown," and that you must be the best in order to be accepted and liked.	Learn to relax. Trust that people will evaluate you on your values and integrity as well as your accomplishments.

Changing Ineffective to Effective Behavior

Individualists

Ineffective	Effective
Express anger at not being seen as special by rebelling against sources of authority, feeling exempt from ordinary rules, procedures, etc.	Recognize that people will not make exceptions and will accept you as they do everyone else; learn to accept rules and norms.
Aggressively defend your unique perspective; convey a dismissive or hostile attitude toward other opinions.	Observe how you judge opinions; allow yourself to listen, and be open to ideas that are not as clever, original, or creative as yours.
Idealize "special" people when they please you—or make a 180-degree reversal—and disparage them when they disappoint you.	Maintain a realistic view and remain honest with people; be aware of your tendency to project special qualities onto some people.
Insist on being an individual contributor, or to do things differently, even when being a team player is what is needed.	Commit to corporate, family, and team goals, work with the best interests of the relationship in mind, and be a team player.
Take things too personally, become hypersensitive, moody, and unproductive, especially when faced with obstacles.	Maintain a positive and realistic outlook, not over-dramatizing problems; nurture a healthy self-image, and remain productive.
Hesitate to make decisions; show anxiety about taking a stand; allow lack of confidence to affect opportunities to express leadership.	Make decisions with confidence; understand and accept your leadership capabilities; express your accomplishments confidently.

Changing Ineffective to Effective Behavior

Observers

Ineffective	Effective
Prefer analysis to action; over prepare, obsess over details, afraid to make a move, as though rehears-ing for life rather than living it.	Realize when you have analyzed enough, know when it is time to stop rehearsing, and time to take action. Learn to "pull the trigger."
Avoid chances to connect with people; emotionally withdraw and feel overwhelmed by the expecta-tions of others.	Nurture relationships and seek out chances to network. Be open and trusting, willing to share your feelings and passions.
Avoid sharing information, not keeping people informed and in the loop, either through neglect or arrogance ("They should know.")	Be generous with information, insights, and opinions. Also, share how you feel, even though you think it is illogical or "useless."
Show off your intellect; compete over facts, theories or esoteric ideas, needing to be a "know-it-all," while avoiding action.	See that philosophical debate can be overdone, and that practical applica-tion and accomplishing results are what is expected.
Become antagonistic toward people who "interfere" with your inner world. Annoy, shock or provoke colleagues with extreme views.	Be patient and accepting of people who don't share your thoughts. Become grounded in the real world.
Avoid conflict, (imagined or real), for example, by ignoring requests for a decision, putting off giving feedback on important issues, etc.	Meet conflict head on. Stay engaged; actively respond to people. Return phone calls, initiate action, and be decisive.

Changing Ineffective to Effective Behavior

Guardians

Ineffective	Effective
Mistrust your thoughts and decisions; vacillate from idea to idea, fear to make a decision on your own.	Trust that you have done your homework. Weigh the pros and cons calmly and make decisions based on your own judgment.
Complain about your situation without doing anything about it; second guess people, and blame others for your situation.	Stop complaining and playing "Monday Morning Quarterback." Be accountable for your situation and take action to remedy it.
Over-commit to people; make unrealistic promises out of fear of disappointing friends, the team or authority figures.	Be realistic about whom you dedicate your time and efforts to. Appreciate your contributions. Answer to your own authority.
Hold back from taking action, expressing an opinion, or giving an answer, even when you know you are correct. Resist taking the lead.	Take risks and speak up. Accept the risks that are always necessary for advancement, improvement and leadership.
Let fear and anxiety run your life, imagine the worst-case scenario, and become scattered, hyperactive and unproductive.	Observe your behavior with a greater degree of objectivity, ask colleagues for feedback and take calm, measured action.
Exhibit displays of defiance, defensiveness and suspicion, holding on to past hurts, and lashing out at perceived "enemies."	Ask for feedback about your responses. Be forgiving rather than defiant; understand that some of your "enemies" are imagined.

Changing Ineffective to Effective Behavior

Enthusiasts

Ineffective	Effective
Become hyperactive and over stimulated; feel bored quickly, losing interest in the task at hand; act distracted, inattentive and scattered.	Be patient, rigorous, and persistent. Remain focused on task at hand, staying with all the details, especially the parts you find boring.
Refuse to look at the negative aspects of things, and keep an unrealistically positive view regardless of the situation.	Face obstacles openly and realistically, staying in the present, avoiding fantasizing and telling "too-good-to-be-true" stories.
Ask for more, not satisfied with the present situation; become rude, and excessive, and demand that your needs be met before those of others.	Practice patience in dealing with people, trust that your needs will be met appropriately, and accept that you can't always be first.
Break promises, fail to follow through on commitments, to do your share of the "dirty" work," and fail to meet deadlines and agreements.	Resist lingering on the fun of "start-ups," "kick-offs," and the planning stage. Follow plans without deviation, and honor promises.
Dominate conversations, ignore what others say, talk too much and too loudly; entertain, joke and clown around at inappropriate times.	Let others speak. Listen attentively. Become comfortable with silence. Know when it is time to be funny and time to be serious.
Live in the future and look for the ideal situation or relationship, as if the present reality is not quite exciting or fulfilling enough.	Accept reality. Live in the present. Realize that your life is what it is and needs no reframing, exaggeration, or enhancement.

Changing Ineffective to Effective Behavior

Challengers

Ineffective	Effective
Seek to be in charge, to dominate, and be the boss, whether you're the legitimate boss or not; force your agenda, ideas, and desires.	Respect others' positions, needs, ideas, and agendas, see them as integral, and accept individual, team, and organizational roles.
Regard empathy, and the expression of feelings as a weakness, and as an impediment to taking action or being decisive.	Understand that feelings have value and convey information, and that managing them is essential to productivity and leadership.
Rebel against the status quo, adopt a "rough around the edges," attitude, enjoy shocking people and creating discord and conflict.	Learn to temper your natural propensity to stir things up. Express your lust for life and passion in more refined, productive ways.
Act impulsively; show disinterest in people's input, unwilling to delay action, expecting others to follow your lead and pace.	Listen patiently, thoughtfully, and with an open mind, and act with care. Be open and accepting of what people have to offer.
See people who don't agree with you as weak, inferior, or stupid; intolerantly ignore, marginalize, or abuse people.	Practice tolerance and appreciate diversity. Accept that anyone can make meaningful contributions to accomplishing group goals.
Express mistrust, and test people's strength, loyalty and intelligence; demand that people continually prove themselves to you.	Try to nurture trust in the good will of others and the inherent goodness of people. Stop demanding a show of loyalty and commitment to you.

Changing Ineffective to Effective Behavior

Peacemakers

Ineffective	Effective
Avoid asserting yourself, holding back from expressing your ideas and taking action. Lack confidence, and healthy aggressiveness.	Assert yourself, communicate your ideas; move past the fear of offending others and let people know what you can accomplish.
Lose your temper, allow unaddressed anger and "forgotten" conflicts to build to an unhealthy climax, and vent frustration through yelling, etc.	Confront potential problems immediately, express yourself, give appropriate feedback, and take pro-active steps to solve problems.
Avoid taking charge, adopt a "Mr. Nice Guy," stance; down play your leadership abilities and allow others to lead when you should.	Take the lead and be self-confident. See that letting less talented people lead does a disservice to your career and to the group.
Act passive-aggressively, getting your way through avoidance and procrastination, allowing others to express your dissatisfaction for you.	Be direct, serious, and factual. Avoid sarcasm, self-deprecation, and making your point by being late, stubborn, dishonest, or vague.
Avoid conflict; prefer to "keep the peace" as if things will take care of themselves. Choose "harmony" instead of addressing problems.	Face conflicts head on. Recognize that unaddressed issues will get worse if not addressed. Take care of minor inconveniences immediately.
Resist change and become stuck in routine; avoid challenges, and see inertia as "peace" rather than stagnation and mediocrity	Embrace change, break with routine, and don't mistake change with conflict. Push yourself to work outside your comfort zone.

TAKE ACTION ON BEING ACCOUNTABLE

Here's a simple and powerful tool to help us be accountable. It involves creating partnerships with people—alignments where we hold each other accountable, where we function as coaches and mentors and "watchdogs" for each other. It begins with understanding the distinction between *having expectations* of people and *creating agreements* with them.

Change Expectations Into Agreements

- No one wants to live up to another's expectations. Expectations are authoritative and one sided. They create resentment and feel oppressive. Expectations are demanding: "This is what I expect from you."
- Agreements, by contrast, are based on equality and are creative and open ended. They involve both parties in a cooperative give-and-take arrangement: "I'll do this if you do that." Agreements are friendly and reciprocal: "What do you need from me for you to accomplish this mutual goal?"
- Agreements create partnerships and strong relationships, a sense of "We're in this together." We can more easily be accountable to each other when we create mutual agreements, when we've both got some skin in the game, and when accountability goes both ways.

Manage Agreements Not People

- Creating an agreement requires bold requests, courage, and clear commitments.
- Both sides must practice trusting, caring communication.
- When agreements are broken, as they occasionally are, don't talk about personal wrongdoing. Talk about agreements and how going forward you can make them stronger.

9

Can We Achieve Mutual Goals?

"Motivating others requires a connection to people's deep desires. It's not just about loading them down with a lot of "how to" information. Transformation is more important than information. Action is everything."

Steve Chandler

Achieving mutual goals involves setting aside individual needs and agendas and dedicating ourselves to what's best for the relationship. This is easier said than done and can feel very counter intuitive to some. Commitment, accountability, and the desire to accomplish objectives for the larger group may mean, "taking one for the team." It is a sign of emotional maturity when we resist the temptation to place personal goals ahead of collective, group success. Individuals who achieve results together minimize self-centered behavior, avoid distractions, keep their eye on the goal, and place relationship and group goals over their own. Achieving results together involves being skilled in the emotional competencies of Cooperation and Optimism.

WAKE UP CALL: USE THE LANGUAGE OF INTENTION–MOVE FROM "HOW TO" TO "WANT TO."

Words like intention, purpose, drive, motivation, and goal imply action. They're connected with things we desire to do because accomplishing them brings us satisfaction and joy. Regarding the power of intention, Steve Chandler writes: "People think that they aren't doing things that would benefit their lives because they don't know *how to*. They are deceiving themselves. The real bottleneck is that they don't (yet) *want* to. The 'how to' can be found everywhere. You can look it up. If you know 'how to' use Google, you can find out how to do anything. The 'how to' is never what's really missing." Shifting our intention so that we are doing things because we intend to, because we want to, and because we choose to creates movement, energy, and the potential for powerful, targeted action.

How often have you said, "I don't know how to do that," or "I can't do that," when what you really mean is you don't *want* to do it? Be honest, and say what you mean: if you don't want to do something, say so, but don't string yourself and others along with this non-committed, weak language. Learn to harness the language of intention, and become positive and enthusiastic about achieving results with a partner. Find your passion. Find what you can be really mutually committed to.

COOPERATION: WORKING WITH OTHERS TOWARD SHARED GOALS

Cooperating in order to achieve results together involves more than agreeing on common goals. It asks us to collaborate and to make sacrifices to reach an identical objective. It means sharing knowledge, building consensus, and solving problems collaboratively. People skilled in Cooperation:

- See the power of synergy and are open to another's ideas.
- Cultivate and maintain relationships.
- Share resources, opinions, and support.
- Look for opportunities to work with others.

Type One: Perfectionists

Normally: Perfectionists see cooperation as the right thing to do and feel it is important to be seen as contributors and team players. Their collaboration depends, however, on whether or not they believe in the correctness and logic of the group's goals. If they disagree with the objectives, they may cooperate half-heartedly or lobby for reform.

Under Stress: Perfectionists can have difficulty working with others. They often feel that no one can do things as well as they can. They can become rigid, aloof, and argumentative if they don't agree with the group's goals. Under pressure Perfectionists would rather work on their own than endure the shortcomings of others.

Type Two: Helpers
Normally: Helpers love to cooperate with others. They are "relationship junkies" and they enjoy roles that require interaction with others. They want to share the best of themselves and to help others be their best; they make people feel appreciated, noticed, and important.

Under Stress: Twos begin to feel ignored or unappreciated by others and complain about doing so much for people. They draw attention to their contributions and the help they have provided in an effort to be acknowledged. Increased pressure causes Helpers to make dramatic attempts to be seen, often through flattery or displays of affection or conversely, frustration.

Type Three: Performers
Normally: Performers enjoy the limelight and prefer not to share it with those who can't keep pace or perform at their high level. They cooperate by being organizers and goal setters, and by inspiring others. Threes may at first cooperate with the group, but if something more personally rewarding comes along, they may be tempted to pursue their individual goals and leave the group.

Under Stress: If working with others doesn't bring them the notice they desire, Performers may abandon the task or relationship. Performers want to be seen as the best and may compete with team members and partners in a relationship. They become frustrated with people they see as holding them back or reflecting poorly on them.

Type Four: Individualists
Normally: Individualists like to cooperate with like-minded people on interesting projects. However, they are soloists at heart and they take pride in being

self-sufficient and independent. Their self-image is based on being unique, and they have strong creative opinions that they often struggle sharing with others, preferring to develop their ideas alone. They often feel misunderstood and hesitate to openly express or expose themselves, a tendency that hinders cooperation.

Under Stress: Individualists avoid cooperation and interaction with others. They withdraw into their own thoughts and feelings. In an effort to express their individuality, Fours may rebel for rebellion's sake and as stress builds they may become depressed or combative.

Type Five: Observers

Normally: Observers are autonomous and resist moving at the pace of others. They'd rather be individual contributors than team players. In relationships, they desire to pursue their own ideas freely and unencumbered. They don't bond naturally with people and often feel like outsiders, even with people they have known for years.

Under Stress: Observers struggle with cooperation. They resist communicating their needs or feelings, and detach under pressure. Stress causes Observers to shut down emotionally and to disengage physically. They may profess to share common goals, but will usually prefer to work on group goals on their own.

Type Six: Guardians

Normally: Guardians find security and contentment by cooperating with others and working toward shared goals. They build bonds based on similar values, beliefs, backgrounds, etc. They see strength in numbers and appreciate the synergy and power of collaboration. Sixes respect the integrity of their relationships and protect the people in them.

Under Stress: Guardians fear doing anything that will endanger their security. They become overly dependent on their trusted relationships and idealize them, seeking things that the group may not be able to provide. Sixes mistrust their own decisions and often relinquish their responsibility to others. As pressure mounts, Sixes seek safety in rebellion rather than conformity, and may defy the group and authority figures.

Type Seven: Enthusiasts

Normally: Enthusiasts enjoy working with others. They bring people together and stimulate team spirit through sheer enthusiasm. They're good at staying in touch, building cohesion, and motivating people. Achieving shared goals can be an exciting game for Enthusiasts and can inspire them to cooperate with others.

Under Stress: Enthusiasts lose interest if the goal is too tedious or too distant, or if cooperation becomes difficult or boring. They become frustrated with people who don't share their enthusiasm, and may see cooperation as an impediment to having their needs met or getting their share of limited resources.

Type Eight: Challengers

Normally: Challengers usually see cooperation as *others cooperating with them* not as them cooperating with others. They prefer to establish goals for others and then convince others to embrace their (the Eight's) goals. More aware Challengers can work toward shared goals, but they still gravitate toward taking the lead. They are able to cooperate in limited partnerships and smaller groups more easily than in larger groups.

Under Stress: Challengers struggle to share goals that are established by others. They question group objectives as an expression of their personal power. Increased pressure (or boredom) causes Eights to become uncooperative, to push their agenda and to sabotage the objectives and efforts of others in order to gain control.

Type Nine: Peacemakers

Normally: Peacemakers value their ability to get along with others and work as part of a relationship or team. They desire to align their goals with the goals of the group and they become energized by a common vision. Nines generally value collaboration, or at least the appearance of collaboration, over competition. For Nines, cooperation and achieving shared goals are clearly aligned with striving to be peaceful.

Under Stress: Peacemakers go back and forth between wanting to be left alone and wanting to be part of the group. If they are not in agreement with the goals of the relationship, stressed Nines may procrastinate and behave passive aggressively rather than express overt disagreement, believing that not objecting is the same as cooperating.

TO IMPROVE IN COOPERATION:

- Cultivate and maintain relationships. Stay in touch and establish a 24-hour "return of message" rule. Some people define being uncooperative as taking too long to return a call or email.
- Seek out opportunities to share ideas, resources, and support.
- Agree with others that mutual, constructive criticism will be the norm, not the exception. Share information about how things are being done. Discuss work and relationship histories, specific skills, success, and talents.
- Help team members to understand, appreciate, and use differences among each other to arrive at better solutions and to do better work.
- Let the mutual goal, not personal agendas, drive your efforts to achieve results.

OPTIMISM: EXPECTING THE BEST POSSIBLE OUTCOME

The pioneering work of Martin Seligman, the author of *Learned Optimism*, and *Authentic Happiness*, has described the benefits of positive psychology, and inspired many to see the power of changing our focus from barriers to possibilities. Kathy Cramer, the author of *Change the Way You See Everything* and the creator of Asset-Based Thinking, gives us the formula for optimistic behavior: Set your sights on what you want/need; move past fear; start exactly where you are with gusto and self-abandon; practice as if no one is judging; build on what you already know how to do—add, shape, edit, expand; when you experience victory, celebrate; set your sights on the next step. People skilled in Optimism:

- Focus on what is good, happy, possible, and positive.
- Expect the best in life and in people.
- Resist being negatively affected by mistakes, accidents, or failure.

Type One: Perfectionists

Normally: Perfectionists struggle with being optimistic because of their focus on what needs fixing. They look for what could go wrong and believe it's their job to give constructive criticism to others—a trait that can jeopardize achieving mutual objectives. Their focus often undermines a positive attitude.

Under Stress: Perfectionists are even more pessimistic. Their need to critique and edit can become severe and obsessive; their negative criticism can drive a wedge in their relationships and the group's ability to achieve results. A Stressed One's negative, fatalistic attitude can be a barrier to achieving team results.

Type Two: Helpers

Normally: Helpers expect the best. They love being upbeat and joyful. They have a positive outlook about themselves and work hard to make others feel positive as well. They are naturals at nurturing the best in people, and are pleasant, cheerful, and generous. Twos help us feel that we are welcome and honored as an important part of a relationship or group. If people around them are not optimistic, Twos will make it their job to make them so.

Under Stress: Helpers are strongly affected by another's unhappiness. They can take a person's lack of joy and enthusiasm personally. Twos may overlook their own needs and force optimism on others through complimenting them and intrusively "helping." They fake being happy and upbeat, believing that this is what people want to see. However, they may ignore working on group goals in favor of making people feel good.

Type Three: Performers

Normally: Performers shine in this competency. They are born optimists and believe they can accomplish their goals and can inspire others to do the same. Threes feel that things will work out fine if they are involved, and are confident that their positive attitude will motivate others to be outstanding.

Under Stress: It's hard to demoralize a Performer. Even under stress they stay optimistic, but often become workaholics, depending only on themselves, feeling that others' self-interests may get in the way of their own goals. They remain optimistic about their abilities but are less trusting in the ability and commitment of others.

Type Four: Individualists

Normally: Individualists are optimistic about meaningful relationships. They use their vivid imagination to envisage the best way to achieve mutual goals. Individualists explore their darker emotions, which may make them appear pessimistic, but in reality they find meaning and richness in introspection and even melancholy. They can transform this exploration into great beauty and deep understanding.

Under Stress: Individualists can fall into a negative mindset, convinced that the world is a dark and unsympathetic place. They feel flawed and unworthy of happiness, and disappointed and pessimistic. When Fours feel deeply unappreciated by others, they become increasingly negative about their capacity to work with others to accomplish mutual goals.

Type Five: Observers

Normally: As their name implies, the Observer's approach to life is not necessarily to engage it but to watch it from a distance. They are normally shy, but with people they trust they can have a childlike curiosity and optimism. However, Fives are apprehensive, don't trust that others have their best interest, and see the world as dangerous. They are not naturally optimistic, but would describe their approach to life as "realistic."

Under Stress: Fives become even more pessimistic, cautious, and withdrawn. They feel hemmed in and stifled if people get too close or relationships become too demanding. Stressed Fives feel vulnerable and withdraw to protect themselves; they find it very difficult to be positive about working toward shared goals.

Type Six: Guardians

Normally: Guardians can be optimistic and loyal if a trusted authority is in the relationship or on the team. They provide a valuable service to organizations by perceiving potential problems that others overlook. Normally, however,

Guardians are more pessimistic than optimistic. They are naturally skeptical and look for what can go wrong in relationships and groups, and are particularly untrusting of untested authority figures.

Under Stress: Guardians become more skeptical, cynical, and uncertain. Pressure makes them doubt themselves and they become increasingly less self-confident. They see things negatively—imagining dangers that aren't there and enemies that don't exist. Rather than focusing on opportunities that can help them achieve mutual objectives, they look for dangers and obstacles.

Type Seven: Enthusiasts

Normally: Enthusiasts may be the most optimistic of the nine personality types. They refuse to let challenges dampen their excitement and imagine achieving goals as "scoring" points in a contest. Their optimism is contagious and they see possibilities where others do not. Sevens prefer to associate with other positive people who will share their enthusiasm and spur them on to even more exciting achievements.

Under Stress: Enthusiasts may work hard to sustain their optimism through imagination, by ignoring the objective facts, fantasizing unrealistic outcomes, and believing that resources and people will materialize to rescue them. They begin to rely on others to boost their optimism, and as stress builds, to do the work.

Type Eight: Challengers

Normally: Challengers are optimistic when they feel they are in charge, in which case their optimism can be huge and inspiring to others. However, if others are in control or have more influence than they do, Eights usually doubt that results will be what they expect. They will be skeptical and will question those in command.

Under Stress: Challengers are pessimistic and paranoid, and look for danger and failure. They misjudge people and groups, imagine the worst, and see potential trouble in harmless people and places. Pressure makes Challengers fearful and angry and they question their closest relationships. Their expression of negativity and aggression often leads to self-fulfilling prophecies and the failure of achieving mutual goals.

Type Nine: Peacemakers

Normally: Peacemakers are positive thinkers who believe the world is safe and benevolent. They trust that people will get along, treat each other fairly, and work toward mutual objectives. Aware Nines are usually undeterred by unexpected obstacles, seeing them as life's lessons. Peacemakers can be overly optimistic, and downplay real problems as a way to stay optimistic.

Under Stress: Peacemakers become indifferent, and lose their optimism without becoming noticeably negative. They have a "who cares?" attitude and adopt a "what will be will be" philosophy. Stressed Nines can settle into a gray, resigned, noncommittal area. Under extreme stress they may be depressed and paralyzed by anxiety.

TO IMPROVE IN OPTIMISM:

- Perceive setbacks as a result of normal, manageable events rather than due to personal shortcomings.
- Look for the good in people or situations before you look for the bad, and make a conscious choice to be positive.
- Be clear on the advantages of being optimistic. Optimism fearlessly opens the mind to possible solutions. Pessimism closes the mind.
- Learn from your mistakes, and trust that your actions can have a positive effect on others.

TAKE ACTION ON ACHIEVING RESULTS TOGETHER

Always Act on the Goal

- Be aware of the goal—of the result we're trying to accomplish together—and act on it. Adopt a bias for action. Consistently remind people what the goal is. Choose to take action rather than gather more information, opinions, or consensus.

- Use the goal as a way to resolve disputes and conflicts: "What agreements have been made, kept, and broken?"
- Enforce natural consequences.
- Lead by example and lead with a sense of urgency.

Move From Awareness to Action

Be aware when someone is *not* focused on the goal but pursues distractions:

- Take action and offer *constructive feedback* in order to correct behavior and get people back on track.

Be aware when someone *is* focused on the goal and is committed and accountable:

- Take action and offer *acknowledgement and praise* in order to encourage them to stay on course.

Part Three: Connecting

"You can make more friends in two months by becoming interested in other people than you can in two years by trying to get other people interested in you."

DALE CARNEGIE

10

How Can We Connect?

"Basic human contact— the meeting of eyes, the exchanging of words— is to the psyche what oxygen is to the brain. If you're feeling abandoned by the world, interact with anyone you can."

Martha Beck

Understanding and accepting the differences in people vastly improves the way we interact. Learning to adjust the way we deal with others takes understanding and acceptance to another level—the level of *connection*—and to the establishment of effective and life-enhancing relationships. Imagine if we never changed our communication or decision-making style. We'd be similar to Mr. Spock, one of the leading characters in TV's original *Star Trek* series. Spock was always predictable, and in his case, always logical, unemotional, and factual. He frustrated his opposite: the passionate, emotional, and intuitive Captain Kirk. Kirk was just as predictable as Spock, but in a different way. They both had strong personalities: determined, willful, and consistent. We could always rely on their reactions. Neither Spock nor Kirk seemed very adaptable, and that was part of the fun of watching them. Week after week we would delight in how their responses to situations got them in or out of trouble. How similar is our life? How predictable or adaptable are we? How open are we to options?

Part of maturing is learning how to adjust our attitudes and behaviors. That's a good thing. It's evolution. The survivors are the ones who adjust most effectively. If we believe we have options, we can adjust how we behave based on the different situations. *But we have to see—and believe—we have options.*

The enneagram teaches how we limit our options and over-rely on one preferred strategy to the neglect of the other eight. It teaches that to be adaptable helps us to live effective, creative lives. When we know that we have options, we can freely and consciously create the best action for the situation. We allow each situation, not our preferred strategy, to determine our behavior. Having the skill and the maturity to adjust to others is a powerful way of being effective with people.

The material in this chapter provides brief, summary descriptions of how to connect with other personality types. It describes how each type is similar (Connections), and how each type is dissimilar (Disconnects). It is written from the point of view of a specific type—in other words, a Type One interacting with a Type Two, a Type Two interacting with a Type Three, etc. This section is not exhaustive and is presented in bulleted format for easy reading and accessibility. I hope that it will be used for both reflection and quick reference when questioning how to connect with another personality type.

ONES CONNECTING WITH ONES
Ones are Striving to be Perfect.

Connections

- Ones share high ideals, a strong work ethic, and a clear focus on achieving goals.
- Ones honor each other's commitments and are good at follow-through.
- They are reasonable, proper, accountable and trustworthy.
- Both prefer to stay focused on work before relaxing or having fun.
- They feel that criticism ("friendly advice") is a way of being helpful.
- Most Ones would not consider their feedback as judgmental or negative, but rather a sign of trust and caring about the success of the project or relationship.
- Ones are more task-oriented than relationship-oriented.

Disconnects

- Ones may have problems seeing the other One's perspective (believing there is only one right way) and may struggle with compromise.
- There may be a tendency to buck heads over small details, getting bogged down in minutia, and being too focused on work to relax.
- There is the inevitable, ongoing comparison: Who's more perfect? Who performs more effectively? Who gets the job done more correctly? Who makes fewer mistakes? Ones can argue about fairness and division of labor (or anything that involves improvement, being perfect, or being logical): Who does more, whose work is superior, whose job is harder?
- Decision-making can be a huge struggle with two Ones because of the fear of making a mistake and being judged by the other.

Connecting With Ones From a One's Perspective

- Ones should appreciate another One's need to be right, and be willing to search for a compromise.
- Get comfortable with the focus on facts over feelings, process over people, and the emphasis on the ideal and the standard of quality. Be direct and logical.
- Emphasize competence, knowledge, reliability, personal integrity, and commitment to quality.
- Ones can help other Ones by being ever vigilant of the tendency toward literalism: the dogged focus on the letter of the law. Help each other to be flexible and open to personal relationships, creative changes, and empathy. Try to see that there are more expansive, often more effective interpretations of the rules. Encourage other Ones to see that there is more than one side to a story.
- When all else fails, allow a third party to help with conflict and anger issues rather than shutting down and becoming emotionally unavailable.

ONES AND TWOS CONNECTING

Ones are Striving to be Perfect; Twos are Striving to be Connected.

Connections

- Like Ones, Twos are good, moral people who want to do the right thing. Twos feel that being perfect is being helpful, nurturing, and in a committed relationship. Ones feel that being in a committed relationship involves offering recommendations for improvement.
- Twos are looking to bond, to gain the One's approval, and appreciate the good that Ones do.
- Ones behave safely and dependably, which is attractive to Twos, who are more spontaneous and emotionally expressive.
- Ones want to help people improve things, and to act responsibly toward the community because these are moral and righteous behaviors. Twos want to do these things because, in addition to being moral and righteous, they make Twos feel connected emotionally to people.

Disconnects

- Ones have a practical, logical, task-oriented focus while Twos have a feelings-based, people-oriented focus.
- Ones may struggle giving Twos all the attention they need.
- Both types are sensitive to criticism, but react to it differently: Twos feel hurt, angry and emotional. Ones feel indignant, angry and self-righteous.
- Twos focus on personal relationships much more than Ones. Twos may seem illogical, codependent, overly sensitive and impractical to Ones.
- Ones focus on task completion, facts, rules and standards. Twos focus on kindness, giving and getting attention, being helpful, and making connections.
- When Ones become too focused on rules Twos may feel neglected and disconnected.

- Ones are more practical and logical than Twos, and can handle the details that Twos are less interested in.
- Twos will flatter and compliment easily. Ones will hesitate to praise or compliment.
- Ones believe in merit and earning what you get through hard work and following the rules. Twos believe more in establishing friendships with people and subscribe to the philosophy "it's who you know" more than Ones.

Connecting With Two's From a One's Perspective

- Ones should be aware that Twos have a big need for approval, acceptance and love.
- Ones should strive to compliment rather than judge Twos, and be willing to talk about feelings and the relationship.
- Get personal and engaged. Talk about people, and acknowledge the Two's contribution to supporting the relationship and their ability to help people.
- Ones should be more open to accepting help from Twos, seeing the help as genuine kindness rather than a judgment from the Two.
- Ones can help Twos stay focused on tangible results that measure up to strict scrutiny—to create something that ultimately serves and connects people with each other.
- Ones should build rapport first by inquiring how the Two is doing, getting along with other team members, etc. before delivering information or challenges.
- Being friendly is as important as being factual, and leads to achieving mutual results.

Connecting With Ones from a Two's Perspective

- Twos should shift from relationship to task orientation to connect with Ones.

- Twos do well to learn to take the One's judgments and criticism with a grain of salt. Their precise, helpful pointers are one of the ways that Perfectionists show they care.
- Twos can respect a One's desire to keep the relationship more formal than Twos would like, and to be patient—appreciation and praise are not given as easily by a One as a Two. Meet at the mutual desire to make things better.
- Twos can help Ones to see that true perfection involves being complete—emotionally present to people, not exclusively focused on tasks—and appreciative of the valuable messages that come through feelings.
- Twos can help Ones to build rapport by being more relaxed and forgiving around people, to resist taking what people say too literally, and to be more tolerant of the "messiness" and lack of precision in others.
- Twos can help Ones to see that trusting coworkers and dealing with conflict depends in part on getting to know people more personally.
- Twos are positive and can help Ones be more light-hearted and empathic.

ONES AND THREES CONNECTING
Ones are Striving to be Perfect; Threes are Striving to be Outstanding.

Connections

- Ones and Threes have much in common and are sometimes misidentified one for the other. Both identify with their work image, are energetic and status conscious.
- They are both hard workers, efficient, and goal oriented.
- Like Ones, Threes care about looking good and what people think about them.
- Both types focus on being at their best, and being productive.
- Both share a focus on task and work, and can be workaholics.
- Both can avoid intimacy and emotionality.

Disconnects

- Threes want to present an image of being outstanding, the best, and a winner, while Ones want to behave properly, appropriately, and correctly.
- Ones focus on correct details; Threes focus on impactful results. Unlike Ones, Threes don't get mired in small details, while Ones can be "nit pickers."
- Ones focus on quality and precision while Threes focus more on quantity and image.
- Threes tend to focus more on the positive than Ones, who focus on what needs fixing.
- Threes can cut corners because they are less focused on perfection than Ones.
- Threes may embarrass or offend Ones if they boast about their accomplishments, connections, and possessions.
- Threes may not engage or debate when confronted or criticized, as Ones do, leaving Ones wondering where they stand. Ones engage in conflict when they experience injustice or see poor quality. Threes avoid conflict, seeing it as nonproductive.
- Ones measure success by how well they follow the rules; Threes measure success by how well they accomplish their goals.
- Threes may be hard pressed to get a compliment from Ones for being a star if that star isn't flawless.
- Threes are pragmatists and want a job done efficiently so they can move on to their next goal. Ones are perfectionists and want a task done perfectly no matter how long it takes.

Connecting with Threes From a One's Perspective

- Ones should define terms and find shared meaning with Threes who focus more on what works than what is the ideal. When Threes talk about "the best" and the "top of the line" they may mean what looks good and what is saleable, whereas Ones may mean what is excellent or flawless.

- Ones should emphasize facts over feelings, and speak with composure.
- Avoid too many personal questions; Threes like to talk about work, goals, accomplishments, awards, prestige, etc. For Threes, being professional is more important than being friendly, which should be easy for Ones.
- Ones can help Threes to appreciate that quality, precision, and completeness are the true marks of an outstanding product, career, or human being, and nothing of value happens without the help of others.
- If Threes are going full throttle on a project and in danger of making mistakes, avoid telling them they are wrong or questioning their competency; instead, use language they can relate to, such as: "We can't sell this," or "This isn't practical."
- Ones should encourage Threes to see that they can accomplish more through group efforts than through individual performance.

Connecting with Ones From a Three's Perspective

- Threes should respect the One's commitment to job excellence.
- Threes can build rapport with Ones by appealing to both type's mutual dedication to competency and achieving results. Try to meet on common ground: efficiency, hard work, and professionalism.
- Threes do well to avoid getting bogged down in the One's slow decision making process (based on fear of making mistakes), but learn from their attention to detail and focus on quality.
- Threes should allow Ones to double and triple check things. They may find mistakes that Threes might overlook.
- Threes can help Ones appreciate the social networking aspects of work. Help Ones to understand that being perfect also involves *being seen* by the right people.

- Threes can coach Ones how to create a successful, professional image by praising the excellence of their products and services. Ones can, by association, attract praise for their personal excellence.

ONES AND FOURS CONNECTING
Ones are Striving to be Perfect; Fours are Striving to be Unique.

Connections

- Like Ones, Fours are ethical and principled; they both have high standards.
- Both types can be perfectionistic and rigid.
- Although Fours express their feelings more easily than Ones, at work both types may appear reserved and aloof.
- Like Fours, Ones can be fastidious, and have a polished, elegant look.

Disconnects

- Feelings are more important than rules for Fours, while Ones see rules as the foundation of efficiency and productivity. Ones follow the established standards, while Fours prefer their own unique standards.
- Ones are more practical and logical than Fours.
- Fours can be rebellious and reckless; Ones uphold the law and are careful and conservative.
- Ones see expressing feelings or being too relaxed as barriers to achieving good work. Fours express feelings freely, and are intense and sensitive.
- Fours, especially when feeling unappreciated, need to process their feelings before going back to work. Stressed Fours can be unproductive, allow their negative moods to curtail working, and feel exempt from rules.
- Ones can be critical and insensitive, which may trigger a Four's sense of not fitting in, or feeling inadequate. Ones prefer to live in a black

and white, logical world; a Four's world is one of color, intensity, and emotions.

Connecting With Fours From a One's Perspective

- Focus less on rules and standards, which can make Individualists feel restrained, and cause them to withdraw.
- Allow Fours to talk about their feelings, and resist the temptation to give advice or criticize creative ideas. Reflect back a Four's intensity. They are looking for a reaction in order to gauge how much they can trust people.
- Emphasize the special quality of the relationship and the desire to build a lasting, exclusive bond with Fours.
- Ones can help Fours to understand that their uniqueness still must fit within the context of the "ordinariness" and the norms and regulations of the world they live in, and that appreciating and mastering the rules of the organization, and the skills of one's craft are necessary before breaking the rules and creating a new, unique paradigm.
- Ones can help Fours to make their creations operational by establishing a structure in which Fours can feel safe to be different and creative.

Connecting With Ones From a Four's Perspective

- Fours can work well with Ones when they appreciate the One's sense of refinement, clarity, elegance, and precision.
- Fours can learn from Ones about order, logic, and discipline and understand that beauty and creativity depends as much on structure as free expression.
- Fours can help Ones to appreciate diversity, to be open to variations on ideas, opinions, and approaches.
- Fours can lower a One's resistance to change, spontaneity, and working "outside the box" by modeling a sane, measured approach to being creative and improvisational.

- Fours should openly discuss their feelings and provide a good example of how Ones can do the same.

ONES AND FIVES CONNECTING
Ones are Striving to be Perfect; Fives are Striving to be Detached.

Connections

- Like Fives, Ones are logical, factual, capable of controlling their emotions, and responsible for accomplishing assigned tasks.
- Fives and Ones are generally well informed about their areas of interest, and more task than people-oriented.
- Like Ones, Fives may insist on "just the facts." Both types prefer clear objectives and are methodical workers.
- Similar to Ones, making decisions for Fives can be a challenge: Fives need more and more data and are afraid of looking uninformed or stupid; Ones are afraid of making mistakes, and being seen as unprepared or flawed.
- Both types are respectful and careful with information and will not hesitate to challenge a source or statistic.
- Both types can be cautious, frugal and socially responsible.

Disconnects

- Fives can be impersonal, distant, and non-responsive. Ones may interpret their silence or detachment as criticism, and their lack of engagement as disagreement.
- A One's anger and expression of frustration may turn off Fives. Fives also can be argumentative when Ones disagree with their grasp of the facts or logic.
- Fives may test a One's patience because Fives tend to process information and express themselves at a slower pace than Ones.

- Ones are more assertive than Fives. Fives can seem unassertive and passive to Ones.
- Ones are respectful of the rules, while Fives can be irreverent and cynical of sacred cows.
- Ones aren't as quiet as Fives (although Fives can be very opinionated about topics of great interest to them). Ones push their agenda more aggressively than Fives.
- Ones tend to be traditional while Fives are more attracted to the unconventional.

Connecting With Fives From a One's Perspective

- Ones should be patient with the Five's slower pace, and what Ones may judge as an unpolished style.
- Ones build rapport with Fives by focusing on safety, practicality, and logic, and by emphasizing facts over feelings.
- Be direct and logical with Fives. Ones can connect by emphasizing competence and knowledge.
- Ones can help Fives by being clear and exact when asking for data. Tell Fives what is wanted, how it should be presented, and how much is wanted. Establish the parameters up front and avoid being critical.
- Be aware that Fives may distribute information at their own pace (and slower than Ones may prefer) and give what may appear as the minimum.
- Ones can help Fives see that real serenity involves appreciating order, and practicing compliance in order to fit into society, the team, and the organization. Fives can avoid being hassled by being responsive.

Connecting With Ones From a Five's Perspective

- Fives should trust that Ones are well prepared, logical, have gathered facts, and have thought about options.

- Fives can build rapport and harmony by emphasizing practicality, logic, correctness, and accountability to rules and norms—be direct and speak logically; emphasize competence, knowledge, and reliability.
- Fives can build trust by being open about their own difficulty with conflict.
- Fives do well to come out of their quiet, reserved comfort zone and initiate conversations with Ones because Ones may interpret silence as criticism.
- Fives can help Ones relax and perform effectively by ensuring that even if mistakes are made, they can be fixed.
- When Fives can model their own intensity around ideas, they can help Ones to be creative, take risks, and find enjoyment in their work.

ONES AND SIXES CONNECTING
Ones are Striving to be Perfect; Sixes are Striving to be Secure.

Connections
- Ones and Sixes both believe that things run smoother if everyone follows rules, procedures, and social norms.
- Sixes and Ones are supportive, loyal, and hardworking.
- Both types have a strong sense of duty, and share a concern for following and upholding family and work traditions.
- Both Ones and Sixes stand behind causes they believe in.
- Ones and Sixes share a strong work ethic, the desire to do the right thing, and fear of going against the rules.
- Both types have a healthy skepticism when first meeting people.
- Both types have a critical eye that looks for what can go wrong and what is risky.

Disconnects

- Stressed Sixes can be erratic and emotional. Ones are steady and logical.

- Sixes express their fear more dramatically than Ones, and can complain and be obsessed with safety and security and disastrous outcomes if proper action is not taken.
- Sixes are more suspicious and reactive than Ones.
- Sixes relate to people well, are empathic, and often have many friends; they can read people and relate to another's joys and anxieties and believe that people should help each other get through the challenges of life. Ones are less empathic, more independent and focused more on discipline and personal resiliency in overcoming challenges.
- While Ones honor authority and its expression through rules, Sixes often question authority unless it is consistently truthful, well established, and reliable.
- Ones may seem overly serious and unfeeling to Sixes. Ones are conservative and seek to be proper and appropriate; they may think that Sixes over react emotionally.

Connecting With Sixes From a One's Perspective

- Ones can practice being supportive and cooperative with Sixes. Emphasize control, safety, reliability, and security.
- Ones should let Sixes know that Ones can be trusted. Don't paint an unrealistically positive picture of anything. Ones build rapport with Sixes by telling them which areas to be cautious of, what could go wrong, and how it could be handled.
- Ones can help Sixes to see that security can be found by balancing their often emotional, anxious, and reactive behavior with a more measured, rational approach.
- Model being unambiguous, fearless, and confidently relaxed for Sixes. Show Sixes that being decisive and direct will provide safety and peace of mind.
- Ones and Sixes should practice checking in with each other to discuss schedules and the safety and viability of projects and events.

Connecting With Ones From a Six's Perspective

- Avoid taking a One's fault finding personally—they do it with others as well. Focus on correctness, practicality, logic, competence, ethics, and reliability. Speak directly but unemotionally.
- Sixes need to be aware of their paradoxical "love/hate," relationship with authority when interacting with Ones because both types are suspicious of hidden agendas and trust issues. Sixes can build rapport by honoring a One's similar tendency, but can help Ones by discussing these issues, dispelling rumors, and establishing the truth. Encourage weekly, informal discussions and reality checks.
- Help Ones to be more open with their feelings in order to establish trust.
- Encourage Ones to listen openly to the views of others, to be willing to change, and to commit to mutual goals.
- Focus on tasks and be honest, serious and rigorous when relating to or leading Ones. Ones are looking for strong leaders and will support and rally around a Six who exhibits strength, ethics, and courage.
- When appropriate, encourage Ones to loosen up, have some fun, and to enthusiastically join the group.

ONES AND SEVENS CONNECTING
Ones are Striving to be Perfect; Sevens are Striving to be Excited.

Connections

- Similar to Sevens, Ones have a desire to accomplish goals and make an impact.
- Both types may be unrealistic: Ones in their idealism and focus on order (the world should be perfect); Sevens in their optimism and focus on options (the world should be exciting).
- Sevens are attracted to a One's precision and clarity, and Ones are attracted to a Seven's healthy expression of spontaneity and optimism.

- Ones often struggle with a Seven's fun loving, relaxed behavior.

Disconnects

- Sevens dislike work that they consider tedious and exceedingly detail-oriented. Ones prefer structure, duty, and tasks that require rigor, reliability, and control.
- Ones believe in following rules and procedures to the letter, whereas, Sevens see rules more as guidelines.
- Ones like to be well prepared, to have a strict game plan, and follow it. Sevens like to improvise, and be creative and spontaneous.
- Sevens favor initiating projects, change, flexibility, options, and variety, and are happy to rely on others to complete tasks.
- Sevens will often feel restricted by a One's perfectionism. Ones may feel frustrated by a Seven's lack of seriousness and preparation.
- Ones are idealists and pragmatists and focused on the present; Sevens are planners and dreamers and focused on the future.

Connecting With Sevens From a One's Perspective

- Ones can get along with Sevens by allowing them to have their freedom and options; avoid making them feel fenced in, and avoid focusing too much on procedures. Let them talk and get engaged and allow them to be creative.
- Emphasize the importance of a Seven's contribution, especially their ability to rally people with their enthusiasm, which is not a One's strong suit.
- Ones should express themselves with energy, humor, enthusiasm, and informality with Sevens.
- Ones can help Sevens to be more selective, to narrow their focus and to practice discipline. Making a clear commitment and following established objectives is an area that Ones can model for Sevens.

- Ones can help by giving Sevens the task of producing a proposal or set of goals or precise instructions. Encourage them to focus on realities versus possibilities.
- Help Sevens to change their *dreams* (that have no action plans and defined outcomes) into *projects* (with exact action steps and measurable goals).

Connecting With Ones From a Seven's Perspective

- Sevens can build rapport with Ones by staying focused on commitments and team results rather than new ideas and exciting innovations.
- Sevens should avoid evasiveness, making excuses, minimizing or rationalizing about mistakes with Ones. A One's black and white thinking will interpret anything but a confession of faults as dishonesty. Sevens can reestablish rapport by admitting to a mistake and correcting it.
- Sevens can help Ones to see that being too serious and reluctant to relax will make it difficult for people to connect and build trust with them.
- Sevens do well to avoid making unplanned and unsolicited changes in directions or plans when connecting with Ones. Ones could interpret this sort of activity as irresponsible, and may resist cooperating. Sevens can learn from the One's objectivity, clarity and discipline.
- Sevens should minimize small talk and get to the facts. Ones are serious and literal and may become sidetracked in searching for faults and loopholes before committing to tasks.

ONES AND EIGHTS CONNECTING
Ones are Striving to be Perfect; Eights are Striving to be Powerful.

Connections

- Like Ones, Eights are not afraid to take a stand, are committed to their ideals, and are self-confident.

- Both types like to be in charge; with Ones it's the "*right* way;" with Eights it's "*my* way."
- Both types are often angry, although Ones may call it "being frustrated," or "annoyed;" Eights may call it something more graphic.
- Both types are achievement-oriented, and like to take the initiative.
- Ones and Eights see things as "black and white," and are convinced they're right.
- Both types have a strong sense of fairness and a love for the truth, and both are more task than people oriented.

Disconnects

- Ones are motivated by perfection, logic, and correctness. Eights are motivated by power, passion, and pragmatism.
- Ones pride themselves in being correct. Eights pride themselves in being strong.
- Ones feel guilty if they haven't followed the rules, whereas Eights are less bothered by guilty feelings as long as their goal has been accomplished.
- Regarding social interactions, a One's standard of behavior is restrained and dignified compared to an Eight's more relaxed, robust style.
- To Ones, Eights can go overboard, show little restraint, and can be embarrassingly inappropriate. To Eights, Ones can seem inflexible, restrained, and fearful of embarrassment
- Under stress both Eights and Ones are quick to debate issues and draw a line in the sand. Eights like to argue, and usually feel they are right, much as Ones do. Eights argue with passion and bravado, while Ones debate with logic and self-righteousness.

Connecting With Eights From a One's Perspective

- Ones should appreciate the enthusiasm and dynamism of Eights, and resist trying to restrain them.

- Feedback from Ones can help "bigger than life" Eights gain a more objective view if the Eight is pushing people too hard, over-stepping boundaries, breaking rules, etc. However, Eights need to be aware enough to ask for feedback and open enough to accept it.
- Ones should be prepared to compromise with Eights, which won't be easy for Ones, because both types have a strong need to be right.
- Ones can help Eights to see the usefulness of rules and procedures in accomplishing their goals and establishing loyal followers.
- Teach Eights that the ability to control their emotions is a powerful and necessary tool. Be conscious that Eights resist supervision, procedures, and being restricted or fenced in.
- Evaluate Eights on their results, (*what* they get done), not on their methods, (*how* they get it done), as long as they are not causing conflict or breaking rules.
- If Eights are performing well, don't insist on the letter of the law, and adherence to procedures; leave them alone. Give them the freedom to be productive, within limits.

Connecting With Ones From an Eight's Perspective

- Eights can learn from a One's restrained approach and do well to appreciate where a Perfectionist's logic trumps an Eight's "shoot from the hip" style.
- Eights should be aware that they might misinterpret a One's insistence on logic, order, and restraint as disagreement and combativeness, rather than a style difference between Ones and Eights.
- Eights can appreciate the One's mastery of impulse control and how it helps in establishing trust, dealing with conflict, and gaining the commitment of people.
- Eights can help Ones be more energetic, to engage fully ("body and soul") in their work and interactions with people rather than rely solely on being proper and conservative.

- Eights can model fun and a healthy love of life, action, and adventure for Ones.
- Eights can help Ones be more decisive and action-oriented—rather than worry so much about making mistakes or appearing flawed. Eights can help Ones to be less concerned about what people think and more concerned about getting results.

ONES AND NINES CONNECTING
Ones are Striving to be Perfect; Nines are Striving to be Peaceful.

Connections

- Both types appreciate predictability and fairness, and a desire for balance.
- Nines are non-threatening, and can create an accepting, nonjudgmental atmosphere that allows Ones to be less critical of themselves, and to relax, kick back, and have fun.
- A Nine's tolerance and ability to see many points of view provides perspective and helps Ones avoid life's minutia.
- Both types thrive on structure and dislike risk and rapid change. Both like to refine and improve established processes rather than reinvent the wheel.
- Both types are slow to make decisions: Nines because they consider many different options, and Ones because they fear making mistakes.
- Both Nines and Ones prefer an organized, regimented work place, and a regular schedule with established expectations.
- Nines and Ones both are concerned with the greater good of the group.
- Both repress anger rather than express it.

Disconnects

- Nines can be as stubborn as Ones; they can argue their point, and refuse to give in. Under stress, both Nines and Ones can allow disagreements to become stalemates.

- Nines can take the path of least resistance, and may minimize problems and resist repairing, improving, or reforming things. Ones tend to seek people and things that need fixing, and start "crusades" that may involve difficult, drawn out battles.
- Ones may judge a Nine's relaxed attitude as a refusal to do the right thing, engage in right action, or as simple laziness.
- Ones are not quick to compliment or forgive. Nines compliment and forgive easily, are self-effacing, give in quickly, and hesitate to defend their own opinions.
- When it comes to taking action, Ones, once committed, are ready to move, whereas stressed Nines, even when committed, can delay, rethink things, and procrastinate.
- Ones can resist compromise and consensus in favor of following policies. Nines seek compromise and consensus as a way to create harmony.
- Ones are very businesslike and impersonal and lack a Nine's personal touch with people. Nines are friendly and likeable and lack a One's one-pointed focus on task accomplishment. Ones are rule driven and task-oriented. By contrast, Nines are creative and people-oriented.

Connecting With Nines From a One's Perspective

- Ones should be clear on deadlines and boundaries, but be open to compromise.
- Ones can build rapport by listening patiently to Nines, who can be verbose and unfocused, and from a One's perspective, may take too long to get to the point.
- Ones should include small talk with Nines. Get personal and engaged.
- Build rapport first before delivering the facts. With Nines, being friendly helps them hear and appreciate the facts.
- Ones can help Nines to see that achieving peace of mind also involves staying focused on details and deadlines, and that dealing immediately with normal conflict before it escalates is a fundamental way to

maintain good relationships, group harmony, and a personal sense of well being.

- Make specific agreements with Nines—brainstorm reciprocal activities and deliverables—and write them down so that they can be reviewed later.
- Ones can help Nines to be successful and happy by keeping positive and negative feedback well balanced, providing structure, clear goals, and clear rewards. Criticism without praise will make Nines less receptive to constructive feedback.
- Remember that Nines have an unspoken desire to be noticed—to be seen, heard and appreciated (although they will not actively seek it out). Avoid criticism and sarcasm. Encourage, compliment, and let Nines know they have been noticed for their efforts.

Connecting With Ones From a Nine's Perspective

- Be patient with Ones' practical, all-business approach, and their focus on finding and correcting flaws, and try to see that it is their way of improving things.
- Understand that Ones feel that expressing constructive feedback (which may come across as criticism) is their way of being helpful and showing empathy.
- Be on guard against your common avoidance of risk-taking and decision-making. Don't get caught in a mutual resistance to change.
- Nines can help Ones establish greater trust, rapport, and likeability by modeling how to use humor and small talk, and to connect emotionally with people.
- Teach Ones that charm and a well-placed compliment can have a greater impact than just the facts. Encourage Ones to provide positive reinforcement, to compliment team members, and to make simple changes in order to be more personal.
- Praise the One's ability to be precise, results-oriented, and accountable.

TWOS AND ONES CONNECTING
See Ones and Twos Connecting on page 170

TWOS CONNECTING WITH TWOS
Twos are Striving to be Connected

Connections

- Twos are on the same positive wavelength and provide the love, appreciation and strong emotional bond that other Twos desire.
- Twos also enjoy nurturing others, staying connected, discussing people, family, friends, and relationships.
- Both are empathic and compassionate.
- Both like to control situations and others by being helpful, indispensable, and "the power behind the thrown."

Disconnects

- Twos may compete for being helpful, indispensable, and appreciated.
- Both may compete with each other for people's attention. Jealousy may arise if they both are seeking to be the favorite.
- Knowing that other Twos can be easily hurt, it may be difficult for a Two to give another Two constructive feedback out of a fear of losing connection and being hurtful.
- A Two may want to gloss over or ignore questionable behavior and even compliment another Two rather than be honest.

Connecting With Twos From a Two's Perspective

- Twos should be tactful, reassuring and cooperative rather than competitive when seeking attention and appreciation.

- Be conscious of the tendency to control other Twos by doing favors, giving unsolicited advice and showering them with attention.
- Appreciate another Two's compassion without over complimenting them. Be aware of the strong desire to connect, and a tendency to manipulate through being kind in order to feel satisfied.
- Twos can help other Twos by encouraging them to set up and follow clear boundaries for behavior.
- Provide feedback on the difference between gaining approval because of political and emotional connections and gaining approval because of consistent, substantive performance.
- Coach Twos to focus as much on details and tasks as feelings and relationships.
- Help Twos to see that practicing self-reflection is not selfish, but a way to be really connected to themselves and others.

TWOS AND THREES CONNECTING
Twos are Striving to be Connected; Threes are Striving to be Outstanding.

Connections

- Twos and Threes both mix well with people, and project a positive impression.
- Both types are energetic and upbeat, and have an enthusiastic approach to getting things done and accomplishing their goals.
- Both types are productive and skilled at promotion.
- Twos and Threes both desire lots of acknowledgment and praise—Twos for how liked and helpful they are—Threes for how productive and successful they are.
- Twos like to give Threes lots of adulation and affection; they are supportive and complimentary.
- Like Threes, Twos are consummate networkers, know how to read a crowd, and know whom the important, influential people are.

Disconnects

- A Three's self-esteem is focused on their success, accomplishments, image, and status. A Two's self-esteem is focused on satisfying the needs of others, being loved, noticed, and admired, and making a difference in people's lives.
- Threes are self-promoters, and work hard to stand out from the crowd; they are consistent individual contributors.
- Twos promote other people through praise, compliments and creating alignments; they are gifted group and community people.
- Threes resist talking about feelings and challenges to their relationships. Twos, on the other hand, find it natural to talk about feelings and consider working on their relationships as a way to get closer to people.
- Threes may have problems with Helpers interrupting work to build rapport and smooth ruffled feathers. Twos will grow weary if a Three ignores the Helper's feelings or is too focused on themselves or their work.
- Twos can complain when they don't get noticed, and may demand attention—attention that Threes think should be devoted to work. A Two's emotionality may be embarrassing to a Three, who prefers to maintain a polished, professional demeanor.

Connecting With Threes From a Two's Perspective

- Twos should accept that Threes find their identity and personal value in work and accomplishment, and that a Three's success extends to his or her partner, team, and/or family.
- Let Threes reveal their more intimate self at their own pace and on their own terms. Be aware that a Three's emotional life may seem unknowable compared to a Two's.
- Both Threes and Twos can benefit from appreciating the importance of balancing task and relationship needs.

- Twos can teach Threes to see that gaining the trust of friends and colleagues involves sharing part of their personal life, and that the trust of people will help Threes achieve their goals.
- Point out to Threes that being likeable makes people want to work with them and follow their lead.

Connecting With Twos From a Three's Perspective

- Threes can work well with Twos by offering praise for the Two's kindness or compassion. Cooperate rather than compete with Twos.
- Threes can learn the value of empathy from Twos. Appreciate how the ability to relate personally and intimately with people can contribute to a Three's ability to be both connected and outstanding.
- Threes can build rapport with Twos by setting time aside to talk, not about work, but about their personal life.
- Help Twos to concentrate on the bottom line. Emphasize the importance of being productive and finishing a project. Teach Twos the importance of details, deadlines, budgets, and productivity.
- Encourage Twos to try to stand out from the crowd for achievement as well as likeability. Help them see that accountability to the team or relationship begins with personal accountability for accomplishing specific, individual tasks.

TWOS AND FOURS CONNECTING

Twos are Striving to be Connected; Fours are Striving to be Unique.

Connections

- Both Fours and Twos like to focus on relationships. Fours value many of the qualities of Twos; both types are warm, caring, and comfortable sharing personal stories.
- Twos and Fours can be dramatic in their expression of emotions, and find comfort and value in being part of another's personal life.

- Twos give Fours the appreciation and understanding that they need and desire. They praise the Four's great taste and creativity.
- Twos are upbeat and can be supportive, patient friends who understand a Four's focus on people and relationships.

Disconnects

- Fours have a greater need for solitude than Twos. Twos have a strong need for community and are be stimulated by people and the outside world, while Fours are introspective, sensitive, and have a rich inner world.
- Twos will flatter, and get personal as a normal way of relating to people they hardly know. Fours may interpret this behavior as inappropriate and inauthentic—that it is exposing too much of one's self. For Fours, getting personal is reserved to special people who have earned their trust and love.
- To Twos, Fours may seem aloof and distant, and may neglect a Two's need for attention and approval.
- Fours may overreact to things and appear negative to Twos, who like to keep things upbeat.
- Both types can be demanding. Stressed Twos feel entitled to special attention because of all the caring things they feel that they do. Stressed Fours are self-absorbed and expect others to be attentive to them because they feel they are more sensitive than others, are easily hurt, and deserve special treatment.
- Fours may feel smothered if Twos don't respect a Four's boundaries and need for autonomy.
- Twos may be more cheerful than stressed Fours can manage, and may talk too much and give too much advice—especially when Fours just want them to listen. Fours often want to stay with the discomfort or pain they are feeling and may be put off by a Two's desire to fix things.

Connecting With Fours From a Two's Perspective

- Twos should take things slowly, show lots of empathy, and give Fours the space they need. Be ever mindful that Fours enjoy their special space (which could be their home, cubicle, or office) and their special status. Build rapport by not being intrusive.
- Twos can help Fours become more committed to accomplishing mutual goals by acknowledging and using their (the Four's) special talents for the good of the relationship or team.
- Avoid assigning mundane tasks to Fours. If possible, single them out for a special responsibility that is connected with some status.
- Encourage Fours to forego their need to put their individual stamp on things and to apply their sense of uniqueness to the relationship or team, not exclusively to themselves.

Connecting With Twos From a Four's Perspective

- Fours can build rapport with Twos by appreciating how Twos focus on others and establish relationships easily. Twos want to connect; Fours want to bond with the special few. Balance is the key.
- Stressed Fours can be self absorbed, which may make Twos feel ignored in the relationship. Fours do well to assure Twos that the Four's moodiness or frustration is a personal thing—often a way they work through emotions—and is not aimed at the Two.
- Fours can help Twos to bring their focal point inside, to be more self-reflective, to become aware of their actions and the impact they hav`e on others.
- Fours can teach Twos that it is all right to have and express one's own needs. Fours can model actions for Twos to be more independent and to avoid psychologically merging with others.
- Fours can help Twos to see that Twos can be even more connected and helpful if they have a stronger awareness of themselves and their independence.

TWOS AND FIVES CONNECTING
Twos are Striving to be Connected; Fives are Striving to be Detached.

Connections

- Fives can be good listeners, are able to give Twos their full attention, and can be calm, quiet, and focused.
- Fives can inspire Twos to appreciate their thinking side as much as their feeling side, and can provide a good example of independence and objectivity.
- Fives and Twos often share a pleasant, gentle quality, despite some of their opposite traits.
- The differences between a Five and a Two can work in their favor: Twos are attracted to people and are agreeable and cooperative—they roll up their sleeves and help out. Fives are attracted to isolation and are also agreeable and cooperative—they are unobtrusive and provide insight and information. Together they can arrive at a committed, mutual work arrangement and personal relationship to achieve mutual goals.
- Twos are positive, kind, and generous. They easily express their feelings and are a great model of how Fives can do the same. Twos like to socialize and, if partnered with Fives, can help alleviate a Five's stress about socializing.

Disconnects

- Twos are outgoing, sensitive, feeling people. Fives are introverted, detached, thinking people.
- Fives avoid socializing and can be overly withdrawn. A Five's emotional distance and lack of attentiveness can leave a Two feeling ignored and unappreciated. Twos can become frustrated by a Five's abstract thinking and lack of connection with them.
- Twos connect on a personal, often intimate, level. They want to know what Fives feel and think, and want to get to know their private

thoughts and feelings, which can feel intrusive to Fives. By comparison, Fives prefer to connect over tasks and ideas, and feel more comfortable engaging in less personal and less intimate discussions.

- Twos can become dramatic and emotional—behaviors that may seem illogical, impractical and uncomfortable to Fives.
- In their desire to get closer to people Twos may seem demanding, intrusive, and controlling to Fives. For Fives, Twos may talk too much and ask too many personal questions.
- Twos tend to show their feelings; Fives tend to hide theirs. Twos go toward people to connect and often to feel accepted, secure and in control; Fives go away from people to analyze the situation, and often to feel safe and in control.

Connecting With Fives From a Two's Perspective

- Twos should respect a Five's need for detachment, and permit them to make contact at their own pace.
- Be aware that the initial attraction between Fives and Twos—the "opposites attract" fascination—may wane without consistent mindfulness and attention.
- Twos benefit from periodically reminding themselves of why they felt drawn to Fives: their depth, honesty, and lack of pretense. Twos must adjust to and accept a Five's emotional unavailability (compared to a Two's eager openness) to build rapport.
- Twos should appreciate how a Five's preference to be quiet and less talkative allows others to express themselves freely.
- Help Fives to begin to collaborate more with others, and to see that they can achieve the security and control they desire by being more connected to others. Teach Fives to invest regularly in personal rapport building.
- Twos can help Fives to practice being accountable and committed to others by staying in contact, and especially *initiating* contact.
- When Fives respond with assertiveness, Twos do well to be supportive and to allow Fives to express themselves emotionally without judgment.

Connecting With Twos From a Five's Perspective

- It is important for Fives to understand how Twos interpret a Five's withdrawing and isolation. Fives see detachment, analyzing, and gaining knowledge as positive, and their way of relating. With this as a starting point, Fives need to reach out to Twos: withdraw less, connect more—compliment Twos, and don't criticize them or act intellectually superior.

- Fives should be willing to talk about their own feelings—or the *Two's* feelings—but at least be aware that Fives can build a connection by *getting personal* with Twos.

- Express the importance of a Two's contribution to the relationship. Speak with energy and enthusiasm. Smile and be informal. Build rapport first before delivering the facts. Being friendly is as important as being factual for Twos.

- Help Twos to focus on their own challenges rather than the challenges or problems of others.

- Coach Twos to be accountable for their own contribution and not expect special treatment. Encourage them to treat people equally, to avoid playing favorites and to cultivate a more detached, objective way of perceiving people.

- Fives can model for Twos how to detach from an overly emotional response and to concentrate on results.

- Fives can tap into a Two's strength by assigning them special projects where they can personally interface with influential people.

TWOS AND SIXES CONNECTING

Twos are Striving to be Connected; Sixes are Striving to be Secure.

Connections

- Sixes and Twos are community-oriented and like to help people.
- Both types appreciate others, and take pride in being committed and reliable.

- Both are good listeners and allow others to express their feelings honestly without judgment. Both are responsive, especially to people's problems and challenges.
- Like Sixes, Twos can be protective, warm, and nurturing. Twos are positive, trusting, and outgoing and can help Sixes be more relaxed.
- Twos value and acknowledge a Six's protectiveness. Twos like to be protective as well, by taking people "under their wings," which can be reassuring to stressed Sixes.

Disconnects

- Sixes can throw a damper on a Two's positive mood by focusing on dangers and personal fears. Stressed Sixes may complain too much for a Two's sensitivities and can be obsessive and negative.
- Sixes can be suspicious or put off by what they consider a Two's neediness, and by a Two's motives when trying to compliment or flatter people.
- Twos tend to affirm people and ignore their negative traits or behaviors, while Sixes are cautious and suspicious.
- Sixes demand loyalty, will test people and try to eliminate disloyalty; Twos try to make friends by being indispensable and doing favors to establish loyalty.
- Sixes believe that trust must be earned. Twos want to automatically trust people; they tend to play favorites with powerful people and authority figures.
- Twos paint an overly positive picture of the world, and can be surprisingly friendly (from a Six's perspective) to people they hardly know, which can make Sixes nervous. Sixes feel that the Two's "rose colored" view fails to look at the dangerous side of things.

Connecting With Sixes From a Two's Perspective

- Twos should be as open as possible about their motives, and reassure Sixes that they see the value in vigilance and safety. Twos need to be especially careful not to be unrealistically optimistic with Sixes.

- Sixes resist accepting others into their circle of trust if they think that people are not following the rules and not respecting group norms.
- Sixes look for fakeness. They may see flattery as a good reason not to trust Twos.
- Twos can help Sixes to remain in action, to avoid getting mired in suspicion and complaining. Let Sixes know that the group needs them to be strongly committed to group results, and to be connected to positive group energy, rather than sitting on the fence, with a 'wait and see" attitude.
- Twos can help Sixes understand that each type achieves safety in their own way; for example, Twos make powerful, personal connections and use their influence to feel safe.

Connecting With Twos From a Six's Perspective

- Be patient and try to understand how important it is for a Two to be liked.
- Unlike Sixes, Twos see little or no value in suspicion or doubt, so try to appreciate their positive attitude.
- Concentrate on the helpful, healthful aspects of the relationship. Make Twos feel special by acknowledging what they do for you and others. Get personal and engaged.
- Sixes should emphasize the importance of a Two's contribution to the friendship, the project, etc. Build rapport first before playing Devil's Advocate.
- Help Twos to deal with conflict openly. Encourage them to be objective with all group members, and to avoid trying to build alliances with favored people.
- Encourage Twos to learn to get in touch with their individual desires and to speak their minds without first gathering opinions.
- Sixes can model a more measured, objective approach to dealing with powerful people by helping Twos to honestly evaluate if their actions are offered to accomplish group goals or if their actions are self-serving and aimed at gaining favor with people.

TWOS AND SEVENS CONNECTING
Twos are Striving to be Connected; Sevens are Striving to be Excited.

Connections

- Sevens and Twos are optimistic, friendly, enthusiastic, and relate well to people; they both have a positive outlook on life.
- Both types like to be engaged, active and where the action is.
- While both types are intellectually curious, each uses a different barometer when relating to people. Twos want to be closer to people and help people feel connected and productive; Sevens want to be stimulated and help people feel enthusiastic and motivated.
- Both types are high-energy people and work well together, especially when Twos can support a Seven by helping turn a Seven's dreams into reality.
- Sevens are great idea and concept people. Twos are skilled at mobilizing people and taking action.

Disconnects

- Sevens can be impatient listeners, preferring to have fun and create excitement rather than listen, especially if they find the topic boring.
- Twos prefer specific leadership qualities in others, such as strong commitment and follow-through. They may misinterpret a Seven's wide array of interests, their spontaneity, and entrepreneurial spirit as a lack of commitment to the Two's special projects.
- Sevens may have difficulty focusing on either the needs of the Two or on the Two's desire to get intimately involved in the lives of others.
- Twos want to solve our problems by giving advice and by being emotionally supportive. Sevens want to help people by planning a brighter future for them, filled with endless, positive possibilities.
- A Seven's behavior may appear scattered, self-focused or inappropriate to a Two. A Two's behavior may appear overly dramatic, controlling, and demanding to Sevens.

Connecting With Sevens From a Two's Perspective

- Twos should not expect Sevens to look out for a Two's needs in the same way that Twos look out for the Seven's needs.
- Twos do well to protect Sevens from boring assignments, to keep them stimulated, learning, and challenged.
- Twos can emphasize mutual commitment by giving supportive feedback and checking that Sevens have met deadlines.
- Twos can help Sevens to understand the importance of people's feelings in building trust and achieving team results, and to concentrate their attention more on results than on entertaining people.
- Help Sevens see that people judge commitment more on how intent and serious one is than on how enthusiastic and lighthearted one is.
- Twos can serve as a powerful model for commitment and accountability by showing Sevens how to be supportive of the group or relationship.

Connecting With Twos From a Seven's Perspective

- Sevens must be especially aware that Twos, who are at their best at supporting strong leaders, may withdraw their support if they sense that Sevens aren't able to sustain their focus over the long haul and produce real results.
- Resist the temptation to take advantage of the Two's helpfulness. Twos can respond negatively if they feel that they are being used and not appreciated.
- Practice sincerely complimenting Twos, and be willing to talk about feelings and the relationship. Appreciate your common ground: being passionately engaged in life.
- Help Twos to focus more on satisfying their own (the Two's) needs and accomplishing tasks, and less on trying to get people to like them.
- Make it a point to regularly appreciate all that Twos do to help people work productively together. They often serve as the glue that holds teams together.

TWOS AND EIGHTS CONNECTING

Twos are Striving to be Connected; Eights are Striving to be Powerful.

Connections

- Both types are strong-willed, like to be engaged and in a pivotal position, and will seize the opportunity to make things happen.
- Under Stress, both Eights and Twos can be dramatic and demanding.
- Eights share a Two's love of life and desire to help and protect others. With friends and intimates, Eights are powerful and protective, but can also be tender and nurturing.
- Eights can make Twos feel supported, special and capable.
- Both types are willful and focused on authority: Eights prefer to *be* the authority, while Twos prefer to *support* authority.

Disconnects

- To Eights, Twos can be overly emotional and overly sensitive.
- Twos want to be connected to gain love and acceptance. Eights connect easily, but use distance to gain control and perspective.
- Eights are suspicious. Twos are trusting.
- Eights naturally express frustration and mistrust. Twos naturally express empathy and support.
- Twos change to meet the needs of others. Eights resist changing for others, and feel that their own needs should come first.
- Eights may see a Two's need for being appreciated and liked as a sign of weakness.
- Twos are trustful and like to help people, even strangers. Eights can be skeptical and believe that people should be independent and self-supporting.
- Eights are task-oriented, competitive, and independent. Twos are people-oriented, cooperative, and inter-dependent.

Connecting With Eights From a Two's Perspective

- Twos and Eights can work harmoniously together when the Eight gives enough attention to the Two, and the Two helps the Eight feel satisfied enough to give up some control.
- Twos should avoid trying to get their way through flattery and bargaining. Eights have very little tolerance for being "played" and will interpret this behavior as manipulation and as an attempt to control them.
- Twos should respect an Eight's very solid emotional boundaries. Don't get too close without permission, and let the Eight make the first move.
- Twos need to keep Eights informed, thus avoiding any surprises which may ignite an Eight's suspicion.
- Help Eights to see that they are most powerful when they are connected to others, and that they are effective as leaders when people trust their fairness, kindness, and restraint.

Connecting With Twos From an Eight's Perspective

- Twos and Eights should have rules of engagement when dealing with each other in public. Eights have less need for approval or need to save face than Twos.
- Eights should learn to see true compassion and helpfulness rather than neediness beneath the Two's striving to be connected.
- Eights can help Twos to be more independent, and to be more focused on achieving results than getting people to like them.
- Eights can help Twos to be more direct, honest, and less manipulative—to ask for and work for what they want—and not expect others to provide it for them simply because they are so pleasant and likeable.

TWOS AND NINES CONNECTING
Twos are striving to be Connected; Nines are striving to be Peaceful.

Connections

- Nines share a Two's desires to be close, positive, supportive, and help-ful. Like Twos, Nines genuinely care about people, are encouraging and engaging.
- Nines are gentle and thoughtful, and provide Twos the attention they need.
- Nines compliment Twos on their efforts and successes, and ac-knowledge what Twos do for them; they make Twos feel loved and appreciated.
- Nines may be drawn to a Two's vibrant, heart-felt energy.
- Both types cooperate and believe in sharing resources.
- Twos compliment and bring attention to Nines who avoid the lime-light but secretly desire it.
- Both types are loyal, empathic, trustworthy, and willing to make strong commitments to the relationship and the group.

Disconnects

- Nines can lack a Two's energy and passion, and can be indirect and unclear about what they want. Twos, on the other, have focused en-ergy, are often dramatic, reactive and intensely personal.
- Twos have a plan, an agenda, want to make things happen, and if need be, to control things. By contrast, Nines may not have a definite plan or agenda, are more willing to allow things to unfold on their own, and don't have a strong need to control things.
- Stressed Nines can be apathetic and unfocused on facts and commit-ments. Stressed Twos are rarely apathetic, and are more focused on feelings and commitments than facts and details.
- Twos and Nines differ in their work pace: Twos get things done and make decisions quicker than Nines; Twos may grow impatient with a Nine's lack of urgency.

- Both like to be supportive, but Twos try aggressively to build relationships and rescue people, while Nines use a "hands off" approach in maintaining peace, harmony, and the status quo.
- Nines can withdraw if they feel the Two is making too many demands, often causing the Two to make more demands for closeness and appreciation.

Connecting With Nines From a Two's Perspective

- Twos should create a peaceful, structured environment for Nines.
- Forcing Nines to deal with conflict won't work; let them engage in their own time and in their own way.
- Be patient when Nines withdraw. Nines need more solitude than Twos. They withdraw to avoid confrontation and also to renew their energy. Nines will appreciate Twos more if Twos allow them their solitude. Nines may interpret a Two's unsolicited advice as bossiness or badgering and will resent it.
- Twos can help Nines to be more confident by acknowledging the Nine's abilities, power, and influence, and by encouraging Nines to talk about their ideas, accomplishments and skills.
- Twos can model a way to be assertive while being pleasant and respectful of people.
- Encourage Nines to focus on important people, to network regularly, and to avoid getting caught up in unnecessary busy work.

Connecting With Twos From a Nine's Perspective

- Nines should accept that Twos are truly trying to be helpful, even if they feel Twos are disturbing their peace of mind by hovering around them or badgering them for attention.
- Appreciate that Twos are natural coaches and cheerleaders and like to give advice and encouragement. They may see a lot of dormant, unused potential in Nines.

- Nines benefit by being open to a Two's ability to initiate action for them. On the other hand, Twos may feel a little too intrusive at times, so Nines should let Twos know when they need space. Nines should set clear directions and boundaries for Twos.
- Build rapport with Twos by complimenting them on their efforts and successes, and acknowledge what they do for people.
- Acknowledge and take advantage of the Two's political savvy and their skill at gathering valuable information.

THREES AND ONES CONNECTING
See Ones and Threes Connecting on page 172

THREES AND TWOS CONNECTING
See Twos and Threes Connecting on page 190

THREES CONNECTING WITH THREES
Threes are Striving to be Outstanding.

Connections

- Threes generally relate well to each other and work well together; they are goal oriented and productive, and really shine when work needs to get done.
- Threes love a fast paced, competitive environment where they are visible, can get praise, and feel a sense of accomplishment. Threes often have great fun working in a dynamic environment together, or engaging fully in a relationship, often with a healthy, playful competitiveness.
- Threes understand people, mix well, and make a positive impression.
- Threes together are generally energetic and upbeat.
- Threes focus on being appreciated for a job well done, and can support each other by assessing each other positively and praising each other's performance.

Disconnects

- Threes working together may push each other too hard, often to the point of exhaustion.
- They're both poor at expressing feelings, and may never get to know each other beyond goals and work projects.
- When challenges to the relationship arise, one or both Threes may withdraw if communication becomes too personal and not work-related.
- Two Threes in a relationship may compete with each other for the spotlight or biggest prize. Under stress both may fail to acknowledge each other's accomplishments.
- If competition between two stressed Threes gets too heated, a stressed Three may refuse to cooperate or try to sabotage the other.

Connecting With Threes From a Three's Perspective

- Threes should find ways to compromise and share the glory rather than compete with each other.
- By respecting each other's energy, positive attitude, and marketing ability, Threes can work very well as a pair or as part of a team.
- Threes need to be aware of the challenge and value of collaboration. Too much competition in a relationship or among group members will cause agitation and burn out. Remember that Threes are individual contributors—compared to more team-oriented people—and may struggle to be effective in achieving group results if they are not adequately noticed for their efforts.
- Threes can help each other by agreeing to provide mutual feedback about their major blind spot: inauthenticity. Threes can practice honesty and focus on how well the other Three is trusted by others.
- Threes can help by asking each other "What is the most effective balance between being an individual contributor and being a team player?"

THREES AND FOURS CONNECTING
Threes are Striving to be Outstanding; Fours are Striving to be Unique.

Connections

- Aware Threes and Fours can find common ground around personal presentation. Fours are elegant, sophisticated, and expressive, and value a Three's appreciation for image and making a good impression.
- Threes know how to "dress for success," and often a have a polished, refined look that Fours appreciate.
- Both types may feel they never receive enough acknowledgment.
- Under stress both types can become angry and demanding when they don't get their way, or they don't get the recognition they desire. However, both types usually avoid conflict.
- Both Threes and Fours have a deep desire to be admired for their special qualities—Threes because they are outstanding and successful, and Fours because they are unique and have special talents.

Disconnects

- Fours focus on making things different, edgy, or unorthodox, while Threes focus on making things practical, acceptable, and mainstream.
- The two types can be opposites when dealing with feelings; Threes prefer to ignore them while Fours feel compelled to discuss them.
- Fours are hyper sensitive to criticism and are conflict averse. Stressed Fours, especially if they feel ignored, can become moody, self-doubting, and sluggish. They can desire to process emotions and disappointments, and can be overly emotional and unproductive.
- Threes also avoid conflict but put off displays of emotions, talking about feelings, and being self-reflective, preferring to think and talk about what they consider to be more productive things such as work and competitive activities such as sports.

- Fours may criticize Threes for being superficial and pedestrian. Fours seek significant, meaningful work environments, and elegant, unique products, people and relationships; Threes seek high visibility, rewarding work environments, and practical, high profit products. Threes generally choose friends and establish relationships based on how they benefit their career or network.
- Threes are masters of convention and social norms, and desire to be shining examples of success. They are fixated on work, prestige, and image.
- Fours are unconventional and often struggle to fit in, or may purposely try not to fit in, often adopting the "rebel without a cause" stance.
- Threes can be impatient with what they see as a Four's aesthetic, introspective interests, while Fours may become bored with what they judge as a Three's disinterest in anything but image, success, and acknowledgement.

Connecting With Fours From a Three's Perspective

- Threes can build rapport by being attentive: ask Fours how their day is going, what they are feeling and thinking. Threes should let Fours know that they are willing to listen to them process their ideas and feelings, without interrupting with "shop talk."
- Threes can help Fours learn to be practical by asking how they intend to apply their ideas, then give them the time and space to respond.
- Threes should value a Four's creativity and encourage them to express themselves. Threes can teach Fours that creativity also means creating something real—useful, marketable, and profitable—not something that is only beautiful and emotionally moving.
- Threes do well to help Fours work in less competitive, less fast paced settings, and to acknowledge the Four's big picture perspective.
- Threes can demonstrate a balanced view of networking for Fours by practicing restraint and avoiding the image of the social climber

(which Fours will resist), while still showing charm and intelligence in social settings.

Connecting With Threes From a Four's Perspective

- Fours must learn that their need for self-expression and emotional connection is not the only way to be inspired and productive. Threes often express themselves, including how they care for loved ones, through long work hours and concentrated effort.
- Fours can learn from Threes how to be productive, to see how Threes use style and image for practical purposes—to impress and influence the right people.
- Help Threes to remember the importance of people's feelings. Be a mirror for them and reflect how they can be seen as inauthentic if they try too hard to impress people and exaggerate or fabricate accomplishments.
- Teach Threes the quality of quiet reflection and careful, active listening. Fours can help Threes see how they may deceive themselves, especially when they fall prey to blind ambition, dominating others, or questionable deals.

THREES AND FIVES CONNECTING
Threes are Striving to be Outstanding; Fives are Striving to be Detached.

Connections

- Introverted Fives and extroverted Threes connect when they complement each other. Together in social settings, Threes charm with finesse and charisma, while Fives charm with their knowledge and wisdom.
- Both types are task-oriented. Fives are innovators and problem solvers. Threes market and sell their ideas and products.
- Both types are efficient, productive, hard workers, and neither sees much value in small talk nor an intense discussion about feelings.

- Both types avoid conflict and prefer the impersonal to the personal. Threes avoid personal conflict by focusing on hard work; Fives avoid conflict through emotional detachment, social avoidance, and silence.

Disconnects

- Fives aren't interested in image and may disappoint or even embarrass Threes with how they present themselves.
- Fives avoid socializing, can become overly withdrawn and irritated if things don't go their way, and may avoid Threes and other people.
- While Threes are sociable, practical and pragmatic, Fives can be withdrawn, minimalistic, and abstract.
- Threes can make quick decisions, and like quick results ("Let's score a win and move on."); Fives prefer a slower pace, belabor decisions, and need more data and preparation time to refine and improve things. Because both types keep so much inside, it can be difficult to assess how stable the relationship is.
- Threes, unlike Fives, don't get mired in small details. Fives and Threes will often have a clash of values. Threes may offend Fives if they boast about their accomplishments, connections, and possessions. Fives are low key and understated.
- Threes are much more conventional about social norms than Fives who often make their own rules.
- Unlike Fives, who like their alone time, Threes have much less need for solitude. Fives prefer isolation and independence. Threes like being in the limelight, and crave praise and appreciation; Fives thrive on time to be quiet, analyze, and process ideas.

Connecting With Fives From a Three's Perspective

- Threes need to understand the Five's slower, measured style and their need to get all of the facts before taking action.

- Although Threes may interpret a Five's slower pace as a roadblock, they can learn from it. Fives often find better, more economical ways of doing things, are innovative thinkers, and may ultimately develop a better, more efficient way.
- A Three should not interpret a Five's lack of attention or enthusiasm as criticism, and do well to temper their need for recognition around Fives because they probably won't get what they're looking for.
- Threes can help Fives to learn to identify and appreciate the important people around them and to make contact with them.
- Threes should emphasize the value of staying in contact with people, especially initiating and answering telephone calls, emails, etc.
- Threes can teach Fives to balance two necessary ingredients for success: knowledge and people. Threes can model one of their own strengths: setting goals and achieving them.

Connecting With Threes From a Five's Perspective

- Fives should take the Three's aggressiveness with a grain of salt, and find common ground in both being efficient and focused on mutual goals.
- Emphasize connections, talk about results, and appreciate Threes for their energy and productivity.
- To build rapport with Threes, Fives can focus on being professional, factual, precise, and to the point. Avoid esoteric subjects and abstract, impractical discussions—emphasize practice over theory.
- Fives can learn from Threes to be polished, appropriately dressed, and sociable.
- Fives can help Threes to be as prepared as possible, to know the details, subtleties, and important aspects.
- Fives can help Threes to slow down and resist rushing too quickly onto the next conquest.

THREES AND SIXES CONNECTING

Threes are Striving to be Outstanding; Sixes are Striving to be Secure.

Connections

- Like Threes, Sixes are hardworking and conscientious. They are committed team players and will praise and support a Three's work and accomplishments.
- Both types like to be active, and Sixes can help balance a stressed Three's fast moving, "more is better" approach with their own focus on safety, discernment and caution.
- Both types are goal-oriented, people savvy, and charming, and can relate well to a variety of people.
- Threes tend to concentrate more on the positive than Sixes do, and can help Sixes focus on what can go right rather than wrong.

Disconnects

- Sixes are trying to fit in, to be part of a group, cause, company, family, or relationship; Threes are trying to stand out, to be stars of the group, cause, company, family, etc.
- Sixes may slow Threes down by focusing on dangers and personal fears. They complain and can blame Threes or others for their mistakes or mishaps.
- Sixes question the motives for a Three's strong need for attention—a quality that Sixes don't share or trust.
- Sixes may see a Three's tendency to exaggerate as dishonesty, bringing shame and negative repercussions to the relationship or team.
- Threes may interpret a Six's desire for security as a fear of taking appropriate risks and a roadblock to being successful.

- Threes are focused on competing to win, taking risks, and achieving individual success. Sixes are concerned with security, playing it safe, and being a team player.
- Threes may underestimate a Six's worries about security and the future, and may not devote adequate time to the relationship because they are busy working and networking.

Connecting With Sixes From a Three's Perspective

- Threes need to be honest with Sixes, to let them know what their personal motives are, and reassure them that they appreciate the Six's focus on vigilance and safety.
- Tell Sixes all the facts, keep them well informed, and avoid painting the most positive picture. Let them know what could go wrong and how it can be fixed or avoided.
- Threes can encourage Sixes to take risks and to stretch for their goals in pursuit of security.
- Threes can share the spotlight with Sixes. Acknowledge their hard work and dedication. Sixes may decline the offer, but offering establishes the trust that Sixes need to work effectively or be in a caring relationship with Threes.
- Threes can help Sixes to be more noticeable. Ease them into seeing that they can still fit in while standing out from the crowd through excellence, commitment, and hard work.
- Teach Sixes the value of achieving individual success as a way of gaining long-term job security, and that achieving individual goals is also a way of accomplishing group goals.

Connecting With Threes From a Six's Perspective

- Sixes and Three have very different work styles, and Sixes do well to observe and evaluate their bias about Threes. Sixes may view Threes as unreliable, with a tendency to take shortcuts and to put a positive spin on things that Sixes often find questionable.

- Sixes can build rapport by trusting a Three's motives and commitment to the relationship. Be less suspicious and give them a chance—they have a different but no less healthy view of competition, drive, and initiative as Sixes.
- Encourage Threes to ask questions and determine if they are in agreement with others rather than assume that everyone is motivated to be "Number One."
- Teach Threes that their success can be bigger and more visible when they are part of the success of an outstanding group.
- Be aware that Threes tend to dismiss negative feedback about them, preferring to focus on their accomplishments and successes. Continue to give Threes constructive feedback.

THREES AND SEVENS CONNECTING
Threes are Striving to be Outstanding; Sevens are Striving to be Excited.

Connections

- Threes and Sevens both have a positive outlook; they are sociable, friendly, and engaging.
- Both are enthusiastic, especially about work and competitive activity, and both prefer to stay busy.
- Threes and Sevens avoid negative thoughts and feelings, avoid conflict, and put the most positive spin on things.
- Both types are doers who believe in being practical, and may cut corners to get something done or avoid boredom. They both like quick results, winning, fast solutions, and having the "latest and the greatest."
- Both types like to plan: Sevens by envisioning a great, exciting future, and Threes on achieving goals that will guarantee them a lucrative future.

- Both avoid conflict and prefer the path of least resistance. Threes take on more projects as a way to exceed expectations, impress others, and be in the limelight. Sevens take on more as a way to stay stimulated, lower anxiety, and be creative.

Disconnects

- Sevens may not be as committed to achieving goals at all cost as Threes, who will do the tedious, boring tasks that Sevens avoid—as long as they lead to success.
- Threes and Sevens are both goal-oriented, with interesting differences. Threes are motivated by goal-completion (not just goal setting), hard work, and acknowledgement, whereas goal setting (the excitement of making plans), freedom, and variety motivate Sevens.
- Sevens may not give Threes the attention and praise that Threes desire.
- Sevens like to let loose and be outrageous at times, while Threes are more proper, and polished, and are too concerned about their image to take the chances that Sevens take.
- Threes may not be receptive to some of a Seven's more creative ideas, seeing them as impractical or frivolous.

Connecting With Sevens From a Three's Perspective

- Threes should be aware that a Seven's enthusiasm should not be mistaken for a willingness to do boring tasks. Threes will need to keep Sevens focused on task completion. Appreciate Sevens for the variety and creativity they can offer.
- Be aware that both Threes and Sevens exaggerate, spin and reframe things with the best of them. Test Sevens when the story they are telling sounds overly optimistic, unrealistic, or too good to be true.

- Threes can help Sevens to stay focused on tasks no matter how long they may take or how tedious they may be. Threes can model their own strong work ethic, and their goal completion approach.
- Encourage Sevens to delay celebrating until the job is done so that people can appreciate the satisfaction of completing the task.

Connecting With Threes From a Seven's Perspective

- Sevens can build rapport by keeping Threes informed of any changes they intend to make, and explain the practical benefit of changes.
- Sevens can learn from Threes how to stay focused on a project until it is completed.
- Sevens like to delegate work once a project is under way, and Threes are eager to oblige in filling this role as long as they get credit for it. The two types can work effectively together—it all depends on how well (practically and specifically) the Seven has defined the tasks and desired results.
- Sevens can demonstrate for Threes the truth of "All work and no play makes Jack a dull boy," to avoid burn out. Model for Threes how to be lighthearted and fun loving and still productive and successful.

THREES AND EIGHTS CONNECTING
Threes are Striving to be Outstanding; Eights are Striving to be Powerful.

Connections

- Eights, like Threes, are self-confident, capable, competitive, and energetic.
- Both like to be in charge and to be acknowledged for their accomplishments.
- Both are pragmatic, assertive, and goal-oriented.
- Both types emphasize product over process and results over intentions ("Do whatever it takes to get the job done.")

- Threes, like Eights, are more task than relationship oriented, and are frustrated when productivity is interrupted. Both hesitate to reveal their more sensitive side, fear being emotionally vulnerable, and prefer facts to feelings.

Disconnects

- Eights can be too aggressive for a Three's more polished approach and the image they prefer to send. Eights are not as concerned with what people think of them as Threes, and under stress, Eights may appear to Threes as overbearing, inappropriate, and crude.
- Eights may be put off if Threes boast about their accomplishments, connections, and possessions, especially if they boast louder and with more conviction than Eights.
- Eights are direct and challenging. Threes are politically sophisticated and compromising.
- Naturally skeptical and always wary of being taken advantage of, Eights may hear in a Three's voice the smooth talk of a salesperson—or worse—a charlatan.
- Threes believe in always presenting their most positive self-image, which may mean leaving out unflattering facts.
- Eights are champions of truth and justice and will have a difficult time if Threes hide facts that may endanger the relationship or group.

Connecting With Eights From a Three's Perspective

- First and foremost, Threes must prove to Eights that they can be trusted. Eights are suspicious, and may need Threes to prove their loyalty every day. Eights have great passion for justice, protecting the underdog, and being authentic.
- Threes can work well with Eights by explaining that they are as competitive and driven as Eights are—and dedicated to the same goal.

- Threes can help Eights to see that their desire to be powerful and express their will can be better accomplished if they make the right connections and have the right people and resources on their side.
- Threes can model their own ability to lead through visibility, likeability, and influence.

Connecting With Threes From an Eight's Perspective

- Eights can benefit from appreciating the Three's mastery of the social arena—their polish, likeability, skill at marketing their ideas, and their charisma.
- To make a connection, compliment Threes on their accomplishments, and let them know you admire their ability to motivate people and to get things done.
- Eights can help Threes build trust with team members by adopting an Eight's honest, "what you see is what you get" attitude.
- Help Threes to avoid projecting a flawless, "poster child" image that's too good to be true. People won't believe it and the behavior will foster mistrust.
- Eights should keep in mind that Eights can be nonconventional, often embodying a maverick quality, whereas Threes thrive in relationships and in organizations that are more conventional. Eights can help by providing Threes a ladder to climb, and an environment where their efforts are regularly rewarded and appreciated.

THREES AND NINES CONNECTING
Threes are Striving to be Outstanding; Nines are Striving to be Peaceful.

Connections

- Nines often admire a Three's degree of activity, focus, and productivity. It can inspire Nines to accomplish goals.
- Nines are thoughtful and sensitive, and can provide Threes the emotional support and attention Threes seek.

- Many Nines have a hidden desire to be seen and admired—a quality that they see and admire in Threes.
- Nines and Threes are both likeable. Nines have a warm, calming effect; Threes have a practiced, often masterful charm. Both are comfortable around people.
- Nines tend to gravitate toward high-energy, self-confident people like Threes.

Disconnects

- Nines are people-oriented and Threes are task-oriented.
- Threes want to stand out from the group or relationship. Nines want to fit in.
- Nines can lack a Three's energy and fast pace, and may frustrate a Three's need to be on the go all the time.
- Nines may not be as productive as Threes would like them to be, and under stress may procrastinate, drag their feet, and bury themselves in unproductive habits and busy work.
- Nines can frustrate Threes by being indirect or unclear about what they want, and unfocused on goals and end results.
- Nines may resent what they perceive as a Three's self-aggrandizement and over-emphasis on their image and accomplishments. Nines judge Threes critically for being "center stagers," whereas Nines avoid the limelight in an effort to be unobtrusive team players.
- Threes like to push their ideas and seek highly visible jobs, relationships, and possessions. Nines often take on another's agenda and downplay their own accomplishments and abilities.

Connecting With Nines From a Three's Perspective

- Threes can build rapport with Nines by keeping their own ego in check and trying to appreciate a Nine's lofty, often philosophical, point of view.

- Be conscious that Threes' natural tendency to market themselves and their accomplishments is often seen by Nines as shallow *attention seeking* and trying to upstage other group members—avoid this around Nines—instead, praise the accomplishments of the relationship or group.
- Threes can help Nines to feel comfortable with wanting to be "Number One." Threes can help Nines to be more competitive, noticeable, and to "sell" themselves more effectively.
- Nines feel that they should be noticed without any effort on their part. Threes can help Nines to see that this is impractical and that real effort is necessary. Help Nines to see how their success serves others— the relationship, the group, or the family.

Connecting With Threes From a Nine's Perspective

- Nines can build rapport with Threes by complimenting their efforts and successes.
- Nines can serve as barometers for Threes for group morale, empathy, and dealing with conflict. Nines, who can see the perspective of other people, can provide feedback to Threes when their task-focus drastically over rides their ability to relate humanely to group members.
- Nines should appreciate the way Threes promote themselves, but should also encourage Threes to be committed to the relationship and to group objectives, not just personal ones.
- Nines can help Threes to resist treating fellow workers as a means to an end, or a cog in the wheel. Nines should encourage Threes to learn to deal with emotional issues, rather than view them as an impediment to getting more work done.
- Nines like to ruminate about process, best practices, theory, research, and team functioning—things that may not interest Threes. Goals, and particularly *short-term* goals, with clearly visible and definable results and rewards, will energize Threes to get into action.

FOURS AND ONES CONNECTING
See Ones and Fours Connecting on page 175

FOURS AND TWOS CONNECTING
See Twos and Fours Connecting on page 192

FOURS AND THREES CONNECTING
See Threes and Fours Connecting on page 208

FOURS CONNECTING WITH FOURS
Fours are Striving to be Unique.

Connections

- Fours value each other's interest in creativity and depth of feelings.
- Both Fours share an ability to discuss things few other people would understand or feel so deeply.
- Fours can support each other's need for being introspective as well as time to discuss experiences together.
- There can be intensity in a relationship between two Fours that can be inspiring, fun, and productive.

Disconnects

- Fours can be resentful and blaming, and when both are focused on processing intense experiences it can be heaven or hell, depending on who feels he or she is being heard and appreciated.
- Fours can compete with each other about creativity, and often have an intense "*I'll show you*" attitude.
- Stressed Fours can over react to the smallest criticism, and often use drama as a way of demonstrating their hurt feelings.
- Conflict can become so escalated in a relationship between stressed Fours that resolution may seem impossible without help from a third party.

Connecting With Fours From a Four's Perspective

- Fours need to be on guard against beginning a relationship or project with passionate interest only to become bored when things hit the routine stages.
- Fours do well to take things slowly, show lots of empathy, and give other Fours the space they need.
- Don't allow mutual needs for creativity and uniqueness get in the way of actually accomplishing something or dealing with day-to-day reality. Try to remain grounded.
- Be aware that other Fours can be caught up in their own feelings and fantasies. Don't interpret this as being ignored.
- Fours should agree to give feedback to each other when they become uninspired and disinterested, for example, when being assertive, and being seen (public exposure) causes them to detach from the group or relationship.
- Help other Fours to see the difference between an unrealistic dream and a viable possibility. Is the relationship based on reality or a fantasy?
- Teach other Fours to see the times when they are stuck in being a visionary or when they need to be more tactical and practical; encourage them to work at the nuts and bolts of the relationship or task and still put their unique touch on it.

FOURS AND FIVES CONNECTING
Fours are Striving to be Unique; Fives are Striving to be Detached.

Connections

- Like Fours, Fives are focused, good listeners and conflict averse.
- Both Fours and Fives have the ability to see things from a different perspective than others.
- Both types can be unconventional, shy, and lacking in self-confidence.
- Fives and Fours prefer a less structured, less established environment, which allows them to create and follow their own path.

- Fours, like Fives, enjoy their independence, are comfortable spending time alone, and have an interesting inner life.
- Both types can be a bit eccentric and like to discuss esoteric and/or aesthetic interests. They are more appreciative of each other's depth and unconventional manner than most other types.

Disconnects

- Fives are not emotionally intense like Fours, and prefer to subdue their emotions. They conserve energy by minimizing contact with others.
- Fours are emotionally intense, dramatic, and are energized by contact with select people.
- Fives may purposely distance themselves from Fours because they feel intimidated or smothered by a Four's emotional intensity and emotional needs. A Five's emotional distance and lack of attention can leave Fours feeling ignored and frustrated.
- Fours can become bored by a Five's abstract thinking (which for Fours may feel mechanical and impersonal), and their lack of emotional connection.
- Although Fours are independent, Fives may see Fours as needy, demanding, smothering, and codependent.
- Fours, especially when feeling unappreciated, can freely express anger, sadness, or self-pity. Fours can be intense in both their expression of joy and sadness. Fives prefer to downplay or keep these issues to themselves.

Connecting With Fives From a Four's Perspective

- To build rapport with Fives, Fours should be less emotional and more logical.
- Fours should give objective data and the rationale for their ideas, because Fives are always looking for more information to support an argument.

- Fours need to be patient with the Five's slower, almost meditative speaking pace and focus on minutia. Both types can find common ground in their mutually unconventional approach to the world.
- Because Fives are the most detached and Fours are the most dramatically expressive of the types, they both can teach each other a lot. Fours should encourage Fives to share their life and their wisdom with others.
- Fives may only want to talk about their ideas, insights and knowledge, but encourage Fives to build trust by being more open, talk about common issues and goals, and avoid the need to show off their intellect.
- Avoid challenging a Five's intellectual contributions, and tread lightly around their grasp of the facts. Try asking what thought process they went through to arrive at their conclusions.

Connecting With Fours From a Five's Perspective

- Fives need to include feelings as a viable way of communicating when dealing with Fours.
- Fives, who prefer a planned structure and agenda, should include more spontaneity and "big picture" thinking into their interaction with Fours.
- Help Fours to practice detachment—to see that not every event personally involves them or has an impact on them. Be sensitive to the fact that Fours can easily feel shamed and appear shy or aloof when even their minor mistakes are revealed.
- Fives can naturally give Fours the space they need to be productive and creative, but should make it a point to arrange for person-to-person meetings rather than emails and phone calls.
- Encourage Fours to cultivate a broader, team perspective and to think in terms of the relationship and group results.
- Encourage Fours to accept, support, and commit to the relationship or team identity without a need to put their individual stamp on it.

FOURS AND SIXES CONNECTING
Fours are Striving to be Unique; Sixes are Striving to be Secure.

Connections

- Aware Sixes and Fours have high ideals and values and are emotionally available.
- Sixes and Fours can be both task and people oriented. They are energetic, trustworthy, and accountable when committed to the relationship or goal.
- Like Fours, Sixes can be rebellious; they can be dramatic and overreactive, and suspicious of authority figures.
- Under Stress, both types can become fearful and imagine worst-case scenarios. Conversely, a healthy understanding of "real" dangers can help both types move into action.
- Fours can create a stimulating, accepting atmosphere for Sixes to explore their more creative side.
- Fours and Sixes are responsive to people and to the environment, and readily show their feelings in a variety of ways.
- Under Stress both are cautious and private when first meeting people (Fours can appear aloof and Sixes can appear skeptical) and test people before they trust and open up to them.

Disconnects

- Sixes see themselves as normal, and the salt of the earth, and they easily adapt to standard, traditional values. Fours see themselves as different, not fitting in, and marching to a different drummer; they struggle with standard behavior and traditional values and may express their uniqueness by being rebellious.
- Fours seek appreciation, praise, and a personal connection from their boss or partner. Sixes seek assurance that their partner is competent, trustworthy, and managing things well.

- Sixes, when playing Devil's Advocate (with its typical mistrust and suspicion), can anger a sensitive Four by challenging the Four's unorthodox creative ideas or abilities. Sixes may think that a Four's special touch or unique approach strays too far from tradition. Fours may see a Six's tastes as ordinary and uninspired.
- Fours know what they want while Sixes question their thinking and struggle with making decisions.
- Fours can allow negative moods to affect their productivity, and may feel exempt from rules. Stressed Fours find fault with themselves, and stressed Sixes can find fault with others—a mix that can drag both types down when interacting with each other.
- Under stress, Fours and Sixes are both reactive, and can be intense—Fours in their disappointment and despair, Sixes in their anxiety and paranoia.
- Sixes prefer being a member or part of something—a team, family, etc. Fours prefer being independent, different, and outside the group.

Connecting With Sixes From a Four's Perspective

- Fours should understand that Sixes like more traditional approaches to work, and that a Four's unique style may conflict with a Six's.
- Help Sixes to feel secure by helping them relax and trust people. Both Sixes and Fours seek a special bond of trust, commitment, and accountability. Provide Sixes with the freedom to be themselves both independently and within the relationship and group. A Four's sincere expression of "I'm here for you," will go a long way in connecting with Sixes.
- Fours can build rapport by adopting a more conventional style of dress and behavior and following normal standards when interacting with Sixes.
- Fours can help Sixes to focus more on what they want, and to allow themselves to feel positive and satisfied with making a decision, voicing an opinion, and sticking with it.

- Show Sixes that taking a stand and dealing with conflict will help them feel more, not less, secure.

Connecting With Fours From a Six's Perspective

- Sixes should place extra focus on remaining positive, uncritical, and loyal.
- Sixes can build rapport with Fours by validating their competence, uniqueness, and contributions without being asked. Fours crave validation and appreciation but feel uncomfortable asking for it.
- Be positive and passionate when letting Fours know that you want to create and maintain a lasting relationship with them.
- Mirror the Four's intensity. Be patient and allow time for Fours to feel and talk about their feelings.
- Try to appreciate a Four's emotional sensitivity and aesthetic point of view.
- Help Fours to fit in by encouraging them to be more receptive of others. Teach them that being a mystery doesn't necessarily help build the trust that is essential for solid relationships.
- Encourage Fours to tone down any hint of elitism or being different just for the sake of being different.

FOURS AND SEVENS CONNECTING

Fours are Striving to be Unique; Sevens are Striving to be Excited.

Connections

- Both types have a sense of being distinct and special, and both types prefer novelty to the routine.
- Beginning something new, including a relationship, energizes both types. Both Sevens and Fours can become bored or disillusioned when the daily routine begins.
- A Seven's variety of talents and interests make it easy for Fours to feel connected to them. Sevens are curious and fun loving. They have their

own unique quality—different than a Four's—but interesting and enjoyable to be around.

- Both Sevens and Fours tend to be connoisseurs. Both types share an interesting relationship with desire. Fours yearn to find something that is missing. Sevens worry that they will miss out on something exciting.
- Sevens often seek "mass quantities" –variety, excitement, joy, and opportunities to satisfy their curiosity and optimism.
- Fours desire quality experiences –deep, meaningful events, feelings, and relationships, and opportunities to be creative and inspirational.

Disconnects

- Sevens may lack the depth that Fours desire.
- Sevens see the glass half full; Fours see it half empty.
- Sevens want variety and lightness; Fours want depth and intensity.
- Sevens and Fours both feel they deserve the best. Sevens feel entitled because of their great expectations and positive thinking—that "Life is for the living, and good times are for the taking". Fours feel entitled because they believe they have suffered more than other people—"No one knows the troubles I've seen!"
- Fours want to discuss negative feelings, and the serious, meaningful, often darker side of life. Sevens like to keep things light, fun, and optimistic.
- Under Stress, Sevens can be self-centered, unfeeling, and oblivious to another's needs. Stressed Fours can be self-absorbed, depressed and unresponsive to others. When both types are stressed, the other may not meet their individual needs.
- Sevens become quickly bored when Fours repeatedly process their deeper feelings and ignore the Seven's desire for excitement and levity.
- Fours become frustrated when Sevens are distracted and unfocused on the Four's need for sensitivity and attention.

Connecting With Sevens From a Four's Perspective

- Awareness goes a long way here. Fours should avoid trying to get Sevens to value the same things as they do, or to dive emotionally as deeply. Fours are on the opposite side of the emotional intensity scale: Fours on the "intense" side; Sevens on the "light" side.
- Fours and Sevens should establish agreed upon ground rules, professional standards, and deadlines because both types have a tendency to evade rules and restrictions. Both types need to focus on real needs with real solutions rather than future fantasies.
- Fours can build rapport by appreciating the Seven's unconventional, irreverent perspective—somewhat like their own—and have fun with them.
- Fours can model how to be dedicated to a goal with passion and intensity.
- Help Sevens to slow down and let things simmer rather than get caught up in nervous activity, impatience and boredom—to commit to doing the hard work of creating viable, researched, data-driven plans and solutions rather than rushing onto the next exciting project.
- Coach Sevens to be accountable for their negative feelings and the value in expressing and working through them.

Connecting With Fours From a Seven's Perspective

- Sevens should be patient, listen openly, and make personal connections with Fours. Be aware of cues that it is time to be serious. Avoid inappropriately timed wisecracking and attempts to keep things light when they should be serious. Fours like to explore the psyche. Build rapport by going there with them.
- Sevens should avoid interpreting the Four's need for emotional intensity as an attempt to limit the Seven's personal freedom. Fours express themselves personally and often intimately through emotional intensity. Sevens do well to realize that giving attention and

empathy to Fours does not rob Sevens of opportunities for satisfaction and fun.

- Sevens can satisfy their own desire for freedom and the Four's desire for attention and appreciation by helping Fours to take the lead, and to represent the group's ideas.
- Teach Fours how their attempts to be seen as different for the sake of being different can cause frustration, conflict and mistrust.

FOURS AND EIGHTS CONNECTING
Fours are Striving to be Unique; Eights are Striving to be Powerful.

Connections

- Eights and Fours engage passionately in life and strive to be authentic and committed.
- Both types are self-referencing and both seek special status. Neither type is a natural team player; both are self-starters and independent. Both have a strong need for autonomy, often preferring to go it alone than depend on others.
- Under stress, both types can be unconventional, intense, and reactive, and believe that the rules don't apply to them—Fours because they feel special and more in touch with pain and emotions than others—Eights because they feel their decisions are wiser, more powerful, and beyond the rules.
- Both types are possessive and territorial.
- Fours and Eights share a passionate commitment to a belief or project, and can push hard, even ignoring social norms to accomplish their goals.
- Fours and Eights know what they want, express their needs and hate to compromise.
- Both types can be volatile and critical when things don't meet their personal needs. They both have a strong internal sense of self and can at times be self-possessed.

Disconnects

- Eights are pragmatists while Fours are idealists and romantics.
- Four are introspective; Eights are more focused on the outside world.
- Fours are sensitive and in touch with their feelings. Eights are somewhat out of touch with their feelings (except for anger) and often reject their tender side.
- Eights are confident; Fours normally lack confidence, at least the way it is normally defined and especially compared to Eights.
- Eights tend to see Fours as weak or vulnerable if they are pensive or too emotional. Fours may see Eights as brutish and insensitive if they are too sarcastic or abrasive.
- Eights may see a Four's need to talk about their feelings as an indulgence and a waste of time.
- Eight's abruptness and directness may put off Fours, who are looking for sensitivity, sophistication and the creation of the perfect atmosphere or tone.
- Stressed Fours may seem silly and strange to Eights. Stressed Eights may seem crude and aggressive to Fours.

Connecting With Eights From a Four's Perspective

- Fours can build rapport with Eights by being honest, stong, and loyal: don't keep secrets or stretch the truth with Eights; work hard, keep your promises, and be consistent.
- Fours should be aware that Eights express caring and support in practical ways—such as keeping commitments, making plans, being decisive, and encouraging and mentoring. Fours express caring and support in more personal ways—such as expressing emotions, thoughtfulness, tenderness, and acts of kindness—when they feel safe with people, and especially when they feel that people are trustworthy and loyal.
- Fours can remind Eights to show more compassion and patience.

- Teach Eights to stop, look, and listen—that their tendency to "ready, shoot, aim," can sabotage the relationship and group efforts.
- Fours can serve as great emotional barometers for Eights by helping them see that their natural style, especially their leadership style, can be intimidating or threatening to others.
- Fours do well to control displays of suffering or negative emotions around Eights. They make Eights feel insecure and vulnerable, and possibly angry and aggressive.
- Give Eights a clear vision of what is desired and provide opportunities for them to be in charge. Let them know they are trusted.

Connecting With Fours From an Eight's Perspective

- Eights should cut back on their normal bigger than life style to build rapport with Fours. Fours resonate with sensitivity not dominance.
- Eights can connect by asking questions, showing interest, and creating a safe, unhurried and unobtrusive environment for Fours to be themselves.
- Curtail skepticism, cynicism, off-color jokes, and coarseness. Both types can find common ground in their passionate approach to life.
- Eights can help Fours gain more confidence by supporting the special contribution that Fours make to the relationship and to their work. Help them to be seen and to gain the individual appreciation that they desire.
- Eights should encourage Fours to take a visionary, strategic, and creative role, ensuring Fours that they will support them through action and commitment.

FOURS AND NINES CONNECTING
Fours are Striving to be Unique; Nines are Striving to be Peaceful.

Connections

- Nines are attracted to a Four's intense energy, drive, and direction. Fours are attracted to a Nine's calmness, acceptance, and sensitivity.

- Nines' open-mindedness and lack of judgment make it easy for Fours to be honest, to process their feelings, and to share intimate thoughts and emotions.
- Both Nines and Fours are empathic and conflict averse. They both fear emotional abandonment. Under stress, each type suffers from poor self-esteem.
- Nines can be good listeners when they want to be, won't try to change Fours, give too much advice, or judge them.
- Both types, especially under stress, can suffer from a lack of confidence.
- Nines and Fours both share a creative, aesthetic side.
- Nines and Fours both entertain fantasy, and have an idealistic, philosophical side.

Disconnects

- Nines won't be able to match a Four's level of intensity or flair for the dramatic.
- Nines dislike change and would rather feel peaceful than stirred up with strong emotions. Fours are fine with change and like emotional intensity. Fours see change as an opportunity for creativity.
- Fours get bored easily. Nines like routine.
- Fours always seem to know what they want, (they also have a deep *yearning* for what they want), can express their wants easily, and can make decisions easily. Nines have trouble knowing what they want, can be fuzzy about expressing their desires, and have difficulty making decisions.
- Nines seek calm and harmony through acceptance, and see little need to change what is going well. They may interpret being asked to change as disapproval.
- Fours seek intensity by challenging the status quo, creating drama, and yearning for what they feel may be missing.
- Stressed Fours seek independence. They want special treatment, special relationships and status, and high profile, inspirational projects.

- Stressed Nines find comfort in the group or relationship, merge with other people, seek consensus and equal treatment of everyone, and prefer the status quo.

Connecting With Nines From a Four's Perspective

- Resist looking for what's missing in Nines and give them the acceptance that they willingly give to others.
- Provide Nines with clear, unambiguous guidelines, and avoid getting "creative" by changing instructions, plans, and procedures. Change for the sake of change stresses Nines.
- Fours can help Nines develop a deeper sense of desire, yearning, and ambition by modeling how Fours do it themselves. Give Nines permission to dream big and to be more personally committed. Teach Nines how to weigh options, reflect on what *they* want—not what would please others or keep the peace—and commit to it.
- Fours can help Nines to find their purpose, to honor their own agenda and vision, and to ignite a fire of passion and energy for their life and work.

Connecting With Fours From a Nine's Perspective

- Nines can build rapport with Fours by accepting a Four's need to change and be creative.
- Be patient with a Four's occasional emotional reactions and their ongoing need to discuss and analyze their thoughts and feelings.
- Encourage Fours to see that dealing with group conflict depends first on building group trust. Help Fours to balance their strong need for autonomy with the group's need for cohesion and commitment.
- Nines can help Fours by supplying a common sense, stable presence that Fours can model, and by encouraging Fours to channel their creative ideas into practical outlets.

- Nines can bring a calm acceptance that is grounded in basic trust and the belief that all will be well. When Nines are focused on their own security and wholeness, they provide Fours with the safety to rest in the quiet equanimity that is the source of the Four's creativity and aliveness.

FIVES AND ONES CONNECTING
See Ones and Fives Connecting on page 177

FIVES AND TWOS CONNECTING
See Twos and Fives Connecting on page 195

FIVES AND THREES CONNECTING
See Threes and Fives Connecting page 210

FIVES AND FOURS CONNECTING
See Fours and Fives Connecting on page 223

FIVES CONNECTING WITH FIVES
Fives are Striving to be Detached

Connections

- Fives together are innovative, independent, efficient, and logical.
- Both are generally well informed about their areas of expertise or interest, and are more task than people-oriented.
- Both Fives will be comfortable spending time quietly together, and/ or giving each other space, and both Fives will naturally respect the other's boundaries.
- Since Fives are comfortable around people who control and contain their emotions, they will be comfortable around each other.

Disconnects

- Fives together may be overly impersonal and even distant.
- Fives also can be argumentative when other Fives disagree with their understanding of facts or logic.
- Fives may reinforce each other's cautiousness, anxiety, and disinterest in being social and may avoid group functions, meetings, initiating contact, and responding to inquiries.
- Fives run the risk of creating animosity and emotional emptiness if they don't make an effort to answer phone calls and respond to requests in a timely manner.

Connecting With Fives From a Five's Perspective

- Fives tend to spend a lot of time analyzing information, so be aware of the "paralysis through analysis" syndrome—look for opportunities to take action.
- Five should practice being responsive to each other. Frustration may result when one Five seeks information from another, and the second Five is reluctant or slow to answer.
- Build rapport with other Fives by presenting ideas with composure and decorum.
- Resist the temptation to send memos or emails or text messages as the preferred means of communication—talk, preferably in person.
- Fives do well when they have the facts and figures in front of them and have time to process them.
- Fives may become disengaged and non-communicative when their specific piece of a project is not being addressed.
- Coach Fives to be more effective and committed to team results by helping them grasp the end goal, or the strategic view of a project.

FIVES AND SIXES CONNECTING
Fives are Striving to be Detached; Sixes are Striving to be Secure.

Connections

- Both Sixes and Fives are mentally quick, curious, and cautious.
- Both types can be suspicious and may struggle to make decisions and take action: Fives because of a desire for more information and to analyze every detail; Sixes because of a fear of deviating from rules or social norms, and anxiety that something may go wrong.
- Both types are basically "low maintenance," with a high sense of resilience, frugality, and persistence in the face of obstacles.
- Fives and Sixes can understand each other's hesitancy to trust people without first getting to know them and testing their loyalty.

Disconnects

- Sixes have a greater need for reassurance about the relationship than Fives.
- Sixes reach to others for security; Fives reach inside, or seek solitude, information or intellectual activity for security.
- Sixes may react to a Five's isolation or need for solitude with suspicion or mistrust. They may misinterpret the Five's behavior as a way of creating boundaries that Sixes may want to eliminate in order to solidify the relationship.
- Sixes are more overtly fearful than Fives and can complain and blame Fives for things they haven't done. They can push Fives for an emotional reaction that Fives can't or won't give. Stressed Sixes can appear illogical and overly emotional to Fives.
- Sixes are more comfortable with relationships than Fives. Fives are more comfortable being alone than Sixes.
- A Five's slower pace or lack of response can test a Six's patience.
- Sixes are comforted by loyalty, and words of emotional support and encouragement, while Fives feel comforted by logic, information, and clarity.

Connecting With Sixes From a Five's Perspective

- Fives can build rapport by making a special effort to support Sixes through regular communication, contact, and emotional reassurance. Let Sixes know that things are under control, safe, and predictable.
- Fives need to be aware of their own tendency to give information sparingly, on a need to know basis. Sixes want lots of meaningful information, especially about any threats to them personally, to the relationship, or to group progress.
- Fives need to be cautious about overwhelming Sixes with factual minutia; instead, keep Sixes informed, especially about unexpected actions and threats. Err on the side of caution when communicating possible concerns.
- Fives can help Sixes to feel more self-assured and effective if Fives provide the opportunity for Sixes to openly discuss concerns, fears, strategies, and work flow. Allow Sixes to question authority, and be available and open to them.
- Fives are loyal and honor their commitments like Sixes, and can help Sixes be more logical and less emotionally reactive to problems.

Connecting With Fives From a Six's Perspective

- Sixes do well to be patient with the quiet, often withdrawn Fives, and should not take the Five's lack of attention as a slight.
- Be direct, avoid drama, and communicate logically with Fives.
- Ask fewer personal, *feeling* questions and focus more on substance and facts.
- Be aware that Fives admire people who can control their feelings, so contain emotional displays and spontaneity. Call first or send an email before meeting a Five in person.
- Help Fives to see that a powerful way for them to establish trust and to practice commitment and accountability is to share their knowledge and insights with people regularly and preferably without being

asked. Coach Fives to avoid assuming that people should know something because they do.

- Help Fives to be more effective and to participate more fully in group efforts by preparing them with To Do lists, agendas, regular "heads up" calls, etc.
- Be aware of a Five's need for lots of time to process things. Consider the extensive analysis that Fives will go through in order to fully commit to a project. Be patient.

FIVES AND SEVENS CONNECTING
Fives are Striving to be Detached; Sevens are Striving to be Excited.

Connections

- Fives and Sevens have a natural curiosity. Both types tend to be interested in a wide range of topics.
- Sevens can be conceptual and can create interesting ideas for Fives to discuss and analyze.
- In social settings and group meetings outgoing Sevens can supply a supportive safety net for shy Fives by taking center stage, allowing Fives the luxury of being quiet and the time and space to access their feelings and thoughts.
- Both types divert attention from their emotions, particularly anxiety: Fives isolate from people; Sevens distract themselves with variety and superficial talk.
- Both types can become caught up in thinking and replace action with dreaming, brainstorming or analyzing, often preferring planning to acting.

Disconnects

- Sevens seem to live on the surface, whereas Fives dive deeply into their thoughts. Both types can more easily answer the question, "What are you thinking?" than, "What are you feeling?"

- Sevens prefer a fast pace, and can jump from concept to concept quickly, while Fives prefer a slower, almost meditative pace, and measure their words and thoughts carefully.
- Fives and Sevens struggle with addressing negative emotions. Fives analyze their feelings and prolong dealing with them through analysis ("I need more info.") Sevens deny, rationalize, or sugar coat them ("Things aren't so bad.").
- Fives prefer to participate in things cautiously and from a distance at first, and then often become experts, gaining security through mastery. Sevens jump in enthusiastically at first, and often remain joyful novices, preferring the "beginner's mind" to mastery, gaining security through excitement and variety.
- Fives may seem too quiet and detached to Sevens. Sevens can seem too loud and over-stimulated to Fives.
- Sevens may become bored with what they see as the Five's over-analysis. Fives may become bored with what they see as the Seven's tendency to talk too much about uninteresting things.

Connecting With Sevens From a Five's Perspective

- Fives need to be patient, allow Sevens to explore their ideas, and to avoid making Sevens feel fenced in.
- Fives can build rapport with Sevens by sharing their mutual sense of curiosity and delight in the world.
- Fives do well to commit time, enthusiasm, and energy to a relationship with Sevens. Fives should try to communicate with energy, emphasizing the positive impact that their relationship will accomplish.
- Fives can help Sevens to focus and to stay with things until they are finished.
- Encourage Sevens to make a commitment to group results, no matter how boring they may seem to Sevens, especially delivering on individual tasks that affect group functioning.
- Help stressed Sevens to see that last-minute changes are not exciting, but are more likely ineffective and problematic for people.

Connecting With Fives From a Seven's Perspective

- Fives will appreciate if Sevens give detailed, logical, written instructions that require little need for interaction with others.
- Sevens can build rapport by asking questions, as long as they are not personally intrusive. Fives will become more engaged when they feel the Seven is interested in their areas of interest.
- To make Fives feel comfortable and more trusting, Sevens should speak half as much as usual, and be patient with a Five's more reflective communication style.
- Teach Fives that they need to learn to accept a cut off point for their requests for information, especially if it delays decisions and is used as an excuse for not making decisions or being accountable to people.
- Sevens should pay close attention to accountability: make sure that information supplied to Fives is complete and on time. Vagueness and a cavalier attitude will frustrate Fives, and give them an excuse to ask for more data, and delay decision-making or task completion.

FIVES AND EIGHTS CONNECTING
Fives are Striving to be Detached; Eights are Striving to be Powerful.

Connections

- Eights, like Fives, value autonomy and self-reliance.
- Both types tend to question authority, Fives less overtly and less aggressively than Eights.
- Both types know what they like and dislike and neither has a high need for personal, emotional approval from people.
- Both like to discuss things in depth and are not afraid to take a stand: Eights take a stand with action ("Let's do it!"), Fives more with analysis ("Here's *why* we should do it.").
- Eights, like Fives, are committed to their ideas, and can be exciting sparing partners for Fives in heated debates.

- Both types tend to be skeptical, suspicious, and wary of being caught off guard.
- Both see knowledge as power, and stay well informed, especially in their area of interest.
- Both types are more task than people oriented. Like Eights, Fives usually insist on "just the facts," and value efficiency over unnecessary rapport building and empathy.

Disconnects

- Eights can be "know-it-alls" (just like Fives) but their communication style can be much more intense and confrontational than the quieter style of Fives.
- Fives are low-impact, low visibility people; Eights are just the opposite.
- An Eight's discussion can feel like an argument to Fives. Eights often challenge the facts, ideas, and commitment of others.
- Eights are passionate and emotional; Fives are neither, so this can be problematic for Fives, who may be intimidated by an Eight's intensity.
- Eights may become frustrated with a Five's slower pace. A big contrast here is between an Eight's action and a Five's analysis.
- To Eights, Fives act too cautiously, and are too impersonal, distant, and in need of unnecessary amounts of information before making a decision. Fives make decisions based in large part on facts—from "the head." To Fives, Eights may act recklessly, without proper information, consideration of consequences, or proper planning. Eights make decisions based in large part on intuition.

Connecting With Eights From a Five's Perspective

- Fives should be prepared for the Eights' need to vent and express their strong opinions and feelings. Eights are looking for a reaction in order to gauge how much they can rely on people.

- Fives can build trust with Eights by being fully present and engaged, and by disclosing information and "gut" feelings rather than having an Eight "tease" things out of them. Be direct and bold with Eights. Speak with confidence and clarity.
- Fives can establish rapport by speeding up their speaking pace, and by being prepared to take action and be decisive.
- Fives should model their own strong ability to be authentic and factual—even brutally honest—with Eights, who will respect them for their honesty. Eights see facts and objectivity as powerful tools.
- Fives can help Eights to be quieter, to be reflective and listen with objectivity and measured, patient discernment. "Counting to ten" before speaking is good advice for Eights.
- Fives can teach Eights the value of detachment—a healthy distance from the action—to gain greater insight on the issues, and ultimately to increase an Eight's influence and power.

Connecting With Fives From an Eight's Perspective

- Eights should avoid showing frustration with Fives for not interacting at the Eight's pace or level of emotional intensity. Eights can build rapport by toning down their forcefulness and abruptness.
- Rely on Fives for their store of knowledge and insight. Appreciate their innovativeness and their ability to come up with new insights. Honor their creativity and give them time for their ideas to develop.
- Eights can teach Fives to move their ideas from the drawing board to the factory floor by coaching Fives to know when a concept is ready to take shape.
- Encourage Fives to believe in themselves, to be confident that they have enough information, and that they are ready to move forward.
- Eights do well to make appointments way ahead of time with Fives; give them time to prepare. Remember—Eights can seem intrusive to Fives—and under stress, disruptive. Fives cherish their privacy and

dislike intrusions. Honor their physical and emotional space to get the most out of the relationship.

• Eights can help Fives feel safe enough to take risks and be more noticeable by running interference for them and dealing with the more emotional team members whom Fives don't want to confront.

FIVES AND NINES CONNECTING
Fives are Striving to be Detached; Nines are Striving to be Peaceful.

Connections

• Both Fives and Nines are non-aggressive and conflict-averse, and tend to cooperate rather than compete with each other. Both types are calm and share a desire to be around calm people and environments.
• Neither type is self-promotional nor status seeking.
• Under stress, both types lack a sense of urgency, initiative, and confidence.
• Fives are usually comfortable with Nines because Nines create an accepting, nonjudgmental atmosphere. Nines are easy going, give Fives the emotional space they need, and don't pressure Fives to engage until they're ready.
• Nines appreciate a Five's ideas, command of the facts, and advice.
• Nines and Fives find common ground in speculation, philosophy, and esoteric topics.
• Both types prefer a relaxed atmosphere, and time to study the facts before making a decision.
• Both Nines and Fives tend to withdraw under stress, and are turned off by bravado, aggressive people, and the "hard sell."
• Both types avoid the limelight and prefer structure, clear expectations, and predictable outcomes.
• Both types, especially under stress, lack an outward expression of vitality. Nines are cautious of expending too much energy. Fives hoard their energy and avoid crowds, which drain their energy.

Disconnects

- Nines are people-oriented. Fives are task-oriented.
- Nines connect easily and are more friendly and outgoing than Fives.
- Fives can struggle to connect with people they don't know or with people they have little in common with.
- Nines can be fuzzy around details and facts, thus frustrating fact-driven Fives who seek precision and data.
- Fives may frustrate Nines with their lack of responsiveness to questions and avoidance or slowness in releasing information.
- Nines want acknowledgement without asking for it. Fives will rarely volunteer praise or give a compliment without a reminder. It's just the facts with Fives, which will frustrate Nines.
- Fives make changes without requesting input from others. Nines, on the other hand, ask for input in order to gain agreement. Nines will expect the same from Fives, but may be frustrated by a lack of response or a delay in responding from the Five.

Connecting With Nines From a Five's Perspective

- Fives can build rapport with Nines by honoring small talk and personal contact first before delivering the facts. Being friendly first creates acceptance, harmony, and trust with Nines.
- Don't give commands and directives to Nines. Instead, ask questions and solicit their opinion to uncover objections—and be aware than Nines can become stubborn and rebellious when they don't feel included.
- Both Nines and Fives are innovative; try to find mutual ideas and solutions.
- Both types are conflict-averse and prefer to ignore problems in hopes that they will go away or be handled by someone else. Fives will need to come out of their comfort zone in dealing with conflicts with

Nines. Don't assume that silence from a Nine means agreement; it rarely does, and may mean indifference or disagreement.

- Fives can create a powerful working relationship with Nines which is built on the Five's needs and the Nine's strengths: a Five's constant need for more data can be satisfied by a Nine's natural gift for reading group dynamics, understanding people, and assessing the political status within groups. Fives need to be willing and aware enough to get the information from Nines.

Connecting With Fives From a Nine's Perspective

- Allow Fives the time and the space (both physical and emotional) they need. Don't misinterpret a Five's quiet nature as aloofness or arrogance. They may simply be thinking, analyzing, or retreating into their comfort zone.
- Nines can build rapport with Fives by connecting in a safe, unhurried environment with relaxed, undemanding people.
- Nines can help teach Fives to be open to feedback, especially concerning their blind spot of *intellectual arrogance*, and to share more of their personal feelings with teammates.
- Encourage Fives to be present with people and to *physically* interact with people, not just through emails and text messages. For Fives, physical presence with a Nine is better than a phone call, but a phone call is better than an email or text message.
- Encourage Fives to attend and participate in team meetings that build rapport and morale and whose purposes are not merely delivering status reports or gathering information. These sorts of meetings are invaluable in building trust, gaining team commitments, and establishing accountability.
- Nines need to be more precise and focused when communicating with Fives, especially in group meetings. Nines prefer exploring issues broadly, and hearing opinions and options from everyone present. Fives prefer concise data with clear end points.

SIXES AND ONES CONNECTING
See Ones and Sixes Connecting on page 179

SIXES AND TWOS CONNECTING
See Twos and Sixes Connecting on page 197

SIXES AND THREES CONNECTING
See Threes and Sixes Connecting on page 213

SIXES AND FOURS CONNECTING
See Fours and Sixes Connecting on page 226

SIXES AND FIVES CONNECTING
See Fives and Sixes Connecting on page 238

SIXES CONNECTING WITH SIXES
Sixes are Striving to be Secure.

Connections

- Sixes can be supportive of each other. They share a common concern for safety and security and can be sympathetic with the other's fears and anxieties. They share a strong sense of loyalty and duty.
- Sixes can stimulate each other's intellectual curiosity and skill at detecting faulty arguments and propositions.
- Sixes work for causes they believe in, and can have great, invigorating conversations and relationships. They are supportive of each other and committed to the relationship or team.

Disconnects

- If not careful, Sixes, especially under stress, can ignite each other's paranoia, fears, and negativity.
- Under pressure Sixes can turn normal events into catastrophes.

- They can doubt each other's actions, dedication, and loyalty.
- Making decisions that affect both can be difficult because both Sixes may be second-guessing the other.

Connecting With Sixes From a Six's Perspective

- Focus on the positive but don't sugar coat things.
- Emphasize control, safety, and reliability.
- Reinforce the desire to be in a workable, loyal, trusting relationship.
- Compliment each other on making good decisions.
- Don't second-guess or revisit the past with "What if" questions.
- Be a barometer for other Sixes by monitoring how much procrastination is going on.
- Help other Sixes to relax and enjoy connecting by establishing some routine tasks where not much thinking is involved. Be aware that over thinking can result in anxiety.
- By sharing fears Sixes can mutually establish the peace of mind that is the hallmark of trust, high performance, and a great relationship.
- Regular meetings with clear information and forewarnings are essential to alleviate worry and establish a sense of security and direction.
- Avoid ambiguous messages and be prompt in communicating deviations in plans.

SIXES AND SEVENS CONNECTING
Sixes are Striving to be Secure; Sevens are Striving to be Excited

Connections

- Sixes and Sevens are often anxious, tend to imagine and live in the future, and use planning to fabricate a sense of safety.
- Both Sevens and Sixes can be anxious about finishing tasks: Six's use doubt to delay completion; Sevens become bored with unexciting details.

- When relaxed, both types can be playful and engaging, and can be great friends.
- Both types share a tendency towards impatience, nervousness, and anxiety, although Sevens will hide it by joking and being light hearted. Stressed Sixes will show caution and anxiety by doubting themselves and others, criticizing, and complaining.
- Both types are energetic, build rapport easily, and are engaging.

Disconnects

- Sevens have little tolerance for bad news, painful memories, or dark moods. Sixes consistently want to know what could go wrong as a way of preparing for the worst.
- Sevens prefer to get up and go, and love to improvise. Sixes prefer to have a well-rehearsed plan and to prepare for all contingencies.
- Sevens like to down play or avoid problems; Sixes like to get problems out in the open (and may inflate them) and focus on duty and hard work.
- Sevens may hesitate to commit, preferring to leave their options open; Sixes prefer to narrow down the options, and find a cause to be loyal to.
- Sixes like to blend into the group, while Sevens don't mind standing out.
- Sevens can have fun by taking chances, changing plans in midstream, and being "wild and crazy." Sixes may see these behaviors as unproductive, inappropriate, or irresponsible.

Connecting With Sevens From a Six's Perspective

- Try to keep things positive when connecting with a Seven, even when delivering bad news.
- Allow Sevens to express their freedom and avoid making them feel fenced in. Emphasize the exciting things you can do together. Get them to visualize a bright, safe, responsible future.

- Sevens avoid facing painful situations and Sixes can provide great support by showing loyalty and resilience during difficult times.
- Be aware that Sevens can make wild promises and not follow through. Help them to make firm commitments to the relationship or the group and to stick to them.
- Sevens may change goals, shift priorities, and try new things without input or permission, but may interpret this sort of behavior as being creative or inspiring. Help Sevens to see that inconsistent behavior endangers the relationship and jeopardizes group efforts.
- Don't demand that Sevens confess their faults, rather, make things clear, and provide safety for them to see your point of view.
- Sevens benefit from reality checks, shared agreements, and mutual To Do lists. They may thank you for holding them accountable.

Connecting With Sixes From a Seven's Perspective

- Sevens can brighten a Six's fearful thoughts by focusing on possibilities rather than problems. They can quell a Six's doubts with their positive outlook.
- Sevens should avoid exaggerating the positives and downplaying the negatives. Be aware that Sixes may become fearful and mistrustful if they sense that information is being withheld or distorted. Don't overwhelm Sixes with unwarranted enthusiasm and optimism.
- Consistency means safety for Sixes, so Sevens do well to avoid making unnecessary changes. If changes can't be avoided, reassure Sixes that the relationship or their job is secure (if this is the case). Keep them informed so they don't imagine the worst.
- Sixes thrive on challenging work, being part of an effective, loyal team, and staying on course with little deviation. Give them the big picture, and regularly communicate the status of how things are going.

SIXES AND EIGHTS CONNECTING
Sixes are Striving to be Secure; Eights are Striving to be Powerful.

Connections

- Both types value loyalty, commitment, and accountability.
- Both types mistrust drama, emotionality, hype, and overly optimistic promises. They both believe that action speaks louder than words.
- Eights, like Sixes, are skeptical, suspicious of authority, and protective of others.
- Both types look for danger, and don't trust people without testing them.
- Sixes seek protection and Eights like to protect people. Sixes are loyal and Eights honor loyalty.
- Sixes feel assured of where they stand with Eights when Eights are direct about actions they plan to take, what could go wrong, and what can be done about it.
- Under Stress, both types can be belligerent and relentless in expressing their will, defending themselves, and blaming others.
- Both types enjoy deflating pretentious bubbles, and challenging weak or flawed arguments.
- Both types distrust and challenge authority, but in different ways and for different reasons. Eights believe they can do better and should be in charge. Sixes fear being taken advantage of and believe that authority figures should be monitored carefully. Sixes, however, don't always seek to be in charge in the direct, assertive way that Eights do.

Disconnects

- Eights see Sixes as overly cautious and indecisive and can become frustrated if Sixes spend too much time complaining.
- Sixes may frustrate Eights because stressed Sixes can be erratic, emotional and indecisive.

- Sixes openly express their fears about uncertainties. They complain, and are concerned about safety and security. Eights feel uncertainties are grist for the mill, and challenges to overcome. Eights may see complaining as a waste of time and a delay in taking action and resolving issues.
- Sixes can be very sensitive and may over react to an Eight's judgments or directness.
- Eights want to make a move, attack the competition, and make something happen, while stressed Sixes want to be cautious, think about things, and wait for reinforcements.
- Sixes tend to have a love/hate relationship with Eights; they admire the Eight's power, yet feel threatened by its expression.
- Stressed Eights can see a Six's desire for protection as a weakness, and treat them disdainfully.
- Eights may try to dominate the Six and the relationship, especially if they think the Six is being indecisive, weak, or unfocused.

Connecting With Eights From a Six's Perspective

- Sixes can build rapport with Eights by concentrating on how to make something happen rather than why it can't be done.
- Sixes should be particularly conscious of their tendency to mistrust authority, especially when an Eight appears pushy. Sixes need to ponder the question: "Is the Eight being pushy simply to dominate or because she has the right answer and appropriate action?"
- Since Eight's often see hesitation as weakness, Sixes do well to stand up for their beliefs, and show their power, passion, and decisiveness. Try to reflect back an Eight's intensity and passion. Eights respect assertiveness and will more readily listen to a convincing argument delivered with authority.
- Appreciate that Eights like to take more risks than Sixes. Sixes see danger in risk taking; Eights see opportunity.
- Sixes need to set clear boundaries and deal with confrontation— Eights see both as signs of good leadership.

- Help Eights to be better partners by coaching them to build trust through patience and cooperation.
- Let Eights know when they make a decision without input from others, and how they make it impossible for others to make and honor group commitments based on the Eight's unilateral decision.

Connecting With Sixes From an Eight's Perspective

- Eights can gain from the insight and strategic vision of Sixes. Eights want to move into action as quickly as possible and can overlook the intricacies and political nuances that are dealt with by more thoughtful, cautious Sixes.
- Eights should support and reassure Sixes as much as possible and resist judging a Six's need for support as weakness.
- Eights need to be especially aware of their forceful impact on Sixes. Be careful not to be seen as someone to be feared, and resist judging Sixes as timid. Sixes are powerful advocates and supporters and want support in return. Eights need to practice being supportive without taking over.
- A good gauge for Eights to determine if they are overpowering Sixes is if Sixes are avoiding them or working around them by communicating and acting through others. Eights should ask for feedback.
- Eight should invite Sixes to meet in person and listen without interrupting. Let Sixes talk and express their concerns. Appreciate that Sixes are keen observers and trouble-shooters who can complement an Eight's bias for action.
- Encourage Sixes to continue to be watchdogs, gatekeepers, and protectors. This is a great way for Sixes to feel more confident and to be valuable partners with Eights. Praise Sixes for this role, which no one can do as well as they can.

SIXES AND NINES CONNECTING

Sixes are Striving to be Secure; Nines are Striving to be Peaceful.

Connections

- Both Sixes and Nines favor cooperation over competition, and both types find it easy to act on behalf of others. Both have a desire for a safe, cooperative, comfortable environment and relationship.
- Neither type likes the limelight, and can struggle to make decisions and take action.
- Both can struggle saying no to requests: Sixes out of a sense of loyalty, and Nines in an attempt to keep the peace.
- Nines create an accepting, nonjudgmental atmosphere that allows Sixes to be more trusting and less suspicious. Sixes help Nines to take action by offering physical support and emotional encouragement.
- Both aware types respond well to deadlines if they are achievable. Deadlines, structure, and action plans push Nines out of inertia and Sixes out of doubt.
- Nines are drawn to the Six's more exuberant, demonstrative style; their hyper-vigilance helps Nine's feel more alive and engaged. Sixes are attracted to the calm, disarming peacefulness of Nines, which makes Sixes feel safe.
- Both types like to cheer for the underdog, value team spirit, and work well with others.

Disconnects

- Nines may see Sixes as skeptical and negative.
- Sixes can see Nines as overly trusting, and can be frustrated by the Nine's lack of concern about potential danger, lack of response in times of crisis, and passive-aggressiveness.
- Sixes prefer Nines to be more decisive, to be more active and to take the initiative more. Nines prefer that Sixes relax and be less reactive and fearful.
- Nines dislike and avoid conflict by looking the other way and trusting people. Sixes may find this behavior questionable and can make them feel nervous. Sixes will question whose side the Nine is on. Loyal,

protective Sixes will want to engage the "outsider," address conflict and reestablish security, whereas a Nine will want the conflict to go away without effort or confrontation.

- Stressed Sixes can have a frantic, anxious focus on problems and daily events, while stressed Nines can be inattentive, forgetful, and uninterested.

Connecting With Nines From a Six's Perspective

- Sixes can initially build rapport with Nines by being patient and allowing Nines to take action at their own pace (within reason) because Nines can be stubborn and will slow down or shut down when they feel they are being pressured to act.
- When the relationship is established, it's helpful to create deadlines and reminders for Nines. Because of their inertia, Nines take time to get into action. Holding them accountable can help Nines get things done.
- Sixes do well to adopt some of a Nine's positive attitudes. Appreciate the ease, and the "no hassle" aspect of the relationship.
- Sixes can help Nines to be more vigilant, to learn to anticipate potential problems, inevitable delays and complications.
- Sixes should appreciate a Nine's value and contributions without being prompted, saving Nine's the discomfort of seeking recognition, and bringing uncomfortable notice to themselves.
- Help Nines to see that they can take a stand, even when it is unpopular, and still maintain their peace of mind.

Connecting With Sixes From a Nine's Perspective

- To build trust with Sixes, be totally honest and make sure to communicate what could go wrong along with contingency plans.
- Recognize that Sixes dislike making decisions, just like Nines, and that this similarity can establish common ground for mutual feedback and support.

- Deadlines apply for Sixes as well as Nines. Establish deadlines or remind Sixes of commitments. Because of their doubt, Sixes hesitate to take action. Deadlines are a way of getting Sixes motivated to act.
- Nines should stay active and engaged in tasks when connecting with Sixes. Be aware that inactivity, ambivalence, and vagueness can engender doubts about the Nine's competence and commitment.
- Nines can help Sixes avoid doubt and anxiety by keeping Sixes engaged with the group. Provide Sixes with consistent feedback, updated timelines, and time to express their concerns. A Six left out of the loop may become fearful, rebellious, and unproductive. Nines can help Sixes feel safer by regularly reassuring Sixes that they are an important part of the relationship and team.

SEVENS AND ONES CONNECTING
See Ones and Sevens Connecting on page 181

SEVENS AND TWOS CONNECTING
See Twos and Sevens Connecting on page 200

SEVENS AND THREES CONNECTING
See Threes and Sevens Connecting on page 215

SEVENS AND FOURS CONNECTING
See Fours and Sevens Connecting on page 228

SEVENS AND FIVES CONNECTING
See Fives and Sevens Connecting on page 240

SEVENS AND SIXES CONNECTING
See Sixes and Sevens Connecting on page 249

SEVENS CONNECTING WITH SEVENS
Sevens are Striving to be Excited.

Connections

- Sevens will delight other Sevens with their spontaneity and enthusiasm. They may compete with each other over who has more ideas, who can accomplish more, win more games, start more projects, get more sales, create more excitement or have more fun.
- Sevens like to socialize and entertain.
- Sevens won't hesitate to exaggerate and embellish things in their efforts to create a light-hearted, fun environment.

Disconnects

- Sevens prefer to work with people who can complement their likes and dislikes. Sevens like partners who can pick up the ball for them, complete tasks and do some of the heavy lifting that they prefer to avoid. Another Seven, who feels the same way, of course, won't fit the bill, and conflict will often ensue.
- If they can't agree on the next fun thing to do, or task to accomplish, Sevens may get on each other's nerves.
- One Seven's impulsiveness may interfere directly with the other's and they may grow weary of each other's company.
- Sevens have high expectations and a sense of entitlement—without a healthy balance of give and take, and adherence to rules, there could be frustration.

Connecting With Sevens From a Seven's Perspective

- In the short run, Sevens working together will do well to focus on short projects.

- Sevens should remind other Sevens of their tendency to overlook details or how their actions affect others when they are caught up in excitement.
- Remind other Sevens to be objective and practical, to keep one foot on the floor and avoid being swept away by the belief that everything is possible. It isn't.
- Try to discipline each other in order to accomplish quality work. Be especially aware of telling tall tales and trying to "out promise" or outdo each other.
- Help other Sevens by providing "reality checks." Encourage them not to make decisions or commitments to impress or excite people.
- Make an agreement to hold each other accountable to follow through on what you say you will do. Sevens like to delegate, but delegating to other Sevens may create a perpetual "passing the buck," if not carefully monitored.

SEVENS AND EIGHTS CONNECTING
Sevens are Striving to be Excited; Eights are Striving to be Powerful.

Connections

- Both Sevens and Eights are enthusiastic and energetic; they like to play hard and are often guilt free.
- Neither type needs excessive time or information to make a decision.
- Both types cherish their independence, like to make their own rules and break them when they see fit.
- Both types are unlikely to question themselves, are self-confident, and assume that their ideas and actions are acceptable to others.
- Eights and Sevens both share a high level of energy and desire for stimulation.
- Both types dislike pessimism, complaining, being restricted by rules and procedures, and things that take too long to materialize.

- Under stress both types can react to unsettling information by denying it. Eights dismiss or forget what they don't want to hear ("Just forget about it."); Sevens distract themselves, rationalize, or sugar-coat things ("Everything will be OK.")
- When both types agree on a plan, Eights can provide the support that allows Sevens the freedom to improvise and be creative.

Disconnects

- Whereas both types can be assertive in getting what they want, Sevens don't like to argue like Eights. Sevens are generally conflict averse; Eights seek out challenges, obstacles to overcome, and a good fight.
- Under stress Sevens become distracted and anxious, while Eights become energized and aggressive.
- Eights like to test themselves and others by debating or testing. Sevens would rather ignore the issue and get back to work or to having fun.
- Eights usually insist on being right and how the rules don't apply to them. Sevens may break the rules but tend not to publicize the fact.
- Sevens may frustrate Eights if they focus exclusively on the positive and ignore obstacles.
- Eights prefer a pragmatic, factual evaluation of people and situations. Sevens prefer to see the positive and to create a happy, utopian world.
- Disagreements can escalate because both types are self-referencing and often don't see the value of another's perspective.

Connecting With Eights From a Seven's Perspective

- Sevens can build rapport by appreciating the enthusiasm and dynamism of Eights.
- Keep commitments with Eights. They judge people heavily by their loyalty and trustworthiness. Be willing to engage in problem solving

and heated discussion with Eights, and don't take their forcefulness personally.

- Help Eights to see the positive side of people. Their tendency is to be suspicious of motives and to be competitive, even with colleagues.
- Encourage Eights to avoid expressing "tough love," and to learn to deliver their messages with empathy and patience.
- Sevens can work well with Eights as long as they establish trust on a constant basis. Keep Eights updated, don't hold back bad news, and don't surprise them.

Connecting With Sevens From an Eight's Perspective

- Eights should be aware of their tendency to see threats and dangers where they may not exist, their impulse to seek out conflict, and the Seven's avoidance of conflict—appreciate the Seven's different style.
- Be aware that Sevens will tune out Eights when they focus too much on aggressiveness, winning at all cost, constant challenges, and negativity.
- Eights should be positive around Sevens whenever possible. Make frequent contact, and support a Seven's positive approach.
- Eights can help Sevens stay results-oriented and goal focused by emphasizing work before play.
- Eights can be single-minded, powerfully focused, and committed to goals. By demonstrating this behavior, Eights can be a great influence on Sevens, who can too easily go off on more exciting, less agreed-to pursuits.
- Encourage Sevens to continue to create inspiring visions, while maintaining a grounded commitment to accomplishing daily tasks.

SEVENS AND NINES CONNECTING

Sevens are Striving to be Excited; Nines are Striving to be Peaceful.

Connections

- Nines and Sevens possess a natural ease, flexibility, and comfort around people. They both share a desire to avoid conflict and to have a pleasant time. They both believe that people work more effectively in a positive environment.
- Both types are accepting, optimistic, and look for the best in people.
- Sevens and Nines prefer that everyone work together as equals. This gives Sevens the freedom to be independent and do what they want. It gives Nines the peace of mind that no one will be controlled, bossed around, or coerced—and that harmony and consensus will prevail.
- Although both types can be as ambitious as anyone else, both Nines and Sevens believe that a realistic life/work balance is preferable to over work and burnout.
- Both types share a big worldview. Sevens see endless options and possibilities for achievement. Nines easily see and appreciate other perspectives.
- Both types can belabor decision-making: Sevens because they don't want to limit their options, Nines because they become overwhelmed by choice.

Disconnects

- Excitable, fast talking, and fast moving Sevens may become frustrated with the Nine's slower, more deliberate, and relaxed style.
- Sevens prefer to communicate with "Cliff Notes," and short, bulleted items; from a Seven's point of view, Nines prefer the detailed, sometimes repetitious "epic tale."
- Nines like a steady pace and resist change, whereas Sevens are impulsive and initiate and embrace change. Nines like routine and the opportunity to stay focused on a task. Sevens prefer variety, become bored with routine, and become distracted by tedious work.

- Nines may see stressed Sevens as insensitive, impatient, and self-centered. Sevens may see stressed Nines as repetitive, stubborn, and resistant.
- Sevens are one of the most self-referencing types with an infectious optimism and personal agenda. Nines are one of the most self-effacing types who are drawn to powerful people, and can merge easily with others and lose their personal agenda. Without vigilant awareness, this partnership can become dysfunctional when Nines focus on Sevens and Sevens focus on themselves.

Connecting With Nines From a Seven's Perspective

- Sevens can model for Nines effective ways to be more energetic, enthusiastic, and confident.
- Sevens do well to resist their impulsiveness with Nines, who respond well to structure, routine, and the pressure of a deadline.
- Ask Nines what they want or what their opinion is. They may not know off hand, but just being asked feels respectful to Nines. Let them know that their input is valued.
- Nines and Sevens can get caught in an unspoken, subtle agreement to avoid unpleasantness and conflict. Nines show their displeasure by passive resistance rather than overt confrontation, and Sevens distract themselves or leave the scene. Both types need to be aware of these cues as a sign that something needs to be addressed.
- Sevens should listen to a Nine's grievances and commit to do something about them rather than dismiss the Nine's concerns as over-reactions or negativity.
- Be honest with Nines. Nines can become stubborn and unproductive if they feel Sevens are in denial, rationalizing, making false promises, or trying to charm their way to a resolution of problems.

Connecting With Sevens From a Nine's Perspective

- Nines should be aware that a Seven's strength is in seeing the big picture. Sevens are idea people. Nines may need to get solid commitments from Sevens in order to move ideas into action.
- Appreciate what Sevens bring to the relationship—their natural likeability, salesmanship, fun, and enthusiasm—and their ability to inspire, plan, and envision a bright future.
- Be aware that beneath a Seven's optimism lies anxiety. Sevens are very sensitive to criticism and have difficulty receiving feedback. However, Nines can help Sevens be aware (through feedback) of the negative impact Sevens have on the group or relationship when they make half-hearted or exaggerated promises without actually delivering.
- Schedule regular reality checks and mutual feedback sessions, and get plans and commitments in writing. This helps both types (who avoid confrontation) to eliminate project creep and to address issues immediately when they go off course.
- Nines can demonstrate a grounded, steady and practical work style for Sevens to emulate.

EIGHTS AND ONES CONNECTING
See Ones and Eights Connecting on page 183

EIGHTS AND TWOS CONNECTING
See Twos and Eights Connecting on page 202

EIGHTS AND THREES CONNECTING
See Threes and Eights Connecting on page 217

EIGHTS AND FOURS CONNECTING
See Fours and Eights Connecting on page 231

EIGHTS AND FIVES CONNECTING
See Fives and Eights Connecting on page 242

EIGHTS AND SIXES CONNECTING
See Sixes and Eights Connecting on page 252

EIGHTS AND SEVENS CONNECTING
See Sevens and Eights Connecting on page 259

EIGHTS CONNECTING WITH EIGHTS
Eights are Striving to be Powerful.

Connections

- Eights together feed off each other's desire to get into action and make things happen.
- Because they are accustomed to being told to hold their energy back, being with another Eight can be an emotional relief because they can be themselves without restraint.
- Both types enjoy irreverent humor, fun-loving repartee, and good-humored competitiveness.
- Both are practical and can accomplish great things if they cooperate.
- Eights like to argue, so this relationship may get loud and rambunctious at times, but it may not be hostile, and may not even involve anger (although Eights don't see anger as negative). Eights debate, argue and fight to test one another, to feel energized, and even to get closer.
- Even after a squabble—what others would consider a serious fight where battle lines were drawn and the gloves came off—Eights can walk away as friends.

Disconnects

- Eights are competitive and controlling and unless the situation is ideal and the Eights are mature, a power struggle will inevitably ensue.
- Since Eights are self-referencing and independent thinkers, they tend to make up their minds before discussing issues—making decisions with another Eight difficult.

- Stressed Eights are strong willed, can be self-centered, and have little sense of guilt or remorse when they offend each other—although most Eights don't consider their normal, assertive communication style as offensive.
- Eights both desire to be in control and dislike being controlled or told what to do.
- Both can be protective and adversarial toward each other, and both are territorial, so unless both Eights are on the same team, there can be conflict.

Connecting With Eights From an Eight's Perspective

- Appreciate the enthusiasm and dynamism of other Eights; resist making it your job to curtail their activities or corral their energy.
- Don't get into a battle of wills. Learn to compromise rather than let hostility escalate.
- Listen. Eights always do well to be self-reflective, to be aware of their tendency to control conversations by interrupting, blaming, and calling for premature action.
- Make sure that the boundaries are clear in the relationship—so unambiguous that there is no doubt about what the rules, roles, and outcomes are.
- Don't withhold any information or surprise Eights.
- Be constantly aware that the other Eight thinks in black and white too, so it's a supportive or adversarial relationship from the beginning. Discerning each other's loyalty is essential.
- Make formal commitment necessary so that both Eights can commit to mutual activities. A third party may be advised to resolve conflict.

EIGHTS AND NINES CONNECTING
Eights are Striving to be Powerful; Nines are Striving to be Peaceful.

Connections

- Eights tend to appreciate a Nine's ease with people and their likeability. Nines appreciate an Eight's vitality and directness.
- At their best, both Eights and Nines share a solid, grounded, authentic quality.
- Both types share a strong sense of integrity and honesty.
- Nines can be as stubborn as Eights; they can argue their point, and refuse to give in.
- Both types seek autonomy and dislike being told what to do.
- Both types have issues with anger, although they deal with anger differently. Eights express it; Nines repress it or express it passive-aggressively.
- Nines admire strong leadership and can commit to Eight leaders who share the Nine's sense of equality, benevolence, and respect.
- Relaxed Eights and Nines can share a desire for creature comforts.
- Stressed Eights and Nines share a desire for excess.
- Nines are often attracted to more dynamic personality types such as aware Eights. Eights find relaxed, non-confrontational Nines easy to relate to and like. Eights are rarely threatened by Nines who are naturally non-competitive, self-effacing, and disarming. Eights can let their guard down around Nines.

Disconnects

- Eights like to be the boss and hate to be bossed around; Nines hate to be bossed around but are contented to play a support role.
- Eights are comfortable with anger. Anger causes stressed Nines discomfort and they numb themselves to it—although when aware Nines allow themselves to feel it, anger can help focus a Nine's attention and commitment.
- Eights can be overly competitive; Nines can be overly cooperative.

- Eights like pressure, a competitor to defeat, and to "turn up the heat." Nines dislike pressure, aggression, conflict, and being rushed.
- Both types are stubborn. When Eights and Nines disagree there may be a war of wills when the irresistible force (Eight) meets the immovable object (Nine).
- A major difference between Eights and Nines lies in *personal control* versus *group consensus.* To solve problems and accomplish tasks Eights assert their will and take charge. Nines assess the will of the group and build consensus.
- Nines like predictable, consistent rules and behavior. Eights follow rules and maintain consistent behavior to the degree that it helps them accomplish their goals.

Connecting With Nines From an Eight's Perspective

- Eights should be clear on deadlines and details, but be open to compromise. Nines will tune out conflict that disturbs their inner calm.
- Eights need to tone down their assertiveness with Nines and try to build rapport with small talk, humor, and graciousness.
- Eights do well to learn how Nines use finesse, charm, and a disarming unobtrusiveness to influence people and gain agreement and control.
- Be aware that a Nine's quiet demeanor does not ensure agreement; better to ask directly, "Are you committed to this?" Eights should appreciate the vast differences between how Eights and Nines express anger—don't mistake a Nine's passive-aggressiveness for mere annoyance—it may be a Nine's version of an Eight's outrage. A safe way to test where a Nine stands on touchy issues is to ask where they are on a scale of 1 to 10.
- Help Nines to see the value of assertiveness in getting their way and getting things done. "The squeaky wheel gets the grease" applies here, and Eights can teach Nines to ask for what they want, and be more demanding rather than ignoring or minimizing problems.

- Don't try to force a Nine's hand. Nines respond negatively to demands, but respond well to requests.

Connecting With Eights From a Nine's Perspective

- Understand what being challenged by Eights may mean. They are looking for information—both factual and emotional. They are seekers after truth and test people to see how determined, passionate, committed, and confident they are.
- Eights will become frustrated if Nines are evasive and avoid problems, so Nines do well to practice precision, logic, and confidence when dealing with conflict with Eights: be direct and be strong.
- Nines should not be afraid to give Eights constructive feedback. Eights assume that they know more and can do more than others. Their confidence can make Nines hesitate to tell Eights when they are over-stepping their bounds, not listening to people, or not showing concern and empathy—all actions that Nines are sensitive to.
- Understand that Eights are not used to people giving them direct, helpful feedback. Eights may not like to hear it, but if it is useful, an aware Eight will respect the Nine's honesty and directness.
- Stay factual when communicating with Eights. Nines can be distracted, noncommittal, and vague. This will frustrate Eights and cause them to question a Nine's awareness and commitment.
- Nines can coach Eights to be more sensitive to the needs of others and practice simple people skills—to be more relationship oriented, to ask others for their opinions, and to compliment people more frequently.

NINES AND ONES CONNECTING
See Ones and Nines Connecting on page 186

NINES AND TWOS CONNECTING
See Twos and Nines Connecting on page 203

NINES AND THREES CONNECTING
See Threes and Nines Connecting on page 219

NINES AND FOURS CONNECTING
See Fours and Nines Connecting on page 233

NINES AND FIVES CONNECTING
See Fives and Nines Connecting on page 245

NINES AND SIXES CONNECTING
See Sixes and Nines Connecting on page 254

NINES AND SEVENS CONNECTING
See Sevens and Nines Connecting on page 261

NINE AND EIGHTS CONNECTING
See Eights and Nines Connecting on page 266

NINES CONNECTING WITH NINES
Nines are striving to be Peaceful.

Connections

- Both Nines appreciate a conflict free, relaxed, cooperative relationship.
- Each one creates an accepting, nonjudgmental atmosphere that allows the other Nine to be less critical, more relaxed, and productive.
- Both will naturally bond together to avoid conflict and establish trust.
- Nines will support each other almost without question, preferring to bond rather than confront or question.
- Both Nines like a fixed schedule, which minimizes decision-making or the need to address changes or conflict. Two Nines, in a conflict-free zone, can buzz along on schedule and produce results.

Disconnects

- "Who's going to make decisions?" is an ongoing issue between two Nines.
- Both hesitate taking the lead, being noticed or assertive, and expressing their needs, so it may be difficult to know who's doing what, and who's being honest rather than agreeable.
- Without an honest exchange about making decisions and taking action, two unaware Nines can float happily into a sea of inertia, maintaining the status quo, doing nonessential tasks, and not making necessary changes to the relationship.
- Two Nines may struggle with finalizing things, making firm commitments, and taking the initiative.

Connecting With Nines From a Nine's Perspective

- Nines should work to get over their fear of making others feel uncomfortable and learn to embrace their own value—to be the expert, the boss, or the elder statesman when necessary—and share their knowledge and experience. Avoid self-effacing and self-dismissive behaviors.
- Encourage other Nines to give clear instructions. Don't leave it up to others to guess at plans and goals as a way of avoiding disagreement. Be direct with each other. Avoid statements such as "Do it your own way," or "You know how to do this. You figure it out." Take a stand.
- When conflict arises, be aware of stubbornness and refusing to hear the other's point of view out of spite ("I always give in, but not this time."). In such cases, Nines do well to ask a third party to help resolve conflict.
- Determine if you have real agreement or just apathy, or worse, fake agreement. Ask.
- Beware of the tendency toward the path of least resistance when change needs to occur. Take the initiative to create change. Don't be

afraid of anger; in fact, welcome it. Anger can create clarity of thinking and initiate purposeful action for Nines.

- Nines can help other Nines to find their own purpose, agenda, opinion, and action plan. Encourage Nines to take what others say as just another opinion and begin to listen to their own voice. Don't agree with people when you disagree.

The Guest House

This being human is a guest house.
Every morning a new arrival.
A joy, a depression, a meanness,
some momentary awareness comes
as an unexpected visitor.
Welcome and entertain them all!
Even if they are a crowd of sorrows,
who violently sweep your house
empty of its furniture,
still, treat each guest honorably.
He may be clearing you out
for some new delight.
The dark thought, the shame, the malice,
meet them at the door laughing and invite them in.
Be grateful for whatever comes,
because each has been sent
as a guide from beyond.

Jelaluddin Rumi, translation by Coleman Barks

A Doorway to Compassion

Over the years I've heard the complaint that the descriptions of the enneagram types focus too much on faults and weaknesses. "Why is it so negative?" I'm often asked. I tell people that looking only at positive characteristics creates an unrealistic picture, that people would not recognize themselves and others if they didn't also consider their less appealing behaviors. The skill in loving and working with people is not to deny the bad stuff, but not to dwell on it either.

All of us are at various stages and degrees of maturation and on an unending journey of discovery and integration. I hope this book has revealed that our personalities and emotions are gifts that help us connect in profound ways, and that accepting our different and common struggles presents a doorway to compassion and deeper, more meaningful relationships.

Appendix A: Framework for Creating Successful Connections

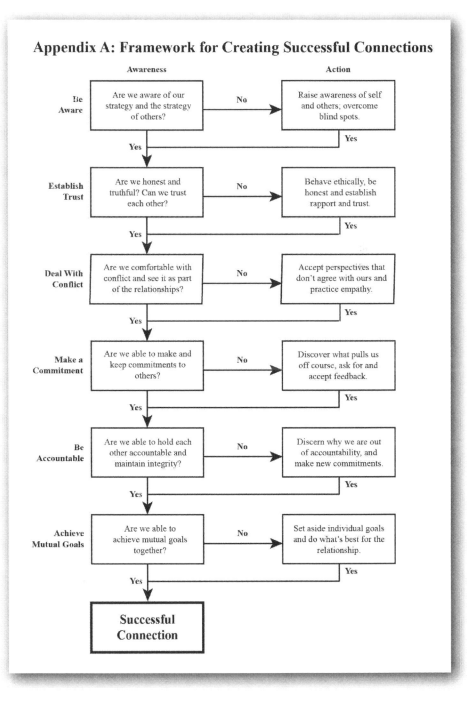

	Awareness		Action
Be Aware	Are we aware of our strategy and the strategy of others?	No →	Raise awareness of self and others; overcome blind spots.
Establish Trust	Are we honest and truthful? Can we trust each other?	No →	Behave ethically, be honest and establish rapport and trust.
Deal With Conflict	Are we comfortable with conflict and see it as part of the relationships?	No →	Accept perspectives that don't agree with ours and practice empathy.
Make a Commitment	Are we able to make and keep commitments to others?	No →	Discover what pulls us off course, ask for and accept feedback.
Be Accountable	Are we able to hold each other accountable and maintain integrity?	No →	Discern why we are out of accountability, and make new commitments.
Achieve Mutual Goals	Are we able to achieve mutual goals together?	No →	Set aside individual goals and do what's best for the relationship.

Successful Connection

Recommended Reading

Almaas, A.H., *Facets of Unity, The Enneagram of Holy Ideas,* Berkeley, CA: Diamond Books, 1998

_____, *The Unfolding Now, Realizing Your True Nature Through the Practice of Presence,* Berkeley, CA: Diamond Books, 2008

_____, *The Pearl Beyond Price, Integration of Personality into Being: An Object Relations Approach,* Berkeley, CA: Diamond Books, 1988

_____, *The Point of Existence, Transformations of Narcissism in Self-Realization,* Berkeley, CA: Diamond Books, 1996

_____, *The Inner Journey Home, Soul's Realization of the Unity of Reality,* Berkeley, CA: Diamond Books, 2004

_____, *Runaway Realization, Living a Life of Ceaseless Discovery,* Boston, MA: Shambala Publications, 2014

Barrett, Frank, J and Ronald E. Fry, *Appreciative Inquiry, A Positive Approach to*

Brach, Sara, *Radical Acceptance,* New York and Canada: Bantam, 2003

Chandler, Steve and Duane Black, *The Hands-Off Manager,* New Jersey and Canada: Career Press, 2007

Chandler, Steve, *Reinventing Yourself,* New Jersey and Canada: Career Press, 2005

_____, *The Story of You,* New Jersey and Canada: Career Press, 2006

_____, *The Life Coaching Connection, How Coaching Changes Lives,* Oregon: Robert D. Reed Publishers, 2011

_____, *Time Warrior, How to Defeat Procrastination, People-Pleasing, Self-Doubt, Over-Commitment, Broken Promises and Chaos*, Anna Maria, Florida: Maurice Bassett, 2011

_____, *Fearless, Creating the Courage to Change the Things You Can*, Oregon: Robert D. Reed Publishers, 2008

_____, *Wealth Warrior, The Personal Prosperity Revolution*, Anna Maria, Florida: Maurice Bassett, 2011

Cramer, Kathryn D, *Lead Positive*, San Francisco: Jossey-Bass, 2014

Cramer, Kathryn D and Hank Wasiak, *Change the Way You See Everything*, Philadelphia: Running Press, 2006

Davis, John, *The Diamond Approach, An Introduction to the Teachings of A.H. Almaas*, Boston, MA: Shambala Publications, 1999

De Llosa, Patty, *The Practice of Presence*, Sandpoint, ID: Morning Light Press, 2006

De Mello, Anthony, *Awareness, The Perils and Opportunities of Reality*, New York, London, Toronto: Doubleday, 1990

Dillard, Joseph, *Waking Up, Using Integral Deep Listening to Transform Your Life*, Berlin: Deep Listening Publishing, 2012

Earley, Jay, PhD, *Self-Therapy*, Minneapolis: Mill City Press, 2009

Goleman, Daniel, *Focus, The Hidden Driver of Excellence, New York: Harper Collins, 2013*

_____, *Working With Emotional Intelligence*, New York: Bantam, 1998

Goldsmith, Marshall, and Mark Reiter, *What Got You Here Won't Get You There, How Successful People Become Even More Successful*, New York: Hyperion, 2007

Katie, Byron, *Who Would You Be Without Your Story?* California, New York, London, Sydney: Hay House, 2008

_____, *Loving What Is*, New York: Harmony Books, 2002

Lencioni, Patrick, *The Five Dysfunctions of a Team*, San Francisco: Jossey-Bass, 2002

Neill, Michael, *Super Coach, 10 Secrets to Transform Anyone's Life*, Australia, Canada, Hong Kong: Hay House, 2009

Pillay, Srinivasan, S, *Your Brain and Business, The Neuroscience of Great Leaders,* Upper Saddle River, NJ: Pearson Education, 2011

Pink, Daniel, *A Whole New Mind,* New York: Riverhead Books, 2006

Rees, Fran, *How to Lead Work Teams, Facilitation Skills,* San Francisco: Jossey-Bass/Pfeiffer, 2001

Reddy, Brendan, W. *Team Building, Blueprints for Productivity,* San Diego: NTL Institute and Pfeiffer & Company, 1988

Riso, Don and Russ Hudson, *Personality Types,* Revised Edition, New York: Houghton Mifflin, 1996

_____, *The Wisdom of the Enneagram, The Complete Guide to Psychological and Spiritual Growth for the Nine Personality Types,* New York: Bantam, 1999

Rohr, Richard, *Immortal Diamond, The Search for Our True Self,* San Francisco: Jossey-Bass, 2013

_____, *Everything Belongs, The Gift of Contemplative Prayer,* New York: Crossroads Publishing, 2003

Rosenberg, Marshall, *Nonviolent Communication,* Encinatas: Puddle Dancer, 2005

Salzberg, Sharon, *Loving Kindness, The Revolutionary Art of Happiness,* Boston: Shambala, 1995

Scott, Susan, *Fierce Conversations,* New York: Berkley Publishing, 2002

Siegel, Daniel, J, *Mindsight, The New Science of Personal Transformation,* New York: Bantam, 2011

Silsbee, Doug, *The Mindful Coach, Seven Roles for Helping People Grow,* Marshall. NC: Ivy River Press, 2004

_____, *Presence-Based Coaching, Cultivating Self-Generative Leaders Through Mind, Body, and Heart,* San Francisco: Jossey-Bass, 2008

Tallon, Robert and Mario Sikora, *Awareness to Action, The Enneagram, Emotional Intelligence and Change,* Chicago: University of Chicago Press, 2006

Tolle, Eckhart, *The Power of Now,* Navato, CA: New World Library, 1999

Wagner, Jerome, *Nine Lenses on the World, The Enneagram Perspective,* Evanston, IL: Nine Lens Press, 2010

Wallace, Alan, *The Attention Revolution, Unlocking the Power of the Focused Mind,* Boston: Wisdom Publications, 2006

Weisinger, Hendrie, *Emotional Intelligence at Work,* San Francisco: Jossey Boss, 1998

_____ *The Genius of Instincts,* New Jersey: FT Press, 2009

Take *The Enneagram Connection* to the next level...

- Download the ESP (Enneagram Strategies Profile), a three-part enneagram personality assessment

- Download the ECA (Enneagram Emotional Competency Assessment), a 360-degree assessment tool with developmental guide

- Download additional enneagram, EQ, team building, and relationship improvement resources at:

www.bobtallon.com

Index

About the Author

Robert Tallon is an author, speaker, teacher and coach. *The Transformational Manager*, his presentation given at the first International Enneagram Conference at Stanford University in 1994, was based on his years of applying the enneagram in business and was one of the first programs to present the efficacy of using the enneagram in the workplace.

Since then, he has developed and applied the enneagram to achieve success in a variety of areas. His practice focuses on executive coaching, life coaching, team building, and mindfulness training.

Robert is the author of *The Enneagram Connection: Using the Enneagram and Emotional Intelligence to Transform Work and Personal Relationships*, (Presence Press, 2016) and co-author of *Awareness to Action: The Enneagram, Emotional Intelligence, and Change* (University of Chicago Press, 2006). He is the co-developer of the *Strategy Approach to the Enneagram*, and the *Awareness to Action Process*.

Robert is the father of Aaron and Lauren. He and his wife, Robyn Helmer, are originally from Philadelphia.

For more information about programs based on *The Enneagram Connection*, as well as other training and coaching offered by Robert Tallon visit www.bobtallon.com

Made in the USA
San Bernardino, CA
28 July 2016